Strategic Ladakh

A Historical Narrative
1951-53
And
A Military Perspective

Strategic Ladakh

A Historical Narrative 1951-53 and A Military Perspective

By
Maj Gen Rajendra Nath, PVSM (Retd.)

Vij Books India Pvt Ltd
New Delhi (India)

Published by

Vij Books India Pvt Ltd
(Publishers, Distributors & Importers)
2/19, Ansari Road
Delhi – 110 002
Phones: 91-11-43596460, 91-11-47340674
Fax: 91-11-47340674
e-mail: vijbooks@rediffmail.com
web: www.vijbooks.com

Copyright © 2016, *Maj Gen Rajendra Nath, PVSM (Retd)*

Paperback Published in : 2017

ISBN: 9789385563393 (Paperback)

All rights reserved.

No part of this book may be reproduced, stored in a retrieval system, transmitted or utilized in any form or by any means, electronic, mechanical, photocopying, recording or otherwise, without the prior permission of the copyright owner. Application for such permission should be addressed to the publisher.

The views expressed in this book are those of the author in his personal capacity. These do not have any official endorsement.

Dedicated to the Noble and Hospitable Citizens of Ladakh.

It was a blessing to be amongst you. Thank You.

and

My Love and My Abiding Pride,

The Indian Army.

and

My Regiment

The 11th Gorkha Rifles

CONTENTS

Introduction		1
Chapter I	Historical Background	7
Chapter II	Geographical and Economic Survey	26
Chapter III	Social Customs and Manners	51
Chapter IV	Health and Hygiene	73
Chapter V	Economic Conditions and Infrastructure	86
Chapter VI	Religion	97
Chapter VII	Political Scenario	112
Chapter VIII	Military Importance	122
Chapter IX	Some Personal Recollections	150
Chapter X	Indo Pak War 1947-1948 Operations in Ladakh	159
Chapter XI	1962 India – China War in Ladakh – Some Background Information	185
Chapter XII	1962 - India China War – Focus on Ladakh	194
Chapter XIII	Siachen Glacier and Ladakh	203
Chapter XIV	China's Future Strategy - It's Impact on Indian Security	209
Index		229

Maps, Appendix and Annexures

1	Appendix A	Area of Ladakh	151
2	Map	Ladakh	2
3	Map	Pakistan Plan of Attack in 1948	162
4	Map	Main Battles in Ladakh	165
4	Map	The Patrol Route to Aksai Chin	169
5	Map	Chinese Attack on Indian Positions	196
6	Map	Chinese Roads	223
7	Scan Copy	CGS Letter 9/8/52	175
8	Scan Copy	CGS Letter 9/6/53	176
9	Scan Copy	MoD Letter 8/6/53	177

Photographs

The Last Nominal King	22
High Mountains	27
Dress of the Women	55
Ladakhi Homes	57
A Gompa	71
Inside a Gompa	72
The Palace	87
Pyonggong Lake	132
Leh Town after Snowfall	203
Col Narendra Kumar	206

INTRODUCTION

Situated in the remote regions of the Himalayan ranges, forming the crest of India's crown, surrounded by lofty mountain massifs, the mighty majestic heights of whose peaks few men have reached to, watered by the perennial springs of the Indus, Shyok and Nubra, inhabited by people whose noble nature and simplicity are paralleled only by their humble living and spiritual thinking, once a centre of the Central Asian trade, paradise of game-hunters and mountaineers, and the melting pot of Chinese, Pakistani and Indian relationships – such is strategic Ladakh.

But today, Ladakh as the haven of Lamas is not important for India; Ladakh as the farthest Northern frontier out post is vitally important for our country's defence. To post partition India, Ladakh is from the point of view of defence, as strategically important as the North West Frontier province was to pre-partition India.

To emphasise the importance of geography, it's pertinent to note what was said about General Allenby; "Certainly no Commander ever gave more careful study to the history and topography of the theatre in which he was operating" writes Field Marshal Wavel in his book 'Palestine Campaign' "than did General Allenby". Two books he consulted almost daily, "the Bible and Adam Smith's Historic Geography of the Holy Land." Nor was it only the natural interest aroused in an acute and exceptionally well informed mind that impelled him to reflect so often on the part of the land. From these reflections he deducted much that was of value to him in planning his operations. That was in 1914-18 when the nature of warfare was not even half as complex as it is today. If even in 1914-18 a distinguished commander like Allenby felt the need to understand the history, geography and religious back ground of the country in which he was operating, it is only imperative that a commander of today has to go much deeper into the problems of the country in which he has to operate. General Eisenhower in his book "Crusade in Europe" also discusses the important political and economic problems he had to face during the campaigns in addition to the pressing military problems, though technically speaking he was only a military commander. Warfare now a days has become so complex that every military commander, in addition to being proficient in his own profession, has to be fully capable of handling political, economic, social and religious problems as well. This a commander can only do if he has thoroughly read and knows the historical background, geography, economic conditions and social customs of the land in which his forces are likely to operate.

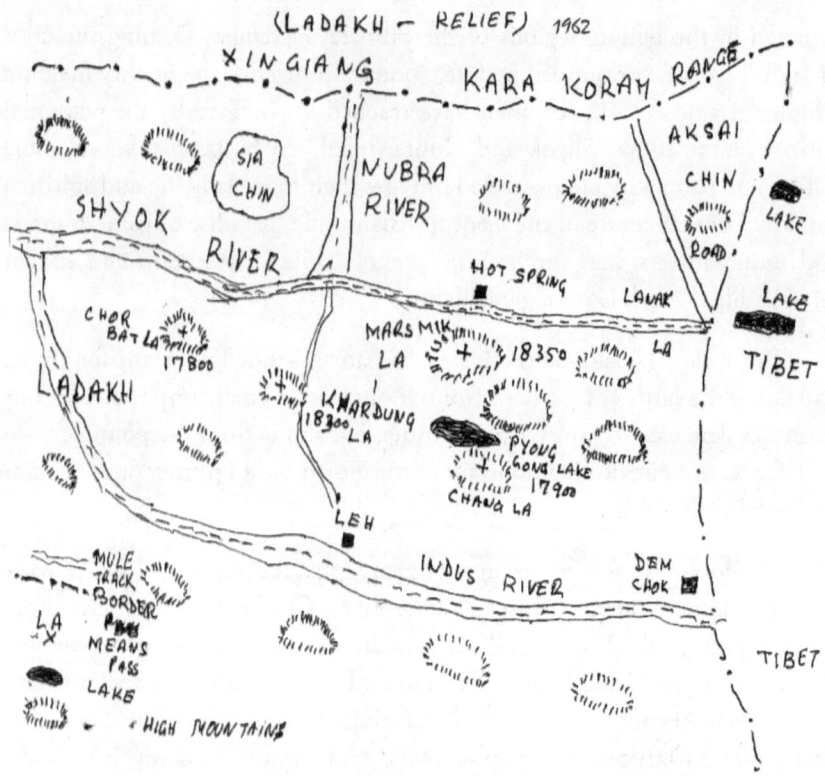

Ladakh is a far flung area and is cut off from the rest of India by lofty mountain ranges. Any commander who has to operate in this area is likely to be a part civil head as well during the operations due to the special characteristics of this area. He will be called upon to make timely political or economic decisions and his relations with the people of Ladakh as well as their leaders will have a great bearing on the conduct of the operations. He cannot possibly tackle these problems unless he has a good knowledge of Ladakh as well as its inhabitants. It has been endeavoured to give a fairly comprehensive picture of Ladakh and its various aspects in this small book. If in times to come, India is again called upon to defend Ladakh from any foreign aggressor, I would venture to state that the study of this hand book by any commander who has to operate in this area is quite likely to be of some use to him.

I wrote this book essentially in 1952-53, when posted in Ladakh as the Army Headquarters Liaison Officer. Readers may place this context, of having written this book in 1953 as a very young officer, while reading the book, a later day context and framework has been brought in too and maybe perused, and its evolution in the military context understood. The chapters and content – especially Chapters I to VII are as I essentially wrote then, in 1953 except for minor editing. I have added some inputs in Chapter VIII and then added some chapters to highlight the progression of events in this sensitive region. Readers may note I have added the 1962 chapter specially to highlight the continuity in military importance of this vital region.

This book is essentially an observation of Ladakh in the early nineteen fifties, after tracing its social evolution from ancient times. I interacted with the local lamas, the elders and the educated amongst the people to trace their roots and habits and culture. Hopefully, this would be found to be a useful input by those engaged in such pursuits.

The nature of my posting enabled me to move amongst the then elite in Ladakh and observe this regions societal structure and socio economic aspects. A simple hospitable people, the people of Ladakh were still grasping way back then the developments around them. I made many friendships; the one I treasure to this day is my friendship and interaction with the Reverend / His Holiness Kushak Bakula, the Ex Head Lama. With him I have discussed mysticism, Buddhism, the characteristics of Buddhism in Ladakh, the political developments etc. It was a major learning experience for me. I also stuck up friendships with the Moravian Mission, specially the heads, the Driver Couple. Mr. Sonam Norbu, the engineer who constructed the Leh Airfield was another. The Army HQ's sanctioned me a generous allowance in those days for a servant, I offered it on arrival to one person, and he said the entire family would work in that money. This was the poverty and simplicity.

I also went out on a major long range reconnaissance patrol to the vital Aksai Chin Area. Incidentally, during the patrol I went off on a tangent to see the exotic wildlife (Snow Leopard and Wild Ass) and was cut off from my patrol party, in thickly falling snow I was debating on how to last the night or if I could last the night or would I have to shoot myself in case warranted. Luckily the patrol party was able to locate me.

I do hope readers would note I was a young Captain (Commissioned from the Indian Military Academy –IMA, at Independence), yet I endeavoured to make notes of what I saw, in as regards the society and specially during my long range patrol, the military aspects and the probable lines of attack by our enemies. Ladakh was then the epicenter of conspiracies, rumours and the Great Game was very much on. It was a serene place in the 1950s, but only apparently, as the local elite jockeyed for a place for Ladakh in a newly independent nation, while war either raged around them or its threat always remained. It was an exciting time to be there and to be intimately involved in the thrusts and counter thrusts. But alas, the issue of confidentiality constrains me from sharing some rather interesting episodes. This aspect to some extent did prevent me from writing this book earlier. However, I can share I took a Militia Officer to meet the Head Lama at Leh. The Head Lama called me aside and told me animatedly that the Militia Officer was not a Buddhist but posing as one. I disbelieved him and we even argued about it but later the militia officer was not identified as a Buddhist. Was it mysticism or previous knowledge, I never could tell.

As I look back, we were a handful of soldiers in 1950-52 where today a Corps Headquarters is located, much has changed, and much is still relevant. Interesting and informal were those times. Once the IAF flight did not come for a few days. I sent a signal to them stating weather was clear at Leh. They responded weather clear at your end does not mean it's clear at Jammu or Banihal Pass! Such were those days. Our dak and newspapers would be delivered by air. I would set the newspapers date wise and then read one newspaper a day starting from the earliest date available. Dakota flights were an adventure by themselves flying through the passes to Leh but that's another story.

We, soldiers, are more often than not disparagingly called "Block heads" by all and sundry. Of course, unlike men in profession such as medicine, science, arts and law, we cannot advertise ourselves for many good reasons, of which two are very significant. Firstly, in our attempt to blow our own trumpet we may disclose some facts, patterns or strategy that would give vital information to the potential enemy. Secondly our ideas can be tested only in the event of war and our judgments vindicated on a battle field. But just in

Introduction

order to prove that the word "Block Head is a misnomer, let me emphasise we do not crave for war, for certainly no doctor would pray for an epidemic to prove his worth in the medical profession. And thus, though we soldiers do not have a chance to advertise ourselves, we must study our profession which is as old as the dawn of history and not yet termed definitely by any one as an art or science. General Sir Charles Napier has rightly remarked "When in a post of responsibility he (the officer) has no time to read; and if he comes to such a post with an empty skull, it is then too late to fill it."

It is but natural that as one studies one is urged to give expression to the final result of his labour by putting it to words. This prompts many of us to attempt to write and then face criticism. But such criticism would do an author no harm; it only rids him of his complacency. This then, is the excuse, if an excuse is needed in the writing of this book.

Last, but not the least, I thank my family for encouraging me to write this book and share my knowledge and experience. My wife, Krishna has always been a pillar of support to me in all my ventures and always encouraged me to write, work and share whatever I would have studied and applied myself to. I thank Col Bedi for his observations and my son Dinesh K Kapila for reading it through. Last but definitely not the least, the staff at the Institute for The Blind are thanked sincerely for their invaluable support, specially Mr Pankaj Sharma.

Finally, as always, I pay tribute to my Regiment, The 11th Gorkha Rifles.

20 July 2016　　　　　　　　Maj Gen Rajendra Nath, PVSM (Retd.)
Chandigarh

PS – I have used units such as maunds, seers, feet, Fahrenheit, miles etc. These were the units in common usage at that time. One Maund is 100 Troy Pounds or 82.82 Pounds or 37.3242 Kgs. A Seer is 09331014 Kgs. A Mile is 1609 metres. A yard is 3 feet or 09144 metres. For Fahrenheit to Celsius Deduct 323, multiply by 5 and divide by 9. For Celsius to Fahrenheit, Multiply by 9, divide by 5 and add 32.

Chapter I

HISTORICAL BACKGROUND

It is said that man cannot get away from his past. The same way nations as well as peoples of different territories cannot break away from their past. In order to study the characteristics of any people, their capabilities and their attitude towards this ever changing world, it is essential to study their past history.

The Ladakh valley has been cut off from the rest of India by the lofty Himalayas. The communications between India and Ladakh are very remote indeed due to highly mountainous terrain, yet it is remarkable to note that contact between India and Ladakh has been very ancient. From Ashoka's time when the first Buddhist's monk came to Ladakh for spreading Buddhism, India has been in contact with Ladakh. The Buddhist monks from India were responsible for converting the Ladakhis to Buddhists. These monks came to Ladakh via Kashmir. However, Buddhism did not remain prominent in India for long time and Hinduism again became predominant. But while Buddhism gradually disappeared from India as well as Kashmir, it has been and still is the predominant religion of Ladakh. After 10th century AD, Kashmir started coming under the sway of Islam. Consequently one finds that the cultural relations between Ladakh and rest of India have not been so strong after 11th century AD. On the contrary Tibet has been a Buddhist country ever since the Indian monks spread Buddhism there dating from Ashoka's time. The Ladakhi's after finding that Buddhism has completely disappeared from Kashmir while it no longer occupied any important position in India either, started having closer cultural relations with Tibet after 10th century AD. The nearness of Tibet might have also been a factor in bringing closer cultural relations between the two regions or nations (as they were then). At present one therefore finds that the present Buddhism of Ladakh has been affected by Lamaism of Tibet. All the Lamas of Ladakh used to go to Tibet for getting their religious education till 1950 when China occupied Tibet and this practice came to an end.

Sources of Information

The sources of information from which one can compile the history of Ladakh are of two kinds; some are foreign and some from Ladakh itself. The latter are of a twofold character. We possess records on stone as well as on paper. Of the former, which cover the period from 200 BC to 1400 AD, only comparatively little has become known up to the present, the reason being that systematic and thorough research in that domain has not yet been made. However, the whole area of Ladakh is full of old remains of 'Chortens', 'Manas', Monastries and other carvings on the stone that throw ample light on its past history. As regards the records on paper, although what is probably the most important work, the chronicles of Kings of Leh (Ladakh) have been edited, much still remains to be done. However, one finds that from 900 AD onwards, the chronicles of the kings of Leh (Ladakh) throw ample light and one can get continuous chronology of events up to the present times. The character of these chronicles is not the same during the different periods it describes. Its most ancient part can hardly be called a history, nor was it apparently meant to be such. It was begun as a pedigree of the kings of Leh, whose chief intention was to prove their descent from the famous line of the ancient kings of Lhasa. Thus the first portion of the work covering roughly the period of 900-1400 AD does not contain much besides mere names. About the year 1400 the account begins to become fuller. Still these accounts leave much to be desired. The writers were 'Lamas', and to them the greatest events during the reign of a king were his presents to 'Lamas' and monasteries or his construction of 'Chortens' and 'Mana' walls. Much ink has been expended on these events, while the campaigns of the kings are treated with extraordinary brevity and of their economic work we hear almost nothing. Thus we see that all these points which go to make a history of the country are missing and yet the native tone of the Ladakhi historians has often a charm of its own.

The other important source is the foreign travellers or writers. Of these Herodotus, Megasthenes, Hieun Tsang and Ctesias are famous and their accounts throw ample light on the past events of Ladakh. Besides the books like *Rajatarangini* and the accounts of Tsing dynasty of China also help in throwing some light on the past history of Ladakh.

An important question is this; are the accounts accurate and state the actual , or is the account distorted partly or wholly, as it often happens. The best test of the veracity of an historical account is its comparison with other entirely independent documents. Only in a very few cases are we able to compare the Ladakhi account of an event with that of a foreign country. In this connection, of great importance are the many inscriptions on rock and stone which are scattered all over the area and enable us to cross-check the events as enumerated in the various chronicles.

Early Inhabitants

The early inhabitants of Ladakh were undoubtedly nomads, who were not civilized as judged from the present standards. They moved from Ladakh into what is now known as Western Tibet and vice versa. There were no villages and no settled life existed. The people were satisfied by leading their simple life. They kept flocks of sheep and goats and that was their chief means of livelihood. They often hunted wild sheep and goats which were found in plenty in this area at that time. Even now the wild goats and sheep are to be found in many parts of Ladakh. They did not believe in any religion as such which exists in the world today. It is quite reasonable to believe that they believed in their own customs which were very strange and queer as per present standards and norms. Since the people were leading a nomadic life, the customs varied from one tribe to another. They wore clothes made out of the sheep or goat skin, while meat and milk were their chief items of food. They lived in tents of yak-hair and utilized the produce of their numerous herds of yaks in multifarious ways.

Their life probably in no way differed from that of Tibetan nomads of the present day. These ancient people had probably the poetical instinct as strongly marked as their children today, and similar songs to the one given here may have sounded through the valleys and hills of ancient Ladakh. A maiden tending flocks on a mountain side sings across the valley to a youth similarly employed (the translation is mine) :-

"In the meadow, in the meadow, in the higher meadow blows
Oh listen, lad, oh listen to my song
A flower, far the sweetest that in field and garden grows
Oh listen, lad, oh listen to my song

Thou mayest kill the flower, sweet-heart,
Thou mayest kill the tender flower
But thou shalt not grasp it rudely in thy hand
Else it will wither in a moment, it will perish in an hour
If thou, ruthless, dare to seize it in thy hand."

The Present Inhabitants

The present population of Ladakh is the result of a long process of blending of atleast three distinct peoples, two of which are of Aryan stock, whilst one which is numerically superior to the other two, is of Mongol origin. The Aryan communities located in regions (then nations) are: the Dards of Gilgit, and the Mons of North India (most probably from Kashmir). The Mongolian is of Tibetan Region / nation. The irrigable valleys of Ladakh were brought under cultivation by the Aryan tribes of Mons and Dards, and the latter especially exhibited an extraordinary skill in the construction of water courses along almost inaccessible cliffs. The products of the fields were as welcome to the Ladakhi nomads as were the produce of the flocks to the Dard peasants, and the lively barter which took place between the two tribes apparently led to many matrimonial alliances as well. So a race evolved which combined the agriculturist and the nomad. What is beautiful, to our perspective, in the features of the present Ladakhis is due to their half-Dard origin.

Spread of Buddhism

It is known from tradition that Emperor Ashoka held the third Buddhist Council at Pataliputra in about 250 BC. It was resolved in that council to send Buddhist missionaries to Kashmir, Tibet, and central Asian countries. Buddhism got such a firm hold in Kashmir that the fourth legendary council, under King Kanishka (125-152 AD) is said to have been held at Jalandara in Kashmir. Either after the third or the fourth council, Buddhism must have been carried to Ladakh and Western Tibet. The strongest proof of the colonization of Ladakh area by ancient Indians are inscriptions in Brahmi characters of about 200 BC which are found in Zanskar (now west of Ladakh) area. Among the ruins of Zangskar one discovers imposing remains of ancient Buddhist art, and more and the more one is convinced that the settlements of the ancient Mons in Zangskar and Ladakh area must have had some connection with the pre-Lamaist Buddhism.

It is interesting and important to note that the religious mission of the Buddhist preachers from India was not only to convert the local inhabitants to Buddhists but it was also an economic mission to better their lot and thus civilize the wandering nomads. Hence this mission was a civilizing and colonizing mission as well. It would have been well-nigh impossible to influence the wandering nomads without founding centres of Buddhist teaching with temples and monasteries. The almost empty land attracted more and more colonists, and the religious settlements grew into villages and towns in course of time. This is why that almost all the large villages and towns in Ladakh valley are situated near the monasteries. That is also the main reason as to why Buddhism which is now a form of Lamaism is so deeply rooted among its inhabitants. The conversion of the wandering nomads into settled Buddhists took centuries and was accentuated by the arrival of Mons and Dards.

The Arrival of The Mons

Though the exact date of the arrival of the Mons into Ladakh cannot be given, it is reasonably accurate to estimate the movement started in about 200 BC. The Mons were residents of North India probably of Kashmir. Some of them are stated to have come as Buddhist preachers. In many villages of Ladakh one finds one or several families who are called Mon. They are treated with little respect by the rest of the population. Their low position makes many observers believe that they belong to a nation or community, originally different from the Tibetans, who were conquered in former days. But to find out who the Mons really were is impossible in most parts of Ladakh, because after the settlement of Mons, and before the arrival of the Central Tibetans, the migration of the Dards took place, and thus the recollection of the people has been obscured. It seems that influence of the Mons was dominant in Western part of Ladakh. Zangskar was probably a great centre of Mons culture in ancient times. Even now one finds numerous ruins of monasteries as well as carvings on the rocks in Brahmi language. The main mission of the Mons was to settle the wandering nomads into small settlements / villages and then try to convert them into Buddhism.

The Migration of the Dards

Although the Mons had, besides preaching Buddhism, founded villages and towns in the almost desert like Ladakh, much arable ground remained uninhabited. This fact was recognized by the Dards of Gilgit.

As already stated Dards were an Aryan tribe, inhabiting the areas round about the present Gilgit. The migration of the Dards took place in about 100 AD. It is quite possible that the colonization of Ladakh by the Mons and the Dards met with little or no opposition from the Tibetan nomads, because their interests lay in different directions; and although a few irrigated plains were occupied by these Aryans, there remained ample pasture-ground for the flocks of the nomads. But it is possible as per accounts that hostilities sprang up occasionally between the Dards and the Mons and that the Mons were subdued in this struggle. Otherwise, it is hardly possible to explain why the position of the Mons in the social hierarchy became so much lower than that of the Dards.

Although no written records of the Dards of Ladakh have been found as yet, we know a great deal more about them than we know of the Mons. This is principally due to the fact that a certain number of them have not yet lost their language, and have withstood the tide of the Tibetan culture that has swept over them. There are two tribes of Dards still existing in the territories of the former Ladakhi kingdom who have preserved their original language. They are the Dards of Dras and the Dards of Da. Those of Dras became Mohammedans about three and a half centuries ago and in consequence most of their original customs and folk lore have been stamped out. Those of Da have become neither Muslims nor have they accepted Lamaism wholeheartedly and thus much of their originality has been preserved. We learn that the Dards were a well built and a warrior tribe. At one time they dominated almost the whole of Ladakh valley, and one can ask with astonishment how it is that they disappeared entirely from most parts of Ladakh. It is not likely that a nation whom Herodotus called the most warlike of all Indians, should have given in very easily to the later attacks of the Central Tibetans and there are tales which speak of the stubborn resistance put up by the Dards.

As regards the religion of the ancient Dards, it was probably the form of Buddhism which was prevalent in the days of immigration at Gilgit. The many stone images without dates which are found all over Ladakh testify to this, and many of them show a particularly strong resemblance of those found near Gilgit. The Dards were very famous for their sports and they are considered as the originators of 'Polo' as a game in this part of the country – probably they were the first to introduce this game in India. However, by the end of sixth century AD the opposition of the Dards had been completely crushed by the Tibetans who had become dominant once again. Unfortunately, though tried for; no historical account or trace or ancient lore is available of a major battle between the Tibetans and the Dards.

The Chinese Occupation of Western Tibet About 600 -760 AD

Though it is stated that the Tibetans were once more dominant in Ladakh by the end of sixth century AD, there are no records available giving any information as to any king ruling over Ladakh or even of any small kingdom. During the seventh and eight centuries AD, several Chinese Buddhists made pilgrimages to the famous Buddhist shrines of North India. The diaries kept by the Chinese Pilgrims on their Indian tours are of the highest value for the study of ancient Indian geography and archeology. Unfortunately, none of them talks about Ladakh in their accounts. However, these references do throw some light on the events that were taking place in Ladakh at that time. Further information regarding Ladakh from Chinese sources is contained in the annals of the Tang dynasty. Those were the days when the Tibetans pushed on towards the West with a great amount of energy. The Chinese claim that during the reign of the Tang dynasty, Turkistan, Ladakh and even Kashmir became a part of the Celestial Empire. But there are no records available to prove the Chinese claim which seems to be rather highly exaggerated and factually inaccurate. Later many small kingdoms of Dards evolved in Western Ladakh, while the Eastern Ladakh region was under Ladakhi Kings. The chronicles of Ladakh make the following remarks about the political state of affairs existing in Ladakh at that time. "At that time Upper Ladakh was held by the descent of Qesar (Kesar), whilst Lower Ladakh was split up into various independent principalities." At Leh there reigned a dynasty of kings who derived their origin from the mythical King Kesar while at Saspool, about 40 miles West of Leh, King Bandel ruled; he constructed the ancient fort of Alchi Kargog. At Khalatsi (the modern Khalsi) a dynasty of Dard kings ruled. The Dard tribes had independent principalities at Da, Garkunu and Lamayaru. There was continuous warfare between these petty kingdoms; particularly difficult were the harvest seasons. It is, however, astonishing to find that even in those unsafe times trade was carried on through Ladakh between India and Sinkiang (now named Xinjiang by the Chinese).

In that period there were two religions co-existent in Ladakh: Buddhism and Bonchos. Bonchos was the age old religion of the Tibetans which was entirely different from Buddhism. Buddhism had entered the region by two channels; the ancient Mons had brought it from India (Kashmir) and the

Dards from Gilgit. During this period Buddhism was strengthened by the emigration of many Buddhist monks from mainly Kashmir and also other parts of India.

The Start of The Western Tibetan Dynasty (About 900-1400 AD)

In most of the inscriptions, the Ladakhi kings call themselves "Descendents of Nyatril Tsanpo", the first king of Tibet, whose reign is placed about 200 or 300 BC. According to the Ladakhi chronicles, the following kings ruled over Ladakh during 900 and 1400 AD:-

S. No.	Name of the King	Period
1.	Lang Darma	(925 – 950 AD)
2.	Ldep Al Kortsan	(950 - 975 AD)
3.	Skyid Ide Nyima Gon	975 – 1000 AD
4.	Lha Chen Gon	1000 – 1025 AD
5.	Dro Gon	1025 – 1050 AD
6.	Lha Chen Dragspa Lde	1050 – 1075 AD
7.	Lha Chen Jang Chub Semspa	1075 – 1100 AD
8.	Lha Chen Rgyalpo	1100 – 1125 AD
9.	Lha Chen Utpala	1125 – 1150 AD
10.	Lha Chen Naglug	1150 – 1175 AD
11.	Lha Chen Gebhe	1175 – 1200 AD
12.	Lha Chen Joldor	1200 – 1225 AD
13.	Trashis Gon	1225 – 1250 AD
14.	Lhargyal	1250 – 1275 AD
15.	Lha Chen Jopal	1275 – 1300 AD
16.	Lha Chen Ngorub	1300 – 1325 AD
17.	Lha Chen Gyalbu Rinchen	1325 – 1350 AD
18.	Lha Chen Shesrab	1350 – 1375 AD

During this period Buddhism spread throughout Ladakh and the Kings spent quite some time of their reigns (and funds) in constructing 'Mana' walls and 'Chortens'. But the most important event of this period is that the authority of Lhasa in Tibet as we know now became paramount in Ladakh. Without the authority of Lhasa nothing of importance could be done in Ladakh. So we find that national literature (i.e. specific to the region of Ladakh), with few exceptions, is not found in Ladakh.

Work of Great Reformer Tsongkapa (1400 – 1580 AD)

The period from 1400 – 1500 AD is well known due to the activities of the great reformer Tsongkapa. The kings of Ladakh from 1400 -1580 AD are hardly heard of as Tsongkapa supersedes everybody. Tsongkapa lived in Tibet from 1378 to 1441 AD. He found the Buddhism of Tibet in a rotten state, and determined to reform it. He sat down to study the writings of the founder of this religion, and soon discovered that there were great discrepancies between what ought to have been and the actual facts. It was due to his efforts that some 'Lamas' started wearing the Yellow dress instead of the Red one. He also tried to raise the morals of the monks to the same standard as that of the Indian Buddhist monks, but their morals could be raised only as high as public opinion would permit them to be. The Kings of Ladakh under his influence erected the famous monasteries of Spitok near Leh, Sangkar and Phiang also near Leh, and the Trigtse monastery about 12 miles away from Leh on the Indus. The Kings of Ladakh under the influence of the great reformer stopped the killing of animals. The edict of Mulbe runs as follows:-

> "Oh Lama (Tsongkapa), take notice of this:
> The king of faith, Bhum Ide, having seen the
> fruit of works in the future life, gives order
> to the men of Mulbe to abolish, above all, the
> living sacrifices, and greets the Lama. The
> living sacrifices are abolished."

King Trashi (1500 – 1530 AD) made the rule regarding the number of children that were to be sent by every village to become 'Lamas' (monks). According to this rule, every family of more than one or two male children had to give up one, not the eldest however, to be made a 'Lama'. Now that this rule is no longer compulsory, there has been a great falling off in the number of 'Lamas'. During this period, King Bhagan also ruled, who was the founder of the Namgyal dynasty which lasted till 19th century when it was finally wiped out by General Zorawar Singh.

The Balti Wars (1560 – 1640 AD)

The population of Baltistan as well as the rest of Western Tibet consists of Aryan and to some extent Tibetan elements also. The Balti is, as history proves, rather warlike than the average Western Tibetan. He is quicker in adopting new methods and is altogether more alert. The Balti can also rightly pride himself on having an ancient alphabet running from right to left.

The Baltis were the first among the Buddhists who became Muslims. Although there is no record to go by, General Sir Cunningham states that this change of religion took place sometime about 1400 AD. The first battle between the Ladakhis and the Baltis took place in the reign of Jamyang Namgyal (1560 – 1590 AD). Although the Ladakhis fought well, the Baltis carried the day. The Baltis being Muslims, destroyed as per their beliefs quite a few monasteries in and around Leh after their victory. However, there was a settlement between the conquerors and the conquered which is unique in history. The daughter of the Balti King was married to Jamyang Namgyal and the Ladakhi kingdom was left intact. It seems that the main idea of the Balti king was to spread Islam in Ladakh valley by this strange settlement. However, this attempt did not achieve much by way of the spread of Islam, though a few Ladakhis did embrace Islam. The following kings ruled over Ladakh during this period:-

Tsewang Namgyal	(1560 – 1590 AD)
Sengge	(1590 – 1620 AD)
Deldan Namgyal	(1620 – 1640 AD)

Although the Baltis had snatched the portions of Gilgit and Baltistan, yet the extent of the kingdom was fairly large. It is very important to note that the Kingdom of Ladakh embraced quite a large portion of what is at present known as Western Tibet. In other words, the history of Western Tibet is closely connected and interwoven with Ladakh. Actually there was no formal border between the two regions.

Namgyal Dynasty (1640 – 1834 AD)

Though the kings of the Namgyal dynasty were ruling over Ladakh as far back as 1560 AD and also during the Balti Wars, yet according to the Ladakhi chronicles the true Namgyal dynasty starts from 1640 AD. The following

HISTORICAL BACKGROUND

Kings ruled over Ladakh during the periods as shown against them:-

Delegs Namgyal	(1640 -1680 AD)
Nyima Namgyal	(1680 – 1720 AD)
Deskyong Namgyal	(1720 – 1740 AD)
Puntsog Namgyal	(1740 – 1760 AD)
Tsewang Namgyal II	(1760 – 1780 AD)
Tsentan Namgyal	(1780 – 1823 AD)
Tsepal Namgyal	(1823 – 1840 AD)

The period of Namgyal dynasty is full of wars which were fought either against the Tibetans or the Muslims. During the reign of Delegs Namgyal (1640 – 1680 AD), the Mongol Army under Gushri Khan seized the whole of Mongolia and Tibet and he thus became king of United Mongolia – Central Tibet. Later on the Tibetan Army under Tsang and with the support of the Mongolian forces attacked Ladakh. Leh was soon over-run and Delegs Namgyal requested the Nawab of Kashmir who after obtaining permission from the Moghul Emperor Shah Jehan, sent an army of 6,000 to help the Ladakhi King against the Tibetans. The combined forces of the Moghuls and the Ladakhis defeated the Tibetans and the Tibetan forces retired eastward. The Tibetans, however, did not retire much but encamped near Pyongong Lake. As soon as the Moghul Army retired to Kashmir, the Tibetans again swooped down upon Ladakh. Deleg Namgyal after offering resistance was forced to make peace with the Tibetans. The terms of the settlement offered by the Tibetans were as hard as the Moghuls had offered before coming to the aid of the Ladakhis. However, there was not much choice and the Ladakhis had to submit to the Tibetan demands. Some of the important terms of the settlement are written below:-

(a) An attempt will be made to define boundary between Ladakh and Tibet along the line of Lhari stream near the Pyong Gong lake.

(b) The king of Ladakh shall send once in three years a mission conveying presents to the clergy of Tibet. On the other hand, the Government of Tibet shall send every year a trade mission to Ladakh carrying 200 loads of brick-tea. This custom strangely enough continued till the 19th century. Though ever since the start of J&K Operations in

1947-48, the people of Ladakh have not been able to send any trade mission to Lhasa due to disturbed conditions, the Government of Tibet sends its trade mission every year. I interrogated the leader of the Tibetan trade mission in January 1952 when he came to Ladakh with Lhasa tea, the stipulated practice much in the same way as was done in the year of 1680 AD. Customs in this strange and charming land change but little. However, this custom came to an end after 1952.

Looking at the kings of this period, the thought cannot be avoided that the dynasty was on the decline. Not one of the kings of this period was great as a warrior or as a politician or a good organizer. Still, judging from the extraordinary multitude of documents on stone referring to these kings, the people of Ladakh seem to have been wonderfully loyal and devoted. A beautiful feeling of loyalty finds expression in the following song:-

> "On the hill in the back there is the 'Chorten' of white crystal;
>
> In the front there is the lake, blue like a turquoise.
>
> On the shore flowers are in bloom.
>
> They grow in my fatherland together with its fortune.
>
> On the shore large yellow flowers are in bloom.
>
> In the castle of Sheh the milk flows.
>
> On the high summit there lives
>
> The eloquent God of the summit
>
> Wherever our gracious prince goes
>
> Oh God, protect his life:
>
> To Deskyong Namgyal, the future Lord of men
>
> Give blessing during his life time."

The Spread of Islam in Ladakh

It is generally said that Islam has usually spread through sword rather than by preaching. Ladakh valley was no exception. The Baltis after defeating King Jamyang Namgyal (1560 – 1590 AD) ransacked the whole of Ladakh. Some of the Buddhist 'Chortens', 'Mana' walls and monasteries were destroyed. Some conversions also took place. Later when the Tibetans attacked Ladakh in the reign of Delegs Namgyal (1640 – 1680 AD) the Ladakhi king was forced to ask the Nawab of Kashmir for help. The Moghul Emperor Shah Jehan ordered his Nawab of Kashmir to help the Ladakhi king but only at very costly terms. The Ladakhi king had to agree to the construction of mosques and give special facilities to the Muslims or to those Buddhists who embraced Islam. Thus the Islam spread in Ladakh. However, due to the greater influence of the Tibetans, Islam as a religion did not have an appreciable effect in Eastern Ladakh and slowly the number of Muslims in Eastern parts of Ladakh diminished. However, in the Western parts, it is paramount.

Fall of Ladakh Kingdom

Tsepal Namgyal (1823 – 1840 AD) was the last independent king of Ladakh. However, he was not considered a capable king. During this period far more important changes were taking place across the Zojila Pass. Maharaja Ranjit Singh, "The Lion of the Punjab", had captured Kashmir with the assistance of Gulab Singh, who was King of Jammu. Jammu was and still is the strong hold of the Dogra tribe. Gulab Singh who was under Maharaja Ranjit Singh decided to enlarge the kingdom which then was restricted to Jammu-Kashmir area. That the Dogra Chief had directed his attention to Ladakh was probably due to the revelation of Tsepal's careless policy. The Dogras were superior to the Ladakhis in that they had better equipment and their participation in several Indian wars had taught them better tactics and discipline. The Ladakhis, on the other hand, had equipment which was many centuries old. However, they had the advantage of severe cold which was certain to reduce the usefulness of the Dogra warriors while the barrenness of the country prohibited the mobilization of a large army.

Dogra – Ladakhi Wars

Gulab Singh sent his famous General Zorawar Singh with about 10,000 men to capture Ladakh through Kishtwar. On 16 August, 1834 Zorawar Singh was opposed for the first time by a Ladakhi force of about 5,000 strong which had been mobilized in haste. It is interesting to note as to how the Ladakhi army was raised at that time. Since the days of Senge Namgyal under whom fire-arms are mentioned for the first time, every household was furnished with a match lock. This old weapon and a certain supply of powder had to be kept in readiness for times of war. When the call to arms was sent around the country, one man with the match lock had to come from every house, carrying on his back provisions to last him for a whole month (chiefly parched grain) and blankets for the night. This load was so heavy that the mobility of the army was considerably impeded by it. There was no artillery. Cavalry it would have been easy to raise, but it was not of much use in the mountainous country. It will be fitting here to cite an ancient "Call to Arms". In this even the women are called to battle and the Ladakhi folk-lore speaks of several women who were able to fight, though in history we do not find any such example. The folk-lore runs as follows:-

> "Thou host of the heaven, come to the fight
>
> And Wangpo Gyabzhin be at thy head:
>
> Thou host of the earth, come to the fight,
>
> And Mother Skybdun be at thy head:
>
> Thou host of waters, come to the fight,
>
> And Water-King Ljogpo be at thy head:
>
> At the head of the heroes of Ling, Palle must ride;
>
> At the head of the Women of Ling, Astag must ride;
>
> You boys who know to use the sling, go to the war;
>
> You girls who know how to use the spindle, go to the war;
>
> March off then towards the land of Hor,
>
> And the king shall march in front of you:"

However, the folk-lore does indicate the sense of patriotism and warrior spirit of the inhabitants. The Ladakhis are good fighters and make for capable warriors, this I did observe in the time spent there.

The Battle of Sanku (1834 AD)

The Ladakhi force numbering about 5,000 had entrenched itself on a hill near Sanku. The Dogra army numbering about 10,000 charged the position. The Ladakhi army defended the position with much vigour for the whole day. Unfortunately, with their very old match locks, they could not do much harm to the storming Dogras. By the evening, the Dogras had over-run many of the Ladakhi positions and consequently the Ladakhis were forced to retire at night. The Ladakhi army thus after the day long fight at Sanku retired during the night across the Russi Pass to Shergol where they halted for eight days.

Thereafter the Ladakhi army continued its retreat Eastward without offering serious opposition to the Dogras till it reached the plains of Pashkyun.

Battle of Pashkyun (1834 AD)

By the time the Ladakhi army reached the plains of Pashkyun, it was expecting reinforcements. The old king had sent his ministers Ngorub and Bangkapa to mobilize all those districts which had not yet sent any warriors, and now a force of about 4,000 men was advancing towards Pashkyun to help the Ladakhi troops already encamping there. However, without waiting for the reinforcements, the young minister of Stog who was in charge of Ladakhi force at Pashkyun attacked the Dorga force. Fierce fighting took place and the fortunes of the day were almost on the side of the Ladakhis when their brave young Captain - the Minister of Stog – was suddenly struck by a musket ball and died. This was for the Ladakhis, superstitious as they are; a signal for a general flight. The Dogras were thus the undisputed winners of the day.

The Battle of Lankartse (1835 AD)

After the battle of Pashkyun, the Dogra army under Zorawar Singh had retired Westwards to seek a place for shelter for the coming winter. The Ladakhis on the other hand did nothing to molest the Dogra army encamping at Lankartse, though it was their opportunity as the Dogras were not in a position to offer any serious resistance in the terrible winter to which they were not used to. However, early in the spring the Ladakhis decided to attack Zorawar Singh. This attempt of theirs was not successful and Zorawar Singh easily beat off their attack. The Ladakhi army was once again obliged to retreat Eastwards – this time with less hopes of stopping the Dogras anymore. The Dogra army under Zorawar Singh then advanced Eastward.

The Treaty of Leh (1835)

The king Tsepal seeing the uselessness of any more resistance requested Zorawar Singh for peace terms when he met him at Basgo – 22 miles West of Leh. However, the treaty was signed at Leh by which the whole of Ladakh came under the Dogras and King Tsepal became a vassal king under Gulab Singh. The Ladakhis rebelled many times against their Dogra masters but each time they were put down with iron hand. Zorawar Singh was always there to do the needful. So thus ended finally the free state of Ladakh once and for all. The Ladakhis have been ruled since then by kingdoms from outside the region, firstly under the Dogras and later on under the British though technically still remaining under the Maharaja of Jammu and Kashmir.

The last nominal king of Ladakh was Kunzang Namgyal. He was 27 years old and was then serving in the 7 J&K Militia as Lieutenant in an honorary capacity when I met him in 1952, at Leh. I found him a thorough gentleman.

"REMNANT GLORY OF LADAKH"
KING KUNZANG NAMGYAL
LAST NOMINAL KING OF LADAKH (1952)

Buddhism of Ladakh

It is of interest to refer here a word about the Buddhism of Ladakh. Really speaking the Buddhism of Ladakh at present is not close to ideals of Buddhist religion. Except for 'Chortens', 'Mana' walls and the statues of Buddha, there is nothing which shows the presence of Buddhism in the country, actually it is Lamaism that is in existence. The influence of 'Lamas' who in the past strictly followed the rituals of 'Lamas' of Lhasa is paramount. The present religion is a complicated system of rituals and hardly follows any principles as laid down by The Buddha. The 'Lamas' who in the past got their education in Lhasa were the religious heads. Now a day's all Lamas get their religious teaching in Ladakh itself from senior Lamas. Every big village now has got its own 'Lama' who gives decisions on religious matters. The monasteries have got lands where the peasants work but the large portion of produce goes to the monastery. Since there is no king nor is there any other important personality in Ladakh to guide the people, the 'Lamas' have got a great hold over the people. The Lamas not only work as religious heads but some of them are now also acting as political as well as administrative heads. However, slowly the Lamas are losing their hold over the Buddhist population.

Ladakhis As Warriors

It will not be out of place if we try to analyze the qualities of Ladakhis as warriors. From about fourth century AD till about the beginning of nineteenth century, historical records indicate that the Ladakhis have been leading an almost free and independent life but for short periods when the foreigners were able to subdue them. However, the foreign domination did not last long. It may be said that due to the lack of communications, shortage of supplies or due to the adverse weather conditions the foreigners were never able to keep their hold over Ladakh for any appreciable time. However, it must go to the credit of the patriotic spirit and ability of the Ladakhis to wage war for their liberty that they kept all foreigners at bay. For unless they had the spirit to fight, they could not possibly keep all foreigners at bay. On the other hand, we find that the Ladakhi kingdom in fifteenth century consisted of a large portion of Western Tibet as well. All this goes to prove that the Ladakhis had been good fighters in the past. The border between Ladakh and Western Tibet has seldom been defined on the ground. It was only after the British took over J&K state and Ladakh that the border was provisionally marked on the maps.

However, while analyzing the character of an average Ladakhi of the present day one finds that he is a very humble, over courteous and a docile person. It seems from his looks as well as behaviour that he is a very peace loving and contented person who just wants to lead his life as comfortable as ever, having no concern with the outside world. One very seldom witnesses any big fight amongst the various tribes nor does one hear of any murder or dacoity taking place in Ladakh area. It seems rather strange that people who were good fighters only a century and a half ago should turn completely a new page of history and become so docile and peace loving creatures. A student of military history, however, cannot help seeking for the reasons which are responsible for bringing about such a drastic change. Below are put down certain important reasons which perhaps were responsible for bringing about this change.

Lethargic effect of Lamaism

When the Dogras had over-run Ladakh and the King of Ladakh had lost his power as well as respect, there was no leader left in the whole of Ladakh who could effectively control and guide the people. The result was that a big vacuum was created in the power structure. The uneducated, innocent and leaderless people had to look to somebody to guide their destiny. The 'Lamas' who had been uptil now only religious heads became leaders of Ladakhis and as already stated almost every big village in Ladakh area has got its own monastery and every monastery has got its own leadership for the people, this is because every big village had to depend upon itself for its improvement and the settlement of law and order as also economic problems. The 'Lamas' fully understood this position and with religious sanction behind them, they started becoming political as well as administrative heads. The leaderless people badly needed somebody to guide them and but for 'Lamas' who were the religious heads as well, there was nobody else who could fill this power vacuum. Consequently the whole of Ladakh was divided into small principalities where the 'Lamas' held supreme power. The 'Lamas' had consequently been the virtual local rulers for the past century and a quarter. The whole of the Ladakh area was thus administratively run almost on the same lines as Tibet. The people hardly went to the courts. Besides the Maharaja of Jammu and Kashmir never had much administrative staff in Ladakh area and all their problems were decided by the local 'Lamas'. Besides the Dogra rulers never recruited Ladakhis in their army.

Long Era of Undisturbed Peace

The Ladakhis fought their last wars against the Dogras in 1834. Ever since the Dogras became their masters thereafter, the Ladakhis never had the occasion nor the opportunity to fight. The British rule of over a century guaranteed perpetual peace. Besides, the Ladakhis were never recruited in the army by the Maharaja of Jammu & Kashmir nor by the British and consequently the people became peace loving and docile.

However, it does not mean that an average Ladakhi cannot become a good soldier or that he has lost the spirit to fight. The circumstances unfortunately have made him peace loving. The Ladakhis fought in a very brave and bold manner when Ladakh was attacked by the Gilgit Scouts of the Gilgit-Skardu area which was commanded by Pakistani officers in the 1947-48 Indo-Pak war. It came as a great surprise to many outsiders and many Buddhist Ladakhi soldiers earned high awards like the Maha Vir Chakra, Vir Chakra in the various battles in 1947-48 and 1965 war, as described in a later chapter.

Chapter II

GEOGRAPHICAL AND ECONOMIC SURVEY

Ladakh is a district of Jammu and Kashmir State. It used to comprise of 3 Tehsils – Leh, Kargil and Skardu. The Tehsil of Skardu is now in the hands of Pakistan while Kargil has become a separate district of J&K while the only one Tehsil now constitutes Leh district. Leh is the district headquarters of Ladakh. The total area of Ladakh is 21,080 square miles. Ladakh is one of the highest mountainous area in the world. The climate being more or less the same as that of a desert, the area can be rightly termed as a Mountain Desert. Next to Tibet, this is probably the highest area in the world where a substantial population exists. The average height of the area is nearly 11,000 feet above sea level and goes upto 18,000 feet. Consequently the area has got certain special characteristics of its own.

There are three important rivers which run through Ladakh, and along the valleys of these rivers are situated the important and most populated towns. These rivers are the Indus, the Shyok and the Nubra.

Ladakh is situated between Tibet, Sinkiang (Xinjiang), Kashmir valley and Himachal Pradesh, and consequently occupies an important strategic position. It is separated from Kashmir by the Zojila Pass, from Sinkiang (Xinjiang) by the Karakoram Pass, from Tibet by an undemarcated border on the ground.

Physical Features and Climate

It has become a trite opinion that the characteristics of a people are generally speaking moulded by the country and climate they live in. This is particularly true of Ladakhis and the land they inhabit has left deep impressions on their life and outlook.

The general aspect of Ladakh is extreme barrenness and if it were to be surveyed from the air, the county would appear a mere succession of yellow plains and barren mountains capped with everlasting snow, with lakes such as the Pong Gong appearing like bright oasis amidst a vast desert of rock and sand. Hardly any trace of men or human habitation would meet the eye and even the large patches of cultivated land and tiny hamlets nestling in the shelter of towering rocks would be but small specks on the mighty waste of deserted world. The yellow plains of the Indus would be seen covered with flocks of goats and sheep. A striking feature in the physical aspect of Ladakh is the parallelism of its mountain ranges which stretch through the country from South-East to North-West. The characteristics lie in the mountains determining the course of the rivers as well as the natural boundaries of the country. An important feature of Ladakh is Aksai Chin in the North-East and Sia Chin in the North-West.

HIGH MOUNTAINS IN NORTH LADAKH

On the North, Ladakh is separated by the Karakoram Mountains from the Chinese province of Sinkiang (Xinjiang). To the East and South-East are the Chinese Tibetan Districts of Rudok and Chumurti, and to the South are Lahaul and Spiti, now Himachal Pradesh. To the West lie Kashmir and Baltistan, the former separated by the Western Himalaya and the latter by an imaginary line drawn from the mouth of Dras River to the source of the Nubra River. The extreme length and breadth of the Ladakh District, however, are about 268 and 191 miles respectively. Its mean length and breadth may be taken at 170 and 124 miles respectively, and the total area about 21,080 square miles. After the 1962 war the area has been reduced due to Chinese occupation though officially the records state otherwise.

The climate of this region is dry and cold, the mean temperature of Leh in summer being 70-75 degrees Fahrenheit and in winter the mercury falls well below zero. Apart from a few showers of rain during the monsoon, precipitation comes in the form of snow, since the altitude of the region ranges from 10,000 to 11,000 feet above sea level. Owing to the intense process of evaporation, which goes on continually in high altitudes, one scarcely ever perspires. The air of the Indus valley is pure and clear, and in summer the rays of the sun are very hot and burn the skin in spite of the high altitude, but indoors the temperature remains very low. There may be a difference as great as 25 or 30 degrees Fahrenheit. At the same time the air is very dry, more so in the valley of Nubra. Atmospheric precipitation being low, the snow line is very high, about 17,000 feet or so.

The long and cold winter and the nature of soil affects the crops considerably. Where, however, there is an abundance of water through irrigation from rivers, and melting of accumulated snow, the crops are fairly good. On the other hand, the high altitude tends to make many of the peasants less assiduous in the cultivation of their crops than should be, and some proportion of the farming population puts in the minimum of personal effort into the cultivation of their holdings, leaving nature to do the rest.

One of the most remarkable phenomena of the area is its winds. They are caused by the high altitude of the area, the rarity of the air and the great mass of rugged mountains that easily get heated under clear sky. The heated air in the day time rises up towards the North and the Southern winds blow with tremendous velocity at times. This is mostly the case from April to October during which period crops mature and the peasant considers these winds favourable for fruit and crop.

Rivers

There are three important rivers in Ladakh. These rivers come from permanent glaciers and consequently are perennial rivers. These rivers are the Indus, the Shyok and the Nubra.

The Indus

This is the most important river of Ladakh. It comes from Western Tibet as its source is Mansarover Lake. It divides Ladakh almost in two equal halves. For a fairly long course through Ladakh, the river runs through rugged mountains and at places makes deep gorges. However, at places the river widens out and makes fairly wide valleys. Such wide valleys are to be found near Hemis, Leh and Nimu. The amount of water in the river is not much in winter but in summer, the water increases manifold due to the melting snows. The river is not navigable for most of its course and the local inhabitants do not possess any crafts either for purposes of navigation. In winter the surface of the river gets frozen for a greater length of its course and men and animals can easily go across. The Indus valley is the most important valley in Ladakh and all big towns are situated in this valley. The important towns along the river are Leh, Nimu, Saspool and Khalsi. After the river enters the Pakistan held Kashmir area, river Shyok joins it just before Skardu.

The Shyok

This is the second biggest river which flows through Ladakh and is an important tributary of the River Indus. Like the River Indus, the source of Shyok is also in Western Tibet. The river flows in the Northern part of Ladakh and runs almost parallel to the course of the River Indus. It is fairly big river and in summer melting snows increase its current manifold. The river runs through rugged mountains and at places makes deep gorges. It is not navigable for most of its course in Ladakh. It enters Pakistan held territory just after Biagdangdo and joins the Indus River near Skardu. Quite a few villages and important towns like Khalsar, Shyok and Biagdangdo are situated along the river. The river Nubra which is its most important tributary joins the River Shyok near Lughzhun.

The Nubra

This is the third biggest river in Ladakh and is the most important tributary of the Shyok River. Unlike the Indus and the Shyok rivers it does not run from East to West. On the contrary, it flows from North to South. Its source lies in the glaciers of Karakoram Range and consequently it is a perennial river. The Nubra Valley is an important valley as the route to Sinkiang goes along this valley. The river Nubra joins the Shyok River near Lughzhun.

Communications

Due to the mountainous terrain and the existence of high mountain barriers, the road system is less developed. In the past less importance was given to development of roads in Ladakh. But keeping in view its strategic importance, the development of better road systems not only in Ladakh but improvements in the road systems connecting Ladakh with Kashmir as well as Himachal Pradesh are required.

The road connecting Kargil with Leh is open throughout the year as both Fotula and Namikala Passes are negotiable during the winter season. However, the road from Leh to Himachal Pradesh remains closed for three months in the winter due to non completion of tunnel north of Manali in Himachal Pradesh. This is indeed unfortunate for proper efforts to construct the tunnel have not been made by the Government of India.

Similar is the case with the road connecting Kargil to Leh though not to such an extent. The two passes, namely, Fotula and Namikala are negotiable only with difficulty in winter season. However, this road remains open the whole year.

The climate of Zanskar being severe, it is accessible during short period only. The spring, summer and autumn together last little more than five months after which snow falls suspending its traffic and communication with different parts of the district. In the spring it causes avalanches to such an extent that the roads get blocked.

From all sides the approach to Zanskar, placed as it is in a maze of mountains, is with considerable difficulty. To the South-East of it the snowy range makes a barrier to cross which is a dangerous business. From the North-West and South-East, roads lead in from Suru and Rupshu respectively, to traverse which is comparatively less difficult but these lead over long uninhabited tracks. That way, communication with Leh by the valley of the Zanskar River is quite impassable, except when the winter frost makes a road over the waters of the river. Likewise, the roads connecting Leh to Nubra and Pyong Gong Lake area remain closed down owing to heavy snow-falls and avalanches rolling down the mountains in winter.

Various mule tracks connecting Leh with adjoining places are described below which have been used for centuries are described for information only as in 1952- 1953:-

Geographical and Economic Survey

Stage	Height	Distance
Route no. 1 – Leh to (Sinkiang) Xingjiang (Winter route in 1953)		
Leh	11,500 ft	
Digar Pulu	15,200 ft	13 miles
Digar	13,080 ft	14 miles
Agham	10,500 ft	8 miles
Pakra	11,000 ft	12 miles
Chimchak	11,600 ft	10 miles
Shyok	12,140 ft	8 miles
Chhong Jangal	11,950 ft	18 miles
Dang Yailak	12,230 ft	18 miles
Yargulak	12,950 ft	20 miles
Kataklik	13,900 ft	18 miles
Sultan Chushku	14,200 ft	15 miles
Kumdun	15,000 ft	18 miles
Gapshan	15,000 ft	9 miles
Karakoram Polu (Pass)	16,900 ft Pass 18,300 ft	18 miles
Balti Brangsa	Xinjiang	20 miles
Baksum Bulaq	16,700 ft	10 miles
Malik Sarai (Aktagh)	15,200 ft	23 miles
Khufelang Aghzi	14,400 ft	15 miles
Igar Saldi	14,000 ft	20 miles
Kugiz Jangal	13,900 ft	20 miles
Kulam Oldi	12,100 ft	15 miles
Tora Oghill	12,000 ft	15 miles
Kizil Ungur	9,300 ft	20 miles
Ishak-art-Aghzi	8,350 ft	20 miles
Akmasjid	8,400 ft	15 miles
Kokyar	6,440 ft	
Besh Terek	5,890 ft	24 miles
Karghalik	5,000 ft	20 miles

Stage	Height	Distance
Yarkand	4,000 ft	40 miles
Kashgar		132 miles
Route no. 2 – Leh to (Sinkiang) Xingjiang (Summer Route)		
Leh	11,500 ft	
Polu	15,252 ft	10 miles
Khardung	13,350 ft	15 miles
Khalsar	10,600 ft	12 miles
Tegar	10,250 ft	15 miles
Panamik	10,600 ft	16 miles
Umlung	12,250 ft	12 miles
Tut-Yenlak	14,150 ft	11 miles
Sasar Brangesa	15,200 ft	10 miles
Murgo	14,600 ft	12 miles
Kizil Langar	16,400 ft	24 miles
Karakorum Polu	16,900 ft	17 miles
From here onwards see route no. 1		
Route no. 3 – Leh to Demchok (Border village on Tibetan – Ladakh Border)		
Leh	11,500 ft	
Chichot	10,750 ft	12 miles
Marselang	11,500 ft	13 miles
Upshi	11,900 ft	10 miles
Gya	13,500 ft	16 miles
Debring	15,780 ft	15 miles
Pongu Napu	15,000 ft	12 miles
Polokongka La	14,600 ft	47 miles
Puga	14,000 ft	11 miles
Nyoma Rap	14,000 ft	20 miles
Mankhang	14,000 ft	23 miles
Hanle	14,280 ft	18 miles

Geographical And Economic Survey

Stage	Height	Distance
Photi La	14,000 ft	11 miles
Koyul	14,000 ft	10 miles
Lagankhel	14,000 ft	10 miles
Demchok	14,000 ft	16 miles
Route no. 4 – Leh to Skardu (POK)		
Leh	11,500 ft	
Nurla	10,500 ft	43 miles
Khalsi	9,700 ft	8 miles
Skirbuchan	9,500 ft	16 miles
Nabi Brangsa	9,000 ft	14 miles
Dah	9,000 ft	13 miles
Urdas	9,000 ft	9 miles
Marol	(POK)	19 miles
Kharmang	8,340 ft	20 miles
Tolti	8,000 ft	12 miles
Parkuta	7,870 ft	18 miles
Gol	7,800 ft	14 miles
Skardu	7,770 ft	20 miles
Route no. 5 - Leh to Himachal Pradesh		
Leh	11,500 ft	
Chichot	10,750 ft	12 miles
Marselang	11,500 ft	13 miles
Upshi	11,900 ft	10 miles
Gya	13,500 ft	16 miles
Debring	15,780 ft	15 miles
Rogchan	15,300 ft	14 miles
Pang	15,200 ft	19 miles
Sumdo	15,520 ft	16 miles
Rachoga	13,400 ft	9 miles
Sarchu	13,950 ft	10 miles

Stage	Height	Distance
Kiling	15,720 ft	11 miles
Zing Zinghar	14,000 ft	12 miles
Patse	12,464 ft	6-1/4 miles
Kyelang	12,464 ft	13-1/2 miles

Agriculture

Agriculture is the main prop of Ladakhi existence. The greater part of Ladakh's population is connected with the soil and the number of artisans is far less. The area of the District is about 1,45,409 acres out of which 23,150 acres only is cultivated. The main characteristic of the area is that the terrain is generally mountainous and the altitudes vary from 11,000 to 14,000 feet. There are, however, some valleys situated at a low altitude which grow more crops. Some of the villages are situated at very odd places but the people have brought at places even barren land under the plough.

The whole of the cultivated area is irrigated and irrigation is generally plentiful, permanent, easy and free of cost. The output is generally good; in good years it beats the record of dry tracts. Due to sufficiency of water for irrigation, many of the crop experiments gave a very high output than in the past. Most of the area returned as uncultivable waste at the time of the last assessment is cultivable provided means were found to bring it under irrigation, but water supply in each village has been fully utilized and there can be little hope of further extension in irrigation except by State aid to find and introduce other means of irrigation. Some of the villages would have also been returned as uncultivable had they not been situated on either side of the Indus and had not irrigation been possible from the waters of the Indus. It is, therefore, considered essential that the system of irrigation to land by other possible means be undertaken to bring under cultivation most of the waste land in the District.

Size of the Holdings

After eliminating the area held by 'gompas' and other big landlords, the remaining area will give an average size of holding at 2.8 acres. It will be noticed that the majority of the agriculturists have very small holdings, with an average size of 1.9 acres. These small holdings will, however, be safe from further fragmentation due to the polyandry custom, which though abolished by statute is still in vogue in some of the villages of the district.

It may, however, be noted that in the second class circle of the District, an average size of holdings is only 3.7 acres, which is larger than that of the first class villages; but the size of an ordinary 'assami' holding is less than this as the general average has been raised to some extent by the very large holdings of the leading 'gompas' and big landlords of Ladakh.

Classification of Land according to Productivity and Fertility

(a) **First Class :-** The first class is much smaller in extent than the second and the third classes. It comprises three villages of Nubra and a few villages of the Indus Valley below Bazgo. Even in these villages the higher localities have been placed in other circles according to their productive capacity. The total cultivated area is about 1329 acres or about 7 percent of the total cultivation. The villages in this circle area are about as good as those in Baltistan and enjoy a moderate climate. Average area per holding is 2.8 acres which is very small. Crops in this circle are sown and harvested much earlier than in other circles. The crops grown are wheat, 'giram', barley, 'matar'(peas), 'kars', and 'trumba'. The principal crops are wheat 22%, 'giram' 31% and 'pulses '31%. The number of livestock is above the average except in Dah, Hanu, Handar and Deshkit which possess large flocks of goats and sheep with extensive grazing areas. The zamindars are distinctly better off in this area than their neighbours in other areas. They are also better cultivators as the longer duration of the working season gives them more time to attend to the field labour. This area may, therefore, well be regarded as a surplus area in respect of produce.

(b) **Second Class :-** This is the largest circle and comprises about one half of the total area. Most of the villages are situated in a line on both sides of the Indus from Upshi to Bazgo and have open valleys with broad fields and plenty of sunshine. The climate is colder than that of the first circle and hence one crop is only grown. Average out turn is about as good in this circle as in the first provided sowing is not delayed by an unusually long winter.

(c) **Third Class :-** This circle is next to the second in extent of its cultivated area which is 7,258 acres. The villages and localities included in this circle are scattered all over in higher attitudes. They are mostly situated in along small streams (called nallas) and are exposed to cold winds. The winter is longer than in the first and second circles and crops are sown late. In exceptionally cold years crops fail to mature in the higher portions of the villages, but on an average crops are pretty secure and in many villages of this class out turn is often as good as in the second class villages. The principal crops are wheat 17%, 'giram 46%, barley 14% and pulses 8%. The number of livestock in the villages in Central Ladakh is rather below average, but the villages Tonktse, Rong and Rupshu areas lying on a higher altitude possess extensive grazing fields and consequently a large number of goats and sheep. The area is regarded as self sufficient in matter of produce though it may go deficit in exceptionally unfavourable weather.

(d) **Fourth Class :-** This is the smallest circle and comprises only 961 acres of cultivated or about 5% of the total cultivated area. The principal crops are 'gram' 77%, barley 5% and pulses 5%. One hundred acres of land grow, on the average, 75% of crops. Cultivation is uncertain in these areas owing to intense cold and early snowfall. The soil is also generally poor. The cultivators generally live in the principal villages lying on a lower altitude, and cannot thus give much attention to these distant and high fields. The three whole villages included in this circle belong to the Rupshu Ilaqa and possess large flock of livestock and extensive pastures. The cultivated area of these villages is most insignificant and cultivation most perfunctory and unprofitable. No trees can grow in the highest fourth class areas of Tonktse, Rong and Rupshu. No general remarks can be given about the cultivators who live in lower localities placed in other circles. The three villages are inhabited by nomads who make a living chiefly by sale of wool and livestock.

System of Cultivation

The following points are worth noting in the system of cultivation:-

(a) **Rotation of Crops:-** There is no customary rotation of crops in vogue here, except that wheat is not grown on the same soil for more than two or three years, as wheat is believed to weaken the soil. Wheat is often followed by 'giram', but if the soil is much impoverished 'matar' (peas) or 'sarshaf' is sown for a year as the roots of 'matar' are believed to strengthen the soil. Moreover, wheat is a crop of the longest duration and allows no time for a second crop. Hence preference is given to 'giram' which is followed by 'trumba', 'china' and 'kangni'.

(b) **Sowing:-** Seed is sown in first class villages at lower altitude but in all villages of other circles it is poured into furrows in much larger quantity. The zamindars say that it is necessary to sow a large quantity of seed in villages at higher altitude to make allowance for possible failures, as a part of the seed grain often fails to germinate on account of cold.

(c) **Ploughing:-** Ploughing is done only twice which is quite sufficient, but the zamindars say that they cannot afford to do more as the number of bullocks is very small. First ploughing is done after the crop is harvested, while the second is done at the time of sowing the seed. The first ploughing is sometimes dispensed with by a poor zamindar who barely scratches the surface of the soil only once at the time of sowing.

(d) **Watering:-** Watering is done very frequently, the first before sowing, the second a month after sowing and the rest after intervals of, say, 8 to 15 days. The crops are sure to dry up if no watering is done for a month.

(e) **Manure:-** Ten to twelve maunds is considered to be the standard manure for one 'Khal' (equivalent to two kanals) of land, but many poor zamindars cannot afford this and go much below the standard. 'Giram' is the best manured crop in all circles, but the zamindars of Leh supply the same amount of manure to wheat. Barley comes next while other crop require no manure. As crops do not flourish here in the absence of manure, it is husbanded with great care and supplied to every field.

(f) **Weeding:-** Weeding is done only in low-lying villages of the first circle, while it is considered detrimental to the growth of crops in higher altitude areas as cold water penetrates into the softened soil and damages the plants.

Crops

The principal crops grown in Ladakh are – 'giram', wheat, barley and pulses, details of which are given below:-

(a) **'Giram'**: – It accounts for nearly one third of the total crops raised in this District and is by far the most important staple food, in all classes of land. 'Giram' being the most popular food and the most important crop of this district, its cultivation is attended with much labour and care. In most villages it is preferred to wheat and sown in the best soil. It is a hardy plant; it is cultivated even at an height over 15,000 feet. This height indeed is exceptional but at heights of 13,700 and 14,500 feet there are villages dependent on its cultivation.

(b) **Wheat and Barley**:- After 'giram' wheat is the most important rabi crop. It is steadily gaining popularity with the progress of trade and civilization. Wheat does well up to 11,500 feet. It is cultivated but with much less success at 13,000 feet. The zamindars do not see any virtue in wheat, but they find that it fetches a better price than 'giram' and is much appreciated by visitors and traders. It is largely grown in second class villages situated along the roads. Wheat is a crop which flourishes well in comparatively hot climate and is always liable to damage in colder regions with higher altitudes.

(c) **Pulses**:- Pulses consist of 'matar', 'kars', 'bakla' and 'masur'. The crop does not flourish better in low lying villages; on the other hand, it is attacked in the warm villages of the first class by a worm called pinze. It requires no manure.

The Kharif crops of 'trumba', 'china', and 'kangni' are of little importance in Ladakh. They are only grown in low lying villages of the first class and in a few villages in other circles. They are much liable to damage from cold winds which set in by the time the crops are harvested. The crops do not thrive well in higher altitudes owing to excessive cold and early winds.

Fodder

'Ul' is a fodder crop of great value to the zamindars. It occupies a considerable area and is indispensable for the maintenance of cattle during the winter. As a purely fodder crop, 'ul' cannot be fairly assessed in terms of area cultivated.

But many villages on or near the road where 'ul' is largely grown, the small farmers make a handsome sale of 'ul' grass to the merchants and traders of Leh. The average output of 'ul' has been assessed by the revenue experts at 500 kilos per acre.

Land Reforms

The Government of Kashmir has almost revolutionized the land tenure system in the state. Some of the outstanding features of the reformed system are as follows:-

(a) For all practical purposes the landlord has been deprived of the power of evicting his tenant.

(b) Landlords owning more than 100 kanals of land are entitled to only one fourth of the produce but they are responsible as before for paying the land revenue in full and delivering to the Government the full quantity of grain due to be realized from them under the Food Control rules.

(c) No single landlord can own more than 182 kanals of arable land. Lands held in excess have been distributed among the tillers concerned. This law does not apply to fruit gardens or areas containing trees used for firewood. Among the Buddhists the land owned by different families has for many centuries remained undivided as under their customary law the eldest brother was recognized as the sole heir of all ancestral property to the complete exclusion of his younger brothers who lived jointly with him if they are happy but had no share in the property. This combined with the custom of polyandry prevented any increase in the number of families which thus remained fixed. The average size of holdings in Buddhist areas is thus considerably larger than in the areas inhabited by Muslims among whom the multiplication of families and the fragmentation of land have gone on uninterruptedly. The average size of Buddhist holdings may be put down as about 100 kanals while the Muslim holdings would approximate to 15 kanals. There are about 23 landlords who have been affected by these laws. There has been a bitter dispute between the Government on the one hand and the Gumpa Association of Ladakh on the other, regarding the application of these reforms to the land owned by the 'gompas'. Various representations by the

Buddhists have been submitted to the Governments of J&K and India for the non application of these reforms to the vast estates of the 'gompas'. The matter is under consideration.

LIVESTOCK

Ladakh:-

Under the orders of the Governor of the J&K a census of livestock was conducted in 1897 for Nubra, Khardung, Tonktse and Rupshu areas only, but no papers are available showing the result of this enumeration. From the grazing fee paid, however, the number of livestock was put approximately (1953) as follows:-

S.No.	Animal	Number of animals
1.	Yak	1876
2.	Dimo	1668
3.	Zo	3281
4.	Zomo	701
5.	Langtu	3935
6.	Balang	4736
7.	Calves	1281
8.	Horses	2672
9.	Colts	695
10.	Mules	32
11.	Donkeys	3376
12.	Sheep and goats	88704

Some of the names in the above table require explanation. Langtu is the common bullock and zo is a hybrid of the yak bull and the common cow. Its female is called zomo while female langtu and yak are called baling and dimo respectively. Ploughing is chiefly done with zo. Yak is also put occasionally to the yoke, but it is not good for the plough and is often used for carrying luggage in higher altitude villages.

The Sinkiang breed of horses and donkeys are very much preferred to the indigenous breed as the former are larger and stronger and more impressive in appearance than the latter. These favourite foreign breeds are to be met with everywhere.

Kargil District

(a) **Zanskar:-** The pony forms the main item in the livestock of the region and belongs to the breed associated with it and celebrated for its pace, patience and endurance. These ponies approximately number 2000 only (1953).

(b) **Rest of Kargil District:-** The livestock of this area falls under the same categories as that of the other parts of the district in general, e.g. goats, sheep, cows, horses. The Zanskar breed of horse is a favourite in this area.

Though the majority of the population professes Buddhist faith, yet they eat mutton probably due to the climatic conditions of the place. The figures of the annually slaughtered livestock are not available and the same is rather difficult to be worked out in the absence of an official record. It is, however, estimated that the number annually slaughtered varies from five to ten thousand sheep or goats.

Yield from land and income from Livestock

In the absence of any subsidiary occupation or industry, yield from land and income from livestock are the only sources of livelihood. Land being of different qualities with varying degrees of output and productivity, careful investigation is necessary to fix the average produce of a family holding. As a rule, crops in respect of which yield is low compensate the peasant by fetching a higher price. The law of marginal utility affecting supply and demand would regulate production and affect prices in a manner to secure a balance in the return obtained for what is produced and sold. Accordingly, to get at the family income the crop is taken to be uniform, i.e. all cultivated land is taken to be land growing wheat or barley or peas. The yield of land of different qualities has also been considered. 24 maunds per acre appears to be safe as the average yield for all cultivated land. It is also agreed that ½ seer of wool and 2 seers butter per head of sheep and goats and 10 seers of butter per head of balang, zomo and dimo would be a safe estimate after making allowance for the young and the dry. Their monetary value as per rates obtaining at present (1953) is: 'giram' or wheat per Rupees 1.50 per seer, butter Rs. 10/- a seer and wool Rs. 4/- per seer.

There are no special stock-farming methods in vogue in the district. The animals are poorly fed and have stunted growth, excepting the Sinkiang (Xinjiang) variety of horses and donkeys. Every colt in Zanskar is castrated before he attains the age of four and this practice is followed elsewhere in the district. The operation is performed by Balti experts as the Buddhists consider it a sinful act. No Buddhist in the town at Leh will take up the profession of a butcher and it is in order to avoid the sin of shedding blood literally that the 'Changpas' (people of Chanthang – Western Tibet) strangle animals to death when they want to kill them for food. The flocks in Chanthang North East Ladakh live under the open sky even in the arctic cold of the winter months.

As there are no pastures worth the name in the district due to its hilly nature, the livestock is generally driven towards the hills in summer where they feed on wild grass. During winter they are fed on dry grass which the peasants obtain after thrashing the crops. Since the people are illiterate, they do not pay much attention to preservation and promotion of species. If breeding is conducted on right and scientific lines, we can hope to have a much healthier and superior stock.

Forests

The district of Ladakh, situated as it is among very high mountain ranges, is naturally devoid of vegetation. There are places where either the high altitude retards growth of trees or where plants do not mature due to the sandy nature of the soil. It is, therefore, natural that one side of the Zojila Pass which is rich in forests should appeal to the human eye while the other side of it has nothing but massive rocks and dignified mountains to offer. Right from Machoi upto Leh no trace of trees can be found except of some solitary ones at different stages. The number of trees being insignificant and the absence of forests is so conspicuous that their future growth and development demands immediate attention.

Importance of Forests in the Area:- The importance of development of forests in this area is very vital both from economic as well as geographical points of view. In the past the State never bothered to conduct a geographical survey of the area and thus explore the possibilities of development of forests. With increased strategic importance of the area, when military troops are indefinitely to be stationed here, it is of prime importance that the wood problem which is so acute here should receive prior attention. If the Government does not immediately foresee future handicaps it will not be surprising if after a few decades not a single tree can be had for fuel consumption. Deficit as the area is in firewood, the increasing demands on the limited number of existing trees are likely to disappoint the consumers in a couple of decades. It is, accordingly, recommended that a team of forest experts be detailed at the earliest to conduct a survey of the area which should be followed by immediate plantation.

This development scheme would not only solve the fuel problem but would do good to this part of the country in other ways also. The existence of forests will aid moisture to the dry and cold climate of the area. In the absence of rains caused by the failure of the monsoons to reach here, the area has to depend entirely on the melting snow for irrigation. The growth of forests would naturally lead to occasional rains and thus be a natural source of irrigation in addition to the existing system.

Possible Areas of Development

The area along the Indus being generally damp offers opportunities for fairly good growth of trees, especially poplar and willow. The whole of Indus valley and some parts of Nubra valley which are rich in alluvial soil are sure to yield good results. Experiments may even be conducted in Rong area and some small streams (nallas) of Line area where the climate is moderate and soil rich enough. The Nubra valley is ideal for development of forests in all respects, and as a matter of fact it is this area alone which is self-sufficient with regard to firewood and may even be able to show some surplus. This area would have been an asset to the district from the fuel point of view, had not the famous Shyok flood swept away many of the trees about a decade ago. We can still hope to have dense forests in this area only if the matter is not delayed and if plantation is taken early in hand.

Plantation Drive

On realizing the pressing need to improve the present deplorable absence of trees in the district, the State Government ordered the Forest Officer, Ladakh in early 1951 to launch plantation drive in the area. The State officials and the locals offered their fullest co-operation and assistance to the Forest Officer in the campaign, as a result of which thousands of trees were planted in Leh. The campaign should have been launched in the suburbs and adjoining villages of Leh also. Moreover, though plantation was conducted on experimental lines, it was nonetheless conducted haphazardly.

The area as has been mentioned required complete economic overhauling and among the development schemes under contemplation by the Government, top priority should be accorded to forest development.

Mineral Wealth

So far as is known no scientific survey of the mineral wealth of the district has been attempted before. The Kashmir Government made an attempt in October 1944 in extracting gold and some precious stones in the area of Skardu but with little success as the sums invested exceeded the value of the out-turn. Another attempt was made in 1951 by the Government of India regarding the extraction of sulphur from Puga in Eastern Ladakh. Due to lack of adequate transport facilities the out-turn proved unprofitable and consequently no more exploration was undertaken. In the absence of a properly conducted survey, it is difficult to furnish information regarding the richness and location of minerals in this area. Tradition, popular belief and in some cases actual knowledge, however, locate certain minerals as stated below but let me hasten to add that though I believe and understand its mostly in traces and is not commercially exploitable, local assertions notwithstanding. The details are as follows -

(a) **Gold:-** The sands of the Indus are said to be prominent in Ladakh for their gold content. It is an established fact that in the past some expert locals have succeeded in extracting gold particles from the sands of the Indus. Though the process is undoubtedly complicated, strenuous efforts put in the past have given encouraging results. It is, however, reported that besides this, gold can be found in Yulchu, Nerak, Cheling, Begu, Sunu, Waris and Phastan. However my inquiries did not bring about any knowledge of commercial scale operations or sales.

(b) **Iron:-** Iron ore is reported to be in Neh, Hanley, Koil, Taru, Wanla, Tangyar and Charasa. It is said that one of the former rajas of Ladakh explored an extensive iron ore in Charasa but no attempts of any description were made for its extraction.

Geographical and Economic Survey

(c) **Asbestos / Silica:-** It is reported to be in abundance in Suru, Zanskar area.

(d) **Copper:-** It is reported to be found in Chilling Sumdo, Yulchu, Nerak, Neh and Depsang (situated on way to Sinkinag (Xinjiang) – own territory). However, copper ore is not being extracted.

(e) **Sulphur:-** As already mentioned sulphur has been located in Puga area. The Puga exploration party discovered many sulphur springs both in Puga as well as in Nubra valley. Nevertheless no sulphur is being extracted due to economic reasons.

(f) **Petroleum:-** About a decade ago an American geologist, one Mr. Dickson by name, visited Ladakh and said that there were some possibilities of petroleum in Tangiri area. Some of the aged locals have a firm belief that the above area is rich enough in petroleum but no attempt regarding its exploration has so far been made. In order to augment the fuel resources, which have been tapped heavily of late due to presence of military troops in Ladakh, it is suggested that urgent steps be taken to find out once and for all the prospects in reality of petroleum.

(g) **Marble:-** Local accounts state that a German geologist, one Mr. Smith by name, explored marble near Pyong Gong Lake in North Eastern Ladakh. It is reported to be generally on hill tops which render its exploration difficult.

(h) **Lead:-** In Kubet (Nubra Valley).

(i) **Salajit:-** In Skildan and Khalsi.

(j) **Mica:-** Found along the Indus, especially She and Hanu.

(k) **Alum:-** In Skampuk (Nubra Valley).

(l) **Shangram:-** It is found in Tirisha (Nubra) but is difficult to explore as it lies on the top of the steep peak there.

The above description regarding the mineral wealth of Ladakh lends a temptation to conduct a scientific mineral survey of the area. There is no doubt that the mountains of this area do possess some minerals and should a survey be conducted a large amount of labour could be brought to the scheme and the people would thereby obtain a livelihood to supplement the meagre living they get out of their crop and cattle. It is, therefore, recommended that among other development plans for this area which might be under contemplation, mineral exploitation should receive serious thought and consideration.

Trade

Since the commercial treaty that was entered into between the Governments of India and Kashmir in 1870, there used to be a British Joint Commissioner at Leh, the nerve centre of the Central Asian trade. His duty was to settle all disputes between the British and the Kashmiris on the one hand, and the Central Asian Merchants on the other hand. The Commissioner was also responsible for the maintenance of the Treaty Road which is now looked after by the State PWD.

Leh, conveniently situated as it is about half way between the markets of India and those of Central Asia, was the terminus for the caravans from both regions. In summer, traders would arrive at Leh from different parts of India and from Sinkiang (Xinjiang), Tibet, and the remotest districts of Central Asia. Here the goods of the South were exchanged for those of the North. It was seldom that a caravan from India goes North of Leh or that one from Central Asia proceeded south of it. The merchants who would travel for months together in either direction would meet here at Leh and dispose of their merchandise mainly by barter. Leh, in the period September to December used to be one of the busiest and crowded places and people derived a lot of benefit out of the trade. The position since 1947 has completely changed in the sense that there has been a trade blockade on account of the Communist occupation of Sinkiang (Xinjiang) and Tibet. The locals did not formerly depend much on import from Kashmir and India as all essential commodities of life would be flooded into Ladakh from Central Asia, besides items of comforts and luxuries. The main commodities imported were carpets, silk, coarse cloth and similar other goods. Trade link with Tibet was also promising and most of the people dealt in wool and pashmina export; since the occupation of the Western Tibet some wool from Chanthang has been diverted towards Tibet.

At present there are hardly any commodities worth mentioning which are exported from Ladakh. According to the recent policy of the J&K

Government, no individual can export wool from this area without the sanction of the Government. Nearly all essentials of life, even the foodstuffs are imported into Ladakh from Kashmir and that too at a high cost. However, trade with India via Himachal Pradesh is now improving as distance involved is much shorter.

Cessation of Trade with Sinkiang and Tibet

For some years Leh, the capital of Ladakh, has been as it were a "City of the Dead", owing to the complete cessation of the Central Asian trade due to Chinese Government's orders in 1952. Very few caravans either from or to Yarkand in Sinkiang (Xinjiang) have passed through the town, thus depriving the people of the means of livelihood either through the exchange of merchandise or the carrying of goods by means of pony transport to Sinkiang (Xinjiang) and Tibet. The traders from India have also become less who visit this region for trading and owing to the lack of free exchange of trade, with Sinkiang (Xinjiang) and Tibet the market prices have risen of essential commodities.

Industrial Establishments

Agriculture is the main prop of Ladakhi's existence and is the chief occupation. Industrial enterprise is conspicuously absent. The Kashmir Government, having felt the need of establishing cottage industries in the area managed to get certain implements from outside and intends to undertake the task immediately. As a matter of fact, the locals especially the women folk here keep themselves engaged in their leisure moments with knitting and weaving. The locals have not so far taken to foreign cloth and have developed a fancy for handmade cloth which due to its durability lasts them for life and is only cast away when it is reduced to its original elements. The richness in wool and pashmina of this area can make possible the manufacture of woolen goods such as 'pattoos', blankets, shawls, namdas and carpets. There are also possibilities of manufacture of drugs from herbs which are found in abundance in the district. The local physicians prepare their medicines from roots and herbs and their method of treatment resembles the Ayurvedic system. As the people have an ingrained belief that their indigenous methods of treatment are more effective, it is worthwhile to encourage development and preservation of herbs in scientifically organized establishments for the extraction of medicines.

Likely Sources of Electricity and Power

(a) **Leh**:- There are great possibilities of installing power houses at various locations in Ladakh provided the Government takes due interest and pains. The waters of the Indus and various streams can with success be utilized for this purpose at various places. Following are the places which are admirably suited for generation of light and power -

   (i) A power house can be built if the waters of the Indus are canalized from Likche or some other place nearby to Bemis, Sharar, Igu or Meeru.

   (ii) If waters of the Indus are canalized from Alchi to Nurla, a power house can be built.

   (iii) If the waters of the Tia Teenugam Stream (Nalla) are harnessed to Teenugam, there a power house can be constructed. From the beginning of June to the end of July the quantity of water in the stream (nalla), however, decreases due to its irrigation of fields. The power house if built here may, therefore, have to suspend work during the summer.

(b) **Kargil**:- Waters of the Pashkum Nala can be diverted through a canal to Kurbathang from where a waterfall can be taken to the lower levels where a power house can be built. This may, however, interfere with the plans of Kashmir Government to irrigate Kurlathang and render it cultivable.

These locations in the two districts are very well suited for installation of power houses and electric plants. No possible development of the area is possible unless and until such power generating plants as will ensure industrialization are installed. It would be in the best interests of the Government and the local people if development schemes for this are earnestly taken in hand in view of abject economic backwardness of the districts.

Population and Area

The area of the entire Ladakh region including Kargil stretches over about 21,080 square miles, almost equal in size to the provinces of J&K State comprising of 27 Tehsils. But the nature of the region, its altitude and severe climate has restricted the size of cultivable land.

The population of Ladakh where the Buddhists are in an overwhelming majority has been kept down by the long prevailing custom of polyandry. In this rather unfertile part of the country where increased population would have been a drain on the impoverished land, credit for keeping the population within reasonable limits undisputedly goes to this unpleasant system of polyandry. The improvident Baltis with their plurality of wives and large families are miserably poor and drag along a pitiable existence. But it is far more necessary to keep down the population in Ladakh than in Baltistan, the reason being that a great portion of the Baltis inhabit valleys at a comparatively low altitude where the summer is almost as hot as in the Punjab and thus the Balti Muslims who are used to this more or less hot climate can easily put up with the heat of plains where they emigrate for labour. But the Ladakhis accustomed to high altitudes only, find it difficult to work in plains. Again, their religion, language and strange ways generally isolate them; they are naturally unwilling to leave their mountains to live among other citizens, and who may not likely be to receive them in too friendly a manner. For this, race emigration is not a feasible relief to over population. So polyandry was perhaps devised as a substitute. But since polyandry has been stopped by Statute, there is every possibility of future growth of population and thus ways and means should be well in advance devised to check this increased rate in population.

Polyandry has a tendency, as is well known, to keep down the population in more than one way and a noticeable feature of this country is the paucity of children. But a Balti village rings with the merry noise of playing children.

Application of Malthusian Law of Population to Ladakh

According to the Malthusian Law of population, population of a country increased in geometrical progression and the food stuffs increase in arithmetic progression. This means that the population has a tendency to increase faster than the means of subsistence. This law has a peculiar application to this land in the sense that the restraint on further growth of population is now more necessary in the case of Ladakh than of Kargil. In the past the institution of polyandry worked imperceptibly as a check on the growth of population in Ladakh and there was no pressure on land either. With the abolition of this practice by State and enforcement of land reforms in the entire State, the pressure on land has increased and in a decade or so the yield from land could be hardly sufficient for the growing population. As the labour of this area is not mobile for climatic reasons, the question of supplementing their meager income by alternative means is necessary.

Belts of Population

The population of Ladakh can be classified into different belts amongst which the Indus Valley belt needs special mention. Density or sparseness of the population can also be described with regard to these belts. The Indus Valley which starts from Khalsi right upto Igu is fertile and is thus comparatively densely populated. The villages are generally located on either side of the Indus and in many cases it is the course of the river which due to natural barriers determines and differentiates one belt from the other. There are some villages along the Indus, for example, Chichot, Thikse and She which are predominantly Muslim while those who live in distant and remote nallas at the foot of mountains constitute a different belt. Among these may be mentioned the villages of Bazgo, Taru, Dah and Hanu. The town of Leh itself constitutes a separate geographic belt where people of all the communities reside.

The area of Rupshu in Chanthang is an entirely separate belt in as much as it is inhabited by nomads known as 'Changpas' who have besides religion no other affinity with rest of the population. Their habits, customs and the mode of living present a striking contrast with the remaining people and as such they don't mix with any other people except on business errands. Similarly, the 'Dokpas' of Dah and Hanu who also profess Buddhist faith have very little in common with the remaining Buddhist community. This element of the local population due to these reasons and geographic considerations of their area may well be said to belong to an entirely different belt or sub region of population.

The valley of Nubra in as much as it is completely cut off from Leh by high mountain barriers may be associated with a different belt. This valley like the Indus Valley being very fertile coupled with favourable climatic conditions is densely populated. Here also habitations can mostly be seen either on the banks of the Shyok or the Nubra rivers. The people of this belt are comparatively contented as their population has so far appreciably kept pace with the growth.

Chapter III

SOCIAL CUSTOMS AND MANNERS

The culture of a people is moulded by various factors such as geographical features of the area where they live, the traditions which they have inherited from their past and the alien influences which they have consciously or unconsciously assimilated from their neighbours and strangers. If one perceives anything strange in the habits, manners and social customs of the people of Ladakh, instead of immediately jumping to conclusions or forming opinions, one should try to seek the reason thereof either in the topography and climate of the area or in the historical tradition of the people or in the alien influences which might have infiltrated into the social and domestic life of the people of Ladakh.

Changes in Ladakh, whether they are cultural, political or economic, always come slowly. It is not because the people are conservative or lethargic, but because the forces that bring about change in this remote corner have literally to climb over high hills and dry wastes. And outside forces, like outside people, find it a hard task to scale or circumvent these natural barriers and reach the heart of the Ladakhi people. The local people, however, are born mountaineers who ascend and descend the mountain slopes as easily as the mountain goats do. To them, the mountains are no barriers. But the people of Ladakh unfortunately love their homes and homeland so much that they seek not any venture beyond their boundaries. Thus forces that stimulate the mind and bring about change rarely reach Ladakh.

But this is all past story. Today the scene is entirely different. Ladakh which has suddenly soared into strategic importance is a prize which many of her neighbours covet. And to get it they are willing to sacrifice quite a lot. The result is that various forces are at work both inside Ladakh and outside.

And these forces are stimulating great changes. What would be the ultimate result of these changes it is hard to foretell.

Dress of The People

From the standards of modern civilization, the dress of the people of Ladakh is rather too basic, greasy and tattered. A pant and a long gown with a typical cap is the normal attire of the men of Ladakh. The dress does not vary very much during the different seasons but in winter there may be two or three layers of them, sometimes even four, to protect oneself from cold. A scarf is rarely used, and when one is, it is usually wound round the neck and thrust inside the gown at the neck, making its presence scarcely noticed.

Cap

The cap worn in Ladakh is not of any uniform pattern. The conglomeration of Central Asiatic cultural influence is seen here in the variety of caps worn by the local people. There is the Chinese cap, round and tight-fitting, covering the back of the neck and with flaps on either side to cover up the ears, and a smaller flap in front to cover the forehead in extreme cold. But even in extreme cold those who wear it fold the flaps up and tie it with an attached ribbon at the top giving the entire head wear a semi-spherical appearance. The second type is the bowl-shaped cap whose rims are slightly upturned and the fur-lining inside, in the third type which is typically the Ladakhi pattern, there is usually no fur inside. This type is mostly cylindrical at the top but with elongated sides about the ears and these protrusions, though evidently meant for protecting the ears in severe cold, are usually slightly tilted and turned upwards, partially fulfilling their function of protecting the ears from chilblains.

Footwear

While the rich and the educated, either through affluence or a sense of decency, prefer to have the normal leather shoes or boots, the common folk in Ladakh go in for the warmth and comfort of the local shoes called 'pabbu', made of hand-spun and hand-woven yarn of wool. These are rough in appearance but the variegated colours of the woollen yarn used in symmetric shapes gives it an appearance of classical beauty and cosy comfort. The front ends of this type of shoes are upturned giving the shoes the shape of country boats with flat or rounded backs.

The socks and stockings worn by the local people are knitted out of rough woollen yarn and in thickness and appearance they approach the jute yarn. But for warmth and comfort in winter there isn't anything to match them. The poorer folk, who cannot be fastidious about shape and show, use ordinary 'namda' which is wound round the feet to form an improvised pair of socks, to protect themselves from the rigours of the sub-zero weather.

The Gown or 'Goncha'

It is rather strange to observe that the people of Ladakh have taken to the flowing gown, which follows the pattern of the Chinese gown. Stretching from neck to ankle, like the Chinese gown, it is buttoned at the neck and the right side of the wearer. The buttons are usually of some shining metal and the gown is fastened by pressing tight thread-insulated cotton loops over them.

While in winter the gown is made of woollen yarn which is as rough as durable, in summer it is usually of dyed cotton. But the colour is invariably the same: dark vermilion or deep grayish-blue. This colour is preferred since the layer of dust that may settle upon it is neither noticed nor does it discolour the material used for the gown. Usually the gown has an inner lining which adds to the warmth and durability of it. The inner lining is sometimes of some attractive colour and sometimes of fine material too.

The people of Ladakh, both men and women, wear a long shawl called 'shiraks' wound round their waist in the form of a belt. This not only gives alertness to the wearer but also saves the bottom ends from sweeping the floor.

In spite of the fact that politically and to some extent culturally Ladakh is now a part and parcel of Kashmir, there is very little in the dress of the local people showing their affinity with the people in the Kashmir valley. Even in severe winter, the people of Ladakh, unlike the people of Srinagar, do not think it necessary or comfortable to wear woollen blankets in the form of shawls. Even the 'Kangadi' (kangri) of Kashmir, a small basket with a pot inside containing glowing ambers to warm the hands, can never be seen in the hands of the local people during the worst days of January and February, the coldest months of the year. The Ladakhis prefer to thrust their hands in the sleeves of each other arm of the gown or into the pant-pockets to keep them warm.

Among the lower classes of society which earn the daily bread through manual labour the gown serves the manifold purpose of a napkin, a handkerchief, a duster and a receptacle to carry things from one place to the other. The last purpose is fulfilled just by lifting the front lower ends of the gown and placing all articles in the cradle-like cavity formed thereby.

Like the Chinese gown again, the Ladakhi gown has its pockets in the inner layer of the gown or in the lining. It is usually located at the space between the chest and the abdomen and it is reached by passing the right hand through two button spaces in the right side of the wearer. Occasionally this pocket too serves as the place where the right hand can be warmed in the warmth of the body temperature.

One point of difference between the Chinese gown and the Ladakhi gown is that while the former, well-cut and well-stitched as it is, gives a noble appearance to the wearer, the latter which is often too loose and locally stitched gives an appearance of ascetic honesty and simplicity. This aspect of the Ladakhi gown is in perfect tune with the innate nature of the people of Ladakh and nothing is more natural and pleasing to the sight than to see a Ladakhi gentleman remaining loyal to the local dress and culture. Even the educated among the people of Ladakh who have taken their degrees in Indian Universities are true to their soil and show no sign of slavish or aping mentality.

The Dress of the Women

But for the hand-dress and the sheep's skin hanging on the back, the dress of the women of Ladakh does not differ very much from that of men. The 'gonchas' that the women wear differ only in minor details from the 'gonchas' worn by men. Of course, there is always an element of artistry and gaudiness in the 'gonchas' worn by women but all the same no attempt is made to bring out the feminine features of the wearer.

An indispensable part of a woman's dress is a sheep-skin hanging on the shoulders and covering the back. This not only gives warmth in winter but keeps her clothes from wear, tear and dust especially when she has to carry loads on her back.

The head-dress of the Ladakhi woman is both unique and cumbersome. Most of the women wear caps which are similar to those worn by men. The

A RICH BUDDHIST LADY WITH ORNAMENTS AND TYPICAL HEAD WEAR

Muslim women do not go in purdah but they can be easily distinguished from the rest on account of the shawl that they put on their head underneath their cap and which flows backwards. The Buddhist women however have what is known as 'pairak' adorning their head. It is a long strip of cloth shaped like a cobra and studded with turquoises or shells. Starting from the forehead it reaches almost the entire length of the back. On the top of the head it is about four inches broad but it gradually tapers on the back. The wealth of a woman or her family is easily judged by the cost of the turquoises or precious stones that adorn her 'pairak'. An inalienable part of this head-dress is a pair of stiff lappets made out of dark sheep-skin. These stand at right angles to the wearer's temples, very much resembling the ears of an elephant. These lappets cover the wearer's ears completely.

Jewellery is something which women all over the world have a mania for, and the women of Ladakh are no exceptions. They wear necklaces made of beads and precious stones and for bracelets they have conch-shell rings. The low economic standard makes gold and silver ornaments prohibitively expensive and a rarity. The best 'gonchas' of every woman are usually embroidered with symmetric designs at the fringes. The younger generation among the women prefers to have a bright-coloured silk shawl to be worn as a waist-band.

Comments of Visitors

Visitors to this part of the globe have often jumped to the hasty conclusion that the people over here are not able to maintain a sensibility of cleanliness. To say so is at best a half-truth. There is no denying the fact that the dress of the Ladakhi people rarely goes to the wash and therefore is dirt-laden and greasy. But the other half of the truth is that the soil here is so hostile to cleanliness that the washerman's efforts are all rendered useless within a day when fine particles of dust floating in the air again settle on the newly washed clothes. Secondly, and this is of vital importance when one talks of cleanliness, the starvation level on which the majority of the Ladakhis live makes it humanly impossible for the people to even think of new clothes or washed clothes. The people who struggle from dawn to dusk to wrest a morsel from the bleak sandy wastes and the rugged Rocky Mountains and still find themselves hungry in the night cannot divert their attention to the smartness of their clothing or the whiteness of their collar. With all their congenital virtues, the people of Ladakh are so woefully handicapped by poverty and economic distress that there are few parallels in the world to match their struggle for existence. Not strange then that they cannot think of buying a cake of washing soap or diverging their precious time for washing their dress. Nor is it strange that every attempt is made to extricate the last bit of service from the most tattered among the gowns or the most worn out among the pairs of shoes. After all one must live first before aiming to live smartly.

It is the low economic standard of the people of Ladakh, which makes their houses unclean and dusty. Cement and fire-burnt bricks are too costly to be used in flooring the rooms and the timber planks are equally expensive. When such is the case, the tread of every man raises a thin cloud of dust from the floor, making one's clothes too dirty in no time. So it is the poverty of the people which makes their rooms dirty like a stable and their dress grey like dust. However, with improving economy, the Ladakhis are changing their habits and are washing their clothes and are keeping their homes quite clean. Rich people have nice houses which are well furnished. The overall trend is certainly of improvement.

Domestic Equipment and Furnishings

The houses in Ladakh are usually ill-lit and ill-furnished. To protect themselves from severe cold in winter, the people when they build the houses reduce the number of windows in each room to the minimum necessary to permit a little light. The size of these windows is such that they resemble more port-holes in a ship than the actual windows in a home in the plains. But the rich people always have their drawing rooms fitted with many glass panes and some are well-decorated. A thick quilt-like curtain usually hangs over these glass panes and these curtains are lowered whenever there is no necessity for bright light in the room or whenever protection is sought from the outside cold. Similar quilt-like curtains also hang in front of the doors, serving a similar purpose.

LADAKHI HOUSES IN LEH (1952)

There is hardly any furniture of the type of chairs and tables in Ladakhi houses but small benches called 'choktse' hardly a foot in height and breadth but two or three feet in length, can be seen in every house as an indispensable piece of the furniture. These benches, usually with paintings or carvings on sides, serve both the purposes of writing and dinner tables. People squat beside them while writing or reading or while taking their meals.

The most artistic and costliest thing usually found in Ladakhi houses is the carpet. Bright-coloured and beautifully designed, these Sinkiang (Xinjiang) carpets add charm and comfort to every house. They are spread on the floor and sometimes also nailed against walls. Even the poorest folk will have one or two of such carpets and to accommodate a guest on the brightest of these is a part and parcel of Ladakhi hospitality.

Serving the same purpose as the carpets but playing a secondary role in the domestic equipment are 'namdas' and cushions. The 'namdas' are Yarkandi woollen blankets with designs embroidered in different colours. The cushions are usually stuffed with rough wool or dry grass and are usually used as seat bases on which carpets are spread.

The drawing room in each house strikes a big contrast with the rest of the rooms. It is usually well lit and well furnished. Sometimes elaborate paintings in different colours can also be seen on the walls or ceiling of the drawing rooms. The paintings are usually in the form of some minute symmetric designs or grotesque shapes involving months of an artist's labour. One rarely sees natural scenes painted on the walls or photographs hung on them.

Most of the rooms are usually equipped with a fire-place for use in winter. Big cylindrical hearths, with connecting pipes for the exit of smoke, can always be seen standing in one corner of the room. Some of the houses have a central chimney through which smoke from different fire-places in different rooms' escapes. In winter, from a distance these houses look like miniature factories with the chimneys smoking. But in some of the houses of the poor people the only smoke-chimney would be an opening in the roof which serves the purpose of the window too in as much as the room is lit by the sun's rays escaping through that hole. In winter this hole is usually covered to keep off snow whenever there is a snowfall.

The poor people, in winter, depend upon the dried dung of the cattle to warm their rooms and the smoke emanating from this often makes the rooms stuffy and dark. But since there is no other alternative, they neither grudge it nor feel it. As a matter of fact, the lower classes mainly depend upon the layers of 'gonchas' they wear to give them the warmth, rather, preserve the warmth of the body, even in the coldest days of winter when the temperature goes down to 20 degrees Fahrenheit below zero. Nor have these people anything like a warm bedding. They just fold themselves in the 'gonchas' that they wear and the quilt would be the only covering. It is also astonishing how these people manage to spend the night by resting their head on a wooden pillow, called 'nyashing' a slightly slanting frame on two props.

An indispensable part of every house is a stable for the pony, donkey, zo or the yak. While the rich people may own several ponies and zos, the poorer classes will have atleast one or two zos, donkeys, ponies or yaks, mostly used, not for riding purposes, but as beasts of burden. Usually no separate rooms are built for storing up fodder. The roof tops serve this purpose and one often sees layers of hay heaped on the parapets of the house tops.

Dogs too are an indispensable part of the domestic possession particularly in out of the way houses and remote villages. A ferocious and huge dog of the Chanthang breed is usually kept as a watch dog, though one or two of the Lhasa breed are kept as pet or pets. The latter breed is full of bushy hair, two or three inches long, but this variety never grows bigger in size than a full-grown cat. As a domestic pet this is ideal and some of the house-holders make regular business by selling these pets. A visitor to Ladakh usually buys one or two and these pets can be easily listed as one of the commodities of export.

The Diet of the People

One of the most interesting and admirable thing about the people of Ladakh is their diet. Their food, like their other creature comforts, is so simple that one almost gets puzzled to know how these people can live on so simple and meagre a diet. 'Sattu' or barley flour prepared from 'giram' (a loose grain type of barley), atta (flour) and 'yoches' or peas, wheat and 'giram' flour are their staple food and 'chheng', a beer like drink, is their staple drink.

Most of the people live on three meals a day. 'Thsana' or the breakfast consists of a handful of 'sattu' and some tea. The tea that the Ladakhi people drink is neither of the Chinese fashion which is just a decoction in boiling water, nor of the Indian type with milk and sugar. Some tea leaves with soda are put into water and boiled until the water evaporates. Water is poured twice again and evaporated until the tea gives a red colour. It is then put into a wooden churn and after adding a little salt, milk and butter, is thoroughly mixed with a churning rod so that a homogeneous mixture is made. This tea is taken as a beverage and occasionally some 'sattu' is also added to it. The mid day meal known as 'zara' consists of 'yoches' and 'lassi' or 'sattu' and tea and 'chheng'. The best meal of the day is the dinner which is taken soon after sunset. Usually meat and 'atta or 'yoches' preparations are taken during this time and those who cannot afford meat take vegetables instead. This last meal of the day called 'ghonzan' is occasionally accompanied with some 'chheng' or 'araq' (another drink). 'Araq' is stronger and more intoxicating than 'chheng' and can be afforded only by the rich.

It is interesting to note how these people prepare 'chheng' and 'araq' out of barley. First some 'giram' or barley is boiled and then it is allowed to cool. When it is cold, some 'fabs' an indigenous preparation of soda and eurotia is added and the mixture is left for three or four days to ferment. When some sour smell appears it is put into a drum which has an outlet at the bottom and hot water is poured from the top. This water after it passes through the fermented barley and draws with it all the essence of it, is collected in a pot of the shape of a flower vase. Hot water is poured three times from above and each succeeding time the 'chheng' collected is inferior to the previous one. 'Araq' is prepared by distilling 'chheng' and it is as strong as 'vodka' or the local Chinese white brew.

Polyandry (Now Much Reduced)

One of the strangest customs prevailing among the Buddhists of Ladakh, who form the majority in the local population, is that of polyandry. Though this is the result of the economic bankruptcy of the people and therefore, so to say, forced upon them, it is, in its turn, the cause of many a social evil. The system of polyandry on this side of the Himalayas is in strange contrast with the custom of polygamy prevailing, or rather that prevailed, on the other side of the Himalayas, in China. The custom is in no measure due to the disproportion among the male and female population, because Ladakh has fairly an equal number of men and women, but it is mainly due to the limited area of the land holdings, too insufficient to permit large families or multiplication of families.

In every family it is the eldest brother who is entitled to a formal marriage and the remaining brothers can only share her affections by turns. There are some families where even two or three brothers will have to seek contentment in sharing only one wife. This system of polyandry is neither an accident nor an exception but is a time honoured custom recognized by the society, state and religion. However, this system is fast changing now.

As a corollary of this system of polyandry comes the law of primogeniture according to which only the eldest son in the family is entitled to inherit the ancestral property while his other brothers are entitled to maintenance from him. This saves the ancestral holdings from being split into tiny bits of land which would increase over all human labour and decrease crop returns. Thus, polyandry and the law of primogeniture go hand in hand, the former trying to restrict the enlargement of the family and the latter trying to check the division of the land holdings. Evidently, the inexorable law of economic necessity sanctions and sanctifies the custom of polyandry which, according to other standards, would be otherwise obnoxious and repellent to that innate characteristic of every man which considers woman to be the most private and personal possession among all his relationships and belongings in the non material sense. But this custom is surely dying out now.

From the point of view of women, the girl who is married to the eldest son in the family evidently occupies a strategic, nonetheless delicate, position in the family into which she is wedded. She becomes a veritable mistress, holding in her hands the reins of the entire family.

While in a family there cannot be more than one 'eldest' son there may be many daughters. Evidently all the daughters cannot be wedded on account of the dearth of 'eldest' sons in the area and their lot cannot but be miserable. They have either to spend their life 'without love' or resort to illicit connection or take to the monastic life of celibacy. Needless to say that all these alternatives would, in some way or other, disfigure their social life, cramp their growth and expansion, and stultify their life in general. There have been instances when girls, out of sheer biological necessity, have married men from other communities, particularly Muslims, thereby giving rise to inter-communal misunderstandings and feuds.

Rich men who are too much attached to their daughters, whether they have sons or not, and who do not like the idea of their daughter or daughters leaving their family would bring in what are called 'magpas' into their family. In consultation with the girl a youth is brought into the family to be her husband and such a person is called 'magpas'. Thus instead of the girl going to the husband's home the process is reversed. Rich men who have no male issues follow this course and wealthy people even when they have sons may occasionally follow suit. This practice has the additional advantage of ensuring that the parents' property, either part or full, goes to the daughter on the demise of the parents.

Luckily for the people of Ladakh, fifteen years ago they saw the wisdom of reforming their society and curing it of its evils. Since then, the practice of polyandry and the custom of primogeniture have been totally abolished by law. Today every man is entitled to marry separately and all the sons have an equal share in the ancestral property.

With the abolition of the system of polyandry the system of 'phorsaks' also stands abolished by law. 'Phorsak' is a man selected as an additional husband by a married man whom she invites to stay with her husband in one and the same house. Of course, a woman who is wedded to the eldest brother in a family did not have this right of inviting a 'phorsak' since she already had the younger brothers of her husband as additional husbands. But a woman who was married to the only son in a family often exercised this right of inviting a 'phorsak' to be an additional husband to her. Usually this 'phorsak' happened to be a relative of her husband. But once he is taken in as a 'phorsak' by her it was her legal husband's duty to treat him as a guest sharing all the chosen favours and precious belongings of the family including the mistress herself, the most precious among them all. The 'phorsak', being one chosen by the woman herself and invited by her loving glances, was in some degree more honoured than the real husband himself and the latter was always expected to give the 'phorsak' the best of hospitality and the utmost of courtesy including the one of privacy and secrecy that he may seek with the mistress of the family. It is a good thing that the 'phorsak' has made an exit for ever from the social life of Ladakh, just as polyandry has done.

Position of the Women in Society

One of the glorious features of the Ladakh society, in spite of many ills already mentioned, is the freedom that women enjoy in the society and the equal rights that they share with men. Women in Ladakh are not confined to the four walls of the kitchen nor do they wear veils when they move about in the streets. Their social freedom is so complete that if the women from rest of India were to know of it they would certainly envy the lot of the local women.

The Ladakhi womenfolk dance freely in public with men, participate freely in all the religious and social functions and partake of 'chheng' liberally in the company of men. They are in no way inferior to men in carrying loads on their back or in doing manual labour on the farms. In the home too they do not play secondary roles to their husbands but equally share the burden of domestic duties and responsibilities with him.

The one apparent handicap that the women of Ladakh suffered was due to the custom of polyandry. But even in this she was not such an absolute and abject slave as one imagines. Because, as the wife of all the brothers she was the central authority wielding considerable influence in the family. She was the dominant figure to whom all the brothers looked for their happiness. When the husband, the eldest of the brothers, dies, a woman automatically becomes the wife of the remaining brothers without and further formal ceremony. But here too, if she does not care to take the remaining brothers as her next formal husbands she performs a small ceremony, immediately on the death of her first husband, by which she disowns her relationship with her deceased husband. One of her fingers is tied by a thread to a finger of her dead husband and then the thread is cut asunder. This done, her relationship with all his brothers automatically ceased. Even under such circumstances, she has still the right to what is known as 'Shrub-Zhing', a piece of land for her maintenance, provided that she is issueless with her deceased husband, that she wants to live in that very house, and that out of inharmonious relationship with her, the remaining brothers are proposing to marry another girl.

A woman, on the demise of her real husband, (the eldest brother in the family) has two choices before her. Firstly, if she is willing, she automatically becomes the legal wife of the remaining brothers. If she or the second brother are not willing to live as legal husband and wife, she disowns her relationship with the deceased husband, immediately after his death, by performing the ceremony described earlier, and simultaneously her relationship with the remaining brothers is severed. But she can still continue to live in the same family and enjoy the piece of land allotted to her as 'Shrub-Zhing', subject to the conditions stated before. But if there is no husband other than the deceased one she has the freedom to marry again and she usually marries a relative of her deceased husband and that too after consulting his parents and relatives. The new husband is called 'magpa' and he has to live with her in her former husband's house. It should be noted in this connection that her 'magpa' inherits the property of his predecessor provided his wife has not got any issues from her previous husband. Ordinarily a widow has the right to remarry. She has also the right to inherit the property of her deceased husband (in case he is the only son of his parents) provided she does not remarry until the demise of both her parents-in-laws.

Prostitution

The custom of polyandry which prevailed so long in this land had forced some girls to remain unmarried, much against their will, as has been noted earlier. While some of them took to the monastic life, the more impetuous and less religious type among them took to prostitution. Though polyandry has been prohibited by law, prostitution continues and may continue until the masses are educated and made to see the sanctity of family life and the value of good health. It is sad, very sad indeed, that in spite of the high religious faith and devotion of the local people this vice of prostitution, the progeny of poverty and polyandry, has survived to this day. But then prostitution exists in all societies in the world, Ladakh can certainly be no exception.

Marriage Customs

There are two ways of contracting a marriage. One is called the 'bagma' and the other 'magpa'. According to the 'bagma' custom, the girl, on marriage goes to her husband's house and gets all her rights there. But according to the 'magpa' custom, the girl stays in her parent's house and it is the husband who comes to stay there. Evidently the first custom is resorted to when the bride's father has too many sons and daughters to be married. But when a man has only one daughter and he does not want her to leave the family then he invites the bridegroom to come and live in his family so that when he dies his daughter and son-in-law can become heirs to the family.

In contracting a marriage alliance it is the boy's family that takes the initiative. The elders in the boy's family first select a family from which they are willing to bring in a bride. This choice is communicated to the 'Onpo' or the astrologer for his verdict. The 'Onpo' on making the necessary calculations would declare whether the proposed marriage, if contracted, would lead to the happiness or not. If he gives a favourable verdict then the relatives of the boy make a formal approach to the bride's parents with some 'chheng' and 'khatak' (ceremonial scarf). The girl's parents, if they favour the proposal, would request the guests to come on some fixed day when other relatives also would be invited to give their opinions. After the possibility of an alliance is ascertained the boy's relations return home with hope and on the appointed day they would again call on the parents of the girl with some quantity of 'chheng' as custom has ordained. The bride's parents arrange a feast if the proposal is accepted and in consultation with the 'Onpo' a day is fixed for the wedding ceremony.

On the day of the marriage the bride-groom's party, with some dancers called 'neopas' goes to the bride's house in a procession. But it must be noted that the bride-groom himself does not go with the procession and instead of him some other boy from the family is sent on his behalf. On reaching the bride's house, a religious ceremony takes place at which 'lamas' officiate and this is followed by a feast. The feast over, the bride-groom's substitute would place a 'khatak' round the head of the bride and holding her hand asks her to go with him to the bride-groom. The bride, at this would start weeping and hugging her relatives whom she is now leaving for ever. All her relatives would then name different things that would be given to her as dowry. These are recorded in a document, a copy of which is given to each party. The mother of the girl then demands formally what is called 'oma-rin' (literally milk-debt) in return for her carefully bringing the girl up. Some small sum is paid by the bridegroom's party as a token of the debt they owe her for having brought up the girl so far. The girl is then taken to 'chotkang' or the family temple where she prays the family deity for the long life and prosperity of her parents whom she is now leaving. She also prays for her own happiness in her new home. Then she departs to her new home. While after her marriage she can come back to her parents' home as many times as she likes or finds convenient, she cannot any more enter the temple of her old home.

Before the bride enters the house of the bridegroom a small religious ceremony is performed by the 'lamas' to ward off all misfortunes that might have accompanied the girl. An earthen pot containing some wastage of 'chheng' or tea is taken round the girl's head and then smashed against a rock. This ceremony is followed by feast, dance and merry-making and huge vases of 'chheng' keep the jubilant world moving and swinging. But the bride will be sitting at the entrance of the bride-groom's house with the pretence of going back to her parents. She would move into the house only when the bride-groom's mother offers her some cash and promise better treatment in the new house. The bride and bridegroom are then taken to the kitchen where they are seated on some grain sprinkled over a white carpet. The boy who had gone to the bride's house to fetch the bride then takes a 'khatak' or 'goras' and places it around the head of the bridegroom. The same boy places similar 'goras' on the heads of those younger brothers of the bridegroom to express their willingness to be secondary husbands to the girl. Such of the brothers as do not consent to the tying of the 'goras' round their head reserve for themselves the right to become 'magpas', by living in a girl's family. The younger brothers who have consented to accept 'goras' together with the eldest brother cannot marry any other girl and become a 'magpa' without the previous consent of the eldest brother's wife who has become their wife too.

On the approaching of night, the bride and the bridegroom are taken to the bedroom where the 'goras' are removed by the very boy who had tied them. A final dance on the next day consummates the marriage ceremony. The groom dances with the males and the brides with the females present. The dance over, male relatives would make some presents to the bridegroom and female relatives to the bride.

The Dards of Dah

These people form a community by themselves. Their habits and customs are very peculiar. They seldom take bath. They never use cow's milk and butter from cow's milk, and they do not eat eggs or chickens. The reason for which they abstain from all these is that their deity has desired like this. The houses of these people are built at a higher level than the ground and to reach up to them one has to climb over a wooden ladder. All the inmates of the house usually sleep together huddled up in one room with their flock of sheep and goats.

Another strange custom prevailing among these people is the one of confining the husband and wife together in one room whenever there is a child birth. The couple are confined together like this for 30 days and during the entire period they consider that the man needs greater care and attention than the woman who has given birth to the child.

Whenever the Dards of Dah want to honour a newcomer or an honoured guest to the village, some women will gather together and wait at the entrance of the village with some 'sattu' in a plate and with musicians playing on a flageolet and "dam-dam-walas" (drummers) in attendance. As soon as the honoured guest comes, the women who have been standing in a line and blocking the way, would bow, present the 'sattu' and then make way for the newcomer. The 'sattu' offered in the plates is only symbolical of their hospitality and the guest is never expected to partake of it. Similar customs, though with greater decorum, prevail among the other people of Ladakh as well, in according formal reception to a guest.

Baths and Hot Springs

The local people are not very particular about the need for a daily bath. This habit, it must be admitted, is partly due to weather and party due to the low economic standard of life. Though spring water is plenty and is available at hand, it is too cold for bath for nearly six months in a year. On account of the high cost of firewood, heating water for bath is something which few people can afford and consequently baths are few and far between.

Luckily for the people of the Nubra valley there are some hot water springs near about Panamik village. These sulphur springs are a great boon to the people nearby and 'Iharjeys' or local physicians sometimes accompany their patients over long distances to have a dip in these springs. A bath in these sulphur springs is considered to be a good cure for various types of diseases particularly rheumatism. The 'Iharjeys' always mixes the hot water of the sulphur spring with cold water, in such proportion as he deems fit, and then the patient takes his bath.

Funeral Ceremonies

The Christians and Muslims of Ladakh, as elsewhere in India, bury their dead and the Buddhists cremate the dead. Unlike the Hindus of India who believe that once the soul has left the body sooner it is disposed off the better, the Buddhists may keep the corpse for a day or so till the death is confirmed. After a death occurs the relatives have no right to touch the corpse and it is the 'phaspuns' who look after the dead body. Soon after a death takes place the head lama is called in at the earliest opportunity. This 'lama' preaches a sermon holding the hair of the deceased person. The sermon over, the 'phaspuns' take charge of the body. The phaspuns are not blood relations but they form a common brotherhood with the deceased person, almost on a reciprocal basis and they play an important role during birth, marriage and death in each other's family. After the last sermon has been preached the 'phaspuns' strip the corps naked and after fixing it in a seated posture, as one sits for a worship, the body is tied tight and it is in this posture that it is slipped into a cloth-sack. Then follows the 'puja' ceremony and the richer the deceased the longer this 'puja' continues. During the days of the 'puja' the 'lamas' before they eat or drink would always reserve the share of the deceased and this food and drink is either given to the beggars or thrown to birds in the belief that it would reach the deceased. After the ceremonies are over the 'onpo' or the astrologer is consulted as to which among the 'phaspuns' should bear the pall. The 'phaspuns' then put the body in a box like bier and carry it to the cremation ground accompanied by friends and relatives of the deceased. On reaching the ground the body is taken out and the final ceremony is performed by the 'lamas'. Then the body is placed on pyre and the 'phaspuns' and relatives of the deceased bow before it after circumambulating three times. But before the pyre is set on fire all except two 'lamas' and the 'phaspuns' turn back homeward.

Character of the People

A good match to the natural charm and the scenic beauty of Ladakh is the simplicity of life and nobility of character of the people who inhabit this land. Friendly and amiable to the very core of their heart, the people of Ladakh are truthful, honest, courteous and hospitable. Their life is untouched and undefiled by the profanity of the modern civilization and their character is untarnished by the vanity of the modern age. Natural and simple as their day to day life is, pure are their sentiments and noble their thoughts. Caste prejudices, narrow bigotry and suspicion of everything alien are unknown in this part of the globe.

Though of late the political consciousness of the local people has roused considerable controversies regarding the future political affiliation of Ladakh and its parent body, Kashmir, and though the different religious Bodies, the only organizations in Ladakh, are embroiled in these controversies, still the local people, whatever their religious creed may be, as individuals, move freely with one another, and personal bickering and squabbles based on religious sentiments, are conspicuous by their absence. It goes to the credit of the people of Ladakh that there is free social intercourse and inter-dining between the people of different creeds; and if their religious tolerance has slightly diminished of late, it is more due to the extraneous elements trying to unruffle the calm waters here with the ulterior motive of fishing at a later stage.

One of the glorious features of the broadmindedness of the people of Ladakh is that they make no difference between a local and an alien. A Kashmiri, a Chinese Turk, a Ladakhi and a European are all equal in the eyes of the local people and nobody is accorded any special rank of honour and nobody is an object of suspicion or contempt. Under the sun everybody is equal and everybody has a right to what Ladakh has to offer by way of hospitality. People of different nationalities have found that the Ladakhis are as good to them as to one another among themselves.

Politeness and Courtesy

The people of Ladakh have made social relationships a fine art. When two peoples meet, be it in a house, a street or a bazaar, there is always something more than a cursory and conventional 'Good morning' or 'Namaste'. They enquire not only about each other's welfare but also about the well being of each and every member of the other's family. These enquiries are made in the most courteous and artistic manner. The smile on each other's face is not artificially got up or simulated but is a genuine reflection of the inner joy at meeting an acquaintance. The hurly-burly of the work a day world does not make the process of greeting each other an unavoidable perfunctory formality; even the busiest day and the busiest hour cannot stop two persons from snatching a few minutes to express the sincerest regards to each other in the most leisurely and courteous way.

The Ladakhi people have coupled their elaborate forms of politeness and courtesy with an unbounded sense of hospitality. This hospitality does not confine itself to the limited sphere of relatives but includes friends and new acquaintances, men speaking other languages, professing other religions or belonging to a different nationality. The best dishes and the choicest drinks are at the disposal of the guest and he is treated with the utmost regard and highest hospitality. Even at the time of his departure the host takes the trouble of escorting him to the outermost gate or door.

It was a common custom among the people of Ladakh, though modern age is driving the habit into disuse, to offer some present called 'dalis' to the respected guest, as token of their esteem. These presents may be in cash or in kind. They are offered in the most ceremonious way and ceremoniously too the guest touches them to show his humble acceptance, but the gift is not actually received. If it is in kind, say, apricots or candies, the guest may taste one or two but he never accepts the gift in its entirely. Though the gifts offered are tokens of one's respect, they are also indicative of the profession or social standing of the man who offers them. Thus a rich man may send a bowl of rupees as present while a poor man may just hold out a rupee coin in his hand. The farmer may present a handful of corn, a gardener may offer a few dried apricots and a brewer may hold out one or two vases of the liquor he produces. But in all these cases usually the acceptance of the gift is formally expressed and the gift is never accepted.

Every body in this remote region of the world seems to have an abundant faith in the goodness of human nature. It is easy for a man to go to the bazaar and get a few things which he needs urgently and tell the shopkeeper that the money will be paid subsequently. It is also absolutely safe to give a rupee or two to the fisherman or the butcher on the understanding that next day he must send to one's house a fish or some meat. People trust each other and have complete faith in each other's bonafides. It is a common occurrence in the bazaar that the shop is kept open when the shopkeeper is away for his lunch or on some personal work. People, whether they run a shop or dwell in a house, pay very little attention to security because of their abiding faith in the goodness of their neighbours and in the trust-worthiness of the strangers. Though one has to admit that there is a little amount of bargaining in the shops and markets here, it is admitted on all hands that rarely this bargaining leads to bickering and seldom any attempt is made by the shopkeeper to cheat a customer.

Predilection For the Mysterious

A characteristic which the Ladakhis possess is the love for the mysterious and abstract. As a matter of fact, Buddhists everywhere over the world have this predilection for the mysterious since it is in marvellous accordance with the spirit of the Buddhist Philosophy. The beautiful and majestic idols of Buddha are worshipped with all reverence no doubt; but it is the grotesque shaped demi-gods, the mysterious symbols and signs that inspire awe and religious veneration in the hearts of the common Buddhist folks. The monasteries and 'lamasseries' would lose much of their sacred awe and air of mystery if they are built on the plains where they are easily accessible to the common folk. Therefore, the founders and builders of these religious monuments have always sought some hilltops, some precipitous rocks to perch them on. The people who live in the valleys close by have always to raise their heads high to have a look at the sacred abode, and have to climb winding roads or innumerable steps to reach the sanctum and worship the divinity. Thus the path leading to God is always long and steep and one should leave behind one's domestic and mundane ties to touch the fringe of the heavenly high and the mysterious.

A GOMPA. THE PATH TO DIVINITY IS LONG, ROUGH AND STEEP.

The high altitude, the inaccessible precipice, the desolate spot, the mysterious symbols, the strange tunes of temple music, the grotesque figures, all these are the necessary concomitances of a religious life. The sanctum sanctorium of each monastery is a veritable den of darkness where queer shaped flags with queer combination of colours ruffle in mysterious waves at the slight puff of air, where idols strange in shape and stranger in emitting facial expression sit solid on raised platforms, where the tiny oil lamps in their twinkling betray the surrounding gloom and where the burning incense permeates the enveloping atmosphere with a benumbing odour. There stays the mysterious one, surrounded in mystery.

"THE ENLIGHTENED ONE" IN THE DIM LIGHT OF THE SANCTUM SANCTORIUM.

This sense of mystery envelopes a person immediately on arrival. Specially as dusk approaches, the sense of living in a desolate, isolated area deepens and that mixed with the sounds from monasteries only adds to the atmosphere. Staying and interacting at monasteries is an experience, and it lives within oneself for a lifetime. Tales and legends abound about mysterious experiences and powers of the lamas. One has to live here and know the people to understand it.

Chapter IV

HEALTH AND HYGIENE

Nature is never unkind to mankind. Seeing the adverse climate combined with high altitude and comparative poverty one may be led to think at first glance that human life as such must be suffering a lot in this land. But very soon one sheds this belief away when going a little deeper one sees the ways in which nature has helped not only the human beings but also the animal life in this land. The people actually look happier and more contented than at many other places of the world. Few people look ill or poor in health. Red cheeks and smiling faces are a common sight.

General Health

General health, both of menfolk as well as women folk, in this district is fairly good. Average height of an adult man is 5' 4" and that of women is 5' 2". They are generally well-built and quite muscular. Chests are comparatively broader shoulders round and necks short and thick. Hardly anybody with a protruding abdomen is seen. Calf muscles are particularly well developed. Such a build of the body is necessarily due to the environment it is facing, the chief factors being a highly mountainous country and a very high altitude. Lack of oxygen at this height necessitates a big chest and the steep mountains a small size to promote ease in climbing, while a small abdomen and big calves are the natural results of the strain undergone in such a hilly land.

The mental development of an average Ladakhi is rather low, because he has got little mental work to do in his usual daily life. In cases he has been made to do some brain work, he has usually responded with a good mental development. Given proper schooling he is sure to develop well mentally. For instance, those Ladakhis who have joined the army have with training learnt very good drill and weapon handling. Put into any trade, they will learn it perhaps only slightly less quickly than people of other parts of India, atleast in the beginning and till awareness levels increase in society.

Water Supply

It is altogether from natural sources on which no artificial devices are superimposed. There are many good springs in the district which yield fresh water throughout the year. This water is clean, delicious, free from any harmful salts or infective matter and adequately rich in Iodine. One, therefore, hardly ever sees a case of goitre. These springs are the main source of drinking water throughout Ladakh. Another source is the streams (nullahs) formed by the down flow of water resulting from melting of snow at the hill tops. The nullah water is mainly used for washing and bathing purposes. A few small villages use it for drinking purposes too, because no springs exist in such villages. Even this water is quite clean and free from any harmful salts or infective material. Some villages even have to drink river water. Because the rivers in this part don't flow through any towns, the water is usually clean and free from any infective matter. Only for a few months in summer the water is muddy, but those who drink it always let the mud and sand settle down before drinking it. In the end it can be said that hardly any diseases due to faulty water supply seem to exist in Ladakh.

Food

Though only one crop is grown in the year, Ladakh is self sufficient in food. Practically every one works on the land and produces enough for himself for the whole year. Undoubtedly he is totally unaware of the proximal principals of food, the importance of a balanced diet and the mineral and vitamin contents of what he eats. Yet what he produces and subsequently eats is reasonably well balanced and wholesome diet. Consequently hardly any deficiency diseases are met with.

Food Constitution

   (a) **Protein:-** The main sources of proteins of animal origin in Ladakh are milk, eggs, chicken, meat and fish. While an average Ladakhi does keep a cow to get his share of milk to provide himself with his quota of animal proteins, other sources of such proteins are usually beyond his means. So he has to make up by consuming a better quality of vegetable proteins which he produces on his land by his own hard work. The chief of these are cereals, pulses and nuts. These vegetable proteins combined with the animal proteins of milk provide an average Ladakhi with adequate growth, energy and tissue repair, because the above combination obtains a fairly effective amino acid supplementation. Therefore, as far as protein content of his food is concerned, he can be compared to a vegetarian in any other part of the world, while a rich Ladakhi can afford all other kinds of animal proteins mentioned above and can be compared to an average non-vegetarian in any part of the world.

(b) **Carbohydrates**:- As in other places, this principal (factor) of food is the most abundant and most economical source of energy in the diet of a Ladakhi. Whereas other places in India depend upon wheat and rice as their main sources of carbohydrates, Ladakh depends upon 'giram' and barley mostly. It is only the rich Ladakhi who can afford wheat or rice. 'Giram' is a sort of poor quality wheat, being less tasty and containing slightly more roughage than wheat. But the quality of carbohydrate contained in it is in no way inferior to that of the wheat; the presence of more roughage in it only helps in obtaining good bowel movement in the absence of enough consumption of vegetables and fruits. Barley is rather a poorer stuff when compared to wheat, yet it serves the purpose of a poor Ladakhi very well who only stands to lose a little bit in the quality and not quantity of carbohydrates.

(c) **Fats**:- The main source of fats in Ladakh is milk, butter, clarified butter - ghee, nut oils, other vegetable oils, meat, fish and eggs. While milk supplies him with only a small quantity of fats, an average Ladakhi mostly depends upon nut and vegetable oils for his fats. Walnuts and apricot (khurmani) are grown in many parts and mustard -'sarson' in some parts of Ladakh. The 'khurmani' (apricot) seeds and walnuts yield the most of the fats while 'sarson' yields a small amount in some parts. These fats are only slightly inferior to butter and ghee and have no baneful effects. The rich Ladakhi can afford imported ghee and other sources of fats mentioned above.

A poor Ladakhi, however, consumes more of carbohydrates which according to medical experts get converted into fat in his body, thus making up the deficiency of consumed fats.

(d) **Mineral Salts:-**

   (i) **Sodium Chloride:-** Very little is obtained in Ladakh itself. Most of it is imported from outside. But thanks to the climate, sweating (one of the chief means of salt loss from the body) is very little throughout the year except from July to September. So salt requirement of an average Ladakhi is not much.

   (ii) **Iron:-** The iron requirement of an average Ladakhi is fulfilled by 'giram', barley, apricot, apple, turnip, cabbage, potatoes and tomatoes. The former two are fairly rich in this mineral and thus stand in good stead for a poor Ladakhi too, who is unable to afford the latter six. The rich Ladakhi, however, affords meat in addition for his iron content.

   (iii) **Calcium and Phosphorus:-** Again 'Giram', barley and milk come to the help of an average Ladakhi for supplying him adequate amounts of calcium and phosphorus, small amounts of which are also derived from apricot, cabbage, turnip and potatoes, according to doctors.

(e) **Vitamins:-** These organic compounds necessary, though in very small quantities, for normal growth and maintenance of healthy life, attract the attention of the modern nutrition expert most. Let us see how an average Ladakhi gets his full requirement of these highly essential components of diet. Here some medical experts feel that no physiological benefit is achieved by consuming very large doses of these compounds under normal circumstances. So one must take into consideration the minimal requirements of vitamins while discussing the food of an average Ladakhi. While summer provides enough of fresh vegetables and fruits and consequently enough of all vitamins, winter seems to be a difficult time when the vitamin content tends to fall down below the least minimal requirement. This applies particularly to the water soluble group of vitamins and Vitamin 'A' which are destructible easily and do not stand storage for any length of time. Yet very few cases of real avitaminosis are seen – a fact which seems rather difficult to explain. It is here one has to confess in completeness of one's knowledge about vitamins, according to some medical experts.

(i) **Vitamin 'A':-** In summer the chief sources are cereals, milk, apricot, nut oils, cabbage and tomatoes though the rich class can afford butter, ghee, meat and fish to obtain a much higher content of this vitamin. In winter the main sources remain to be cereals, milk and nut oils. Though dried apricots and cabbage are stored and well preserved for the winter, it is doubtful if they retain even half of their Vitamin 'A; content. Because no cases of avitaminosis 'A' are met with, it is considered that cereals, nut oils and milk provide the least minimal requirement even in winter.

(ii) **Vitamin 'B' Complex:-** Thiamine (B1) – More than required amount is supplied throughout the year by 'giram' and barley.

Riboflavine (B2) – Again enough is provided by 'giram' barley and milk throughout the year.

Nicotinic Acid (B7) – Adequate amounts are supplied by 'Giram' barley, and walnuts throughout the year.

(iii) **Vitamin 'C'** – In summer enough of this easily destructible vitamin is provided by green chillies, cabbage, tomatoes, potatoes, turnip, apricots and apples. But in winter none of these vegetables and fruits are available fresh and as this vitamin cannot stand storage for more than a few days, the vitamin 'C' content of the food naturally falls below the least minimal requirement. Yet one finds only a few cases of gum bleeds and nose bleeds during the whole winter. This fact is very difficult to explain. Perhaps the adrenals of an average Ladakhi are accustomed to storage of adequate quantities of Vitamin 'C' during the summer to last him throughout the winter without showing any signs of avitaminosis 'C' or perhaps an automatic and unknown process of sprouting keeps on working in the stored 'giram' thus increasing its Vitamin 'C' content.

(iv) **Vitamin 'D'** – Sunlight, nut oils are the chief sources, though the rich can afford much higher quantities in the form of butter, ghee and meat.

(v) **Vitamin 'E'** – The cereals, 'giram' and barley are the chief sources.

Caloric Value:- The minimal caloric requirements of an average Ladakhi doing average amount of strenuous work in this mountainous country having a height of 11,550 feet would vary from 2800 to 3200 calories. He makes it up as follows:-

Proteins	8%	56 gm	224 calories
Fats	10%	70 gm	630 calories
Carbohydrates	82%	574 gm	2294 calories
Total	100%	700 gm	3148 calories

Hence it can be clearly seen that an unbalance of food factors occurs where comparative poverty makes an average Ladakhi prefer quantity to quality in making up for its daily caloric needs. But this unbalance really does not matter at all. Carbohydrates is the current coin of our bodily needs and its combustion is always going on to give heat energy for all the work we do. Moreover, when lot of carbohydrates is taken some of it gets converted into fats in the body; so that if somebody is fed on carbohydrates and minimal requirement of protein only without giving any fats, yet he will grow fat owing to the conversion of carbohydrates into fats inside the body. Thus low quantity of fat in diet does not matter at all. Unlike carbohydrates, proteins are never stored in the body to fall back upon in hours of need (i.e. stress and strain). So that all that one must consume should be equal to the minimal daily requirement and containing the amino-acids necessary for promotion of growth and tissue repair. As already discussed, the diet of an average Ladakhi contains quantitatively and qualitatively the same amino-acids as are present in the diet of a vegetarian anywhere else and its protein content does not go below the minimal requirement.

Hygiene and Sanitation

A Ladakhi is not fond of bath. A cold climate combined with very cold nullah water and inability to afford wood for warming it will naturally deter any man, not to speak of a Ladakhi, from taking bath. Due to the same circumstances he does not wash his clothes also very often; the question of being able to afford soap is also there. Thank God, flies are not met with in any abundance here.

But now slowly a Ladakhi is learning the importance of personal hygiene and is trying to improve it. This he is mainly learning from the army. I am sure in due course of time he will be as conscious of personal hygiene as others are in the plains.

House Hygiene

Small semi-kuchha houses are a common sight. There is only one main room which is used for all purposes including cooking and sleeping. This is the only room which is kept clean. Outside this room is usually a small lawn which is seldom cleaned. This lawn is used for keeping Cattle, dried cow dung and other kinds of fuel. On one side of the lawn is the latrine-cum-urinal which is just a modified form of deep trench latrine. It has a small room as super structure, through which a small hole (usually 2-1/2 feet X3/4 foot) leads to the main latrine cavity, which in itself is a small room having an excreta clearing exit in one of its walls. This kind of latrine makes a permanent and lifelong type of deep trench, the excreta being cleared from it from time to time. Dry earth is always stored in the superstructure and when the excreta drops into the latrine cavity below, the dry soil is shoveled over it in sufficient quantities. This method has a twofold purpose:-

(a) The emanation of stench is minimized if not completely eliminated.

(b) The earth mixed excreta becomes a valuable stenchless manure which, in spring, is carried in baskets and bags to the farms and spread over evenly on them, thereby insuring better crop and greater yield during the harvesting season. Ladakh seeks to enrich her depleted soil in this way, obviating the necessity of buying costly chemical manure and at the same time keeping the village clean and tidy. This method of sewage disposal very much approaches the Chinese method except that while in China the latrines are dug into the ground, in Ladakh they are built over it.

This type of latrine is quite good for this place because it works cheap in the long run; requires no sweeper system as every house clears its own latrine as and when necessary for use as manure, in its own fields. Fly breeding in such a latrine is almost negligible.

Ventilation and lighting of the whole house is rather poor. Not to speak of the latrine, even the main room does not have more than a door for entrance and a small window which is also mostly kept closed due to cold weather. At cooking time the whole room is filled with smoke. The black roof of the room bears testimony to this fact. Sunlight hardly enters the room during the day and there is no electric or hurricane lamps to give it enough light at night. But a Ladakhi seldom sits inside his room during the day and does no reading or writing work at night. With the availability of electricity the hygiene will improve in Ladakh also. As it is the deep trench type latrine system is better than most Indian villages have. The availability of electricity will enable them to read and write also at night.

General Sanitation of Towns and Villages:- But for the fact that Leh forms one of the arteries of Central Asian Trade, it cannot be considered a town in the modern sense of that term and can very well be looked upon as a big village. Except for some roads and the bazaar, Leh is covered all over the farms and arid mountain strips. But the scenario is fast changing.

Handicapped as the people of Ladakh are on account of the shortage of fuel, the poor class among the local population depends upon dry cow-dung to augment the meager supply of fuel. Thus, cow-dung sometimes is deprived of its legitimate role of being good manure on the farms and is made to play the more precious role of the kitchen fuel. This has indirectly but considerably helped in keeping the streets and the bazaar clean. It is a common sight in the bazaar of Ladakh that cow-dung is brought into the market for the sale to the poor folk. It is not strange that there are many buyers if one remembers that firewood in this corner of India sells at much higher rate as compared to India.

Chances of Improvement:- Large number of Ladakhis who have joined the army have certainly learnt personal and house hygiene. Seeing them their neighbours are also picking up the same. So it is expected that in due course of time the Ladakhis will have a good personal and house hygiene. And if the civil health authorities do their bit, the general sanitation of the towns and villages will also improve soon.

Some public latrines at important corners of the town for the general use of the traveller or man on the street may also be constructed. The night soil collecting in these can be given to the highest bidder who in turn can be made responsible for keeping these latrines clean and in good condition.

Effects on A New-Comer to the Place

In the summer a new-comer only suffers from effects of height. The usual symptoms noticed are breathlessness, feeling of weight on head and shoulders, sleeplessness, headache and in some cases vomiting and epistaxis (mountain sickness). These symptoms pass off in two or three days and the new-comer slowly completes acclimatization in about a week's time.

In winter he is in an additional danger of catching cold, getting bronchitis and in occasional cases Pneumonia. Localized effects of cold in the form of frost-bite and trench foot may occur in about 0.5 percent of the new-comers. Fibrositis is more commonly met with. In winter about 10 to 12 days are required to get acclimatized.

The body responds to the height (which means oxygen lack) by a quicker breathing, a quicker and enhanced circulation throughout the body and particularly through the lungs, increased number of red blood corpuscles and increased percentage of hemoglobin in the blood. All the organs of the body and particularly the heart and lungs have to work much more. The result is a high metabolic rate, i.e. greater bodily wear and tear so that the appetite and thirst both start increasing as soon as acclimatization starts. The heart and lungs tend to undergo some degree of hypertrophy which is reversible on going back to the mental condition of a new-comer is that of depression and lack of interest in work. But in a few days he gets over it.

Every individual before coming to this place should undergo a medical examination as regards the condition of his lungs and heart and blood pressure. People who have ever suffered from any kind of lung disease like TB, Bronchitis and Pneumonia should be prevented from coming to this place. Owing to the excessive stress and strain undergoing by the lungs at such a height, the dormant foci of TB may burst open, the bronchitis may start advancing further and pneumonia may easily occur due to excessive cold in those who have already suffered from them in their past.

People with fatty constitution or high blood pressure are also unfit for the place. A fat man usually takes a much longer time to get acclimatized. A hypertensive will suffer marked breathlessness, complete insomnia, more bleeds, and loss of appetite, vomiting and marked restlessness. His blood pressure goes higher which means excessive strain on the heart.

Diseases

While in the rest of India, Malaria, Tuberculosis and Enteric Group of Fevers take the heaviest toll of human life, Ladakh is entirely free from these deadly enemies. The mosquito vector conveying Malaria cannot exist at such height, the germs of TB and Enteric Group of Fevers are quite unknown to the place. Again epidemics of plague, cholera and dysenteries and diarrheas of infective nature have seldom been known to occur in this district. The plague-carrying vector, the Ratflea, cannot exist in the cold climate of the place though rats do live here. The absence of cholera, enteric, dysenteries and infective diarrheas only points to a faultless water supply and absence of flies for most of the year.

But Ladakh is not altogether free from disease. The main ailments found here are VD, Typhus, Chickenpox, Mumps, and Worm infestations, dental caries and pyorrhea. One may find a few stray cases of goitre (simple). Dyspepsia and sore throats occur only in those who have joined the army and started eating and drinking the army way. Fortunately, few surgical emergencies like acute appendicitis and intestinal obstruction are met with. Cancer, the dilemma of the whole modern civilization, is hardly met with here.

(a) VD – It is the most common disease. About 3% of the whole population of Ladakh is infected with it. It was the Sinkiang trader who brought this disease about two centuries back. Due to the practice of polyandry the disease has procured many victims since then. The Ladakhi does not seem to worry much about it except when it shows itself in acute exacerbations. The women folk in many cases do not know themselves that they are having VD and quite unintentionally marry and convey the disease to their husband(s).

The army is always in a potential danger of the disease. Most of the men are locals and therefore are quite unmindful of the horrors of VD. The rest who are from India or Kashmir are sometimes tempted by the local women who, out of poverty, may be ready to mix with men. Therefore, the army must enforce rigorous training about horrors and prevention of VD and also provide lot of amenities for the men.

(b) Typhus – It is supposed to be endemic in some parts of Ladakh. Sometimes it has taken up an epidemic form also. Whenever there is even a single case of typhus in the civil population, the army is always in danger of an epidemic. Because all the army personnel live together at one place, if a single case occurs amongst them and timely delousing of all other personnel and all stores is not done, the louse born typhus can spread.

Prevention being always better than cure, rigorous training about the horrors of this disease is essential throughout the year.

(c) Chicken and Small Pox – These are also endemics in some part of Ladakh, and many a time small epidemics of chicken pox have also been reported. Though primary vaccination in infancy is done in most of the cases, nobody seems to bother about vaccination for the rest of the life thereafter. However, there has hardly ever been an epidemic of small pox in this place, though a few cases of chicken pox occur almost every autumn and spring.

(d) Mumps – In some or other part of Ladakh mumps is always lurking throughout the year. Usually it is accompanied by no serious complications endangering life or the sex glands.

(e) Worm Infestations – It is quite common in the whole area. The most common worm is the Ascaris Lumbricoides (the round worm) though stray cases of Taeniasis (flat worm infestation) also occur. The most potent cause for this is bad hygiene and sanitation where upon the eggs of these worms are infested by human beings through unwashed hands after working in the fields and eating unwashed vegetables and fruits. Improvement of hygiene and sanitation is the only way of getting rid of these worms.

(f) Dental caries and Pyorrhea – Due to poor oral-dental hygiene, dental caries and Pyorrhea are quite common.

(g) Dyspepsia and Sore throats – These occur mostly in those who have joined the army and started partaking of rich and spiced diet and drinking rum. In civilian Ladakhis one comes across abdominal discomfort, mild diarrhoea and constipation due to worm infestation only.

Suggestions For Prevention and Cure

It is clear from the above that almost all the diseases occurring in Ladakh can be prevented by proper education in personal and house hygiene and general sanitation. It is only the medical authorities who have to get up and exert a lot towards bringing home to the public the importance of hygienic ways of living, the horrors of all diseased endemic in the area, and the sense of reporting to civil medical authorities on falling ill.

Unfortunately, the medical facilities existent at present are meager for the whole area. There is one civil hospital in the town of Leh. In addition, there is a Moravian Mission Dispensary which is also situated in the town of Leh. In the rest of the district there are minimal medical facilities. The result is while Leh itself gets some scientific medical aid, most of the district has to depend upon the flukes (chance) of local 'hakims'. Two dispensaries do exist in Nubra in Ladakh and one in Chushul Sector. These civil dispensaries should teach a few intelligent persons the principles of hygiene and prevention and thus form a sanitary squad in each village. The duties of such a squad should be:-

(a) To look after the general sanitation of the village.

(b) To impart to the whole of the village the importance and principles of personal and house hygiene.

(c) To teach preventive measures against Typhus, VD, Chicken pox, Worm infestations and Mumps.

(d) To ensure that every man who falls sick in the village is at once sent to the civil dispensary for timely and proper aid.

(e) To report at once on the occurrence of a single case of any of the endemic infectious diseases.

(f) To do vaccination whenever required.

The main civil dispensary at Leh should be properly equipped to diagnose and treat all those diseases at least which are endemic in the area. Therefore, it should have complete facilities for urine and faeces examination, routine blood tests, blood tests for VD and Typhus. It should also have an X-Ray plant because broken limbs are not altogether unknown. Further, it should have all the modern antibiotics for the treatment of VD and Typhus and enough surgical instruments to deal with all kinds of surgical emergencies. It should infact become a proper hospital.

All the dispensaries should be well equipped with drugs required to treat worm infestations and should have enough of anti-louse powder at all times.

Chapter V

ECONOMIC CONDITIONS AND INFRASTRUCTURE

The economic conditions of a country are largely conditioned by the geographical factors and climate. How far the geographical factors in Ladakh govern and condition the economic life of the people is already seen in the second chapter of this book. In this chapter, however, an attempt will be made to study the economic conditions as such prevailing here.

Though in extent Ladakh including Kargil is as large as the provinces of Jammu and Kashmir comprising over 27 individual Tehsils and niabats, the mountains regions and dry lands have considerably restricted the area that could be brought under cultivation. It is estimated that in Ladakh there are just about 20,000 acres of cultivated land. For the entire area of Ladakh this figure would give one acre of cultivated land for one square mile. This gives one a rough idea as to how barren a land Ladakh is.

When Ladakh is such a barren country one can easily gauge the struggle for existence of the local people. Though the size of families varies, on an average the Ladakhi family can be taken to be composed of 6 members. Because, while the Buddhists who practise polyandry have comparatively few children in the family, the Muslims practicing polygamy have many children – thereby each offsetting the other, so to say. For a population of 36 thousand and odd, therefore, there would be roughly 6 thousand families, assuming an average of 6 members for each family. Thus, six thousand families have to depend upon about 20 thousand acres of cultivated land for their livelihood. That would mean that each family of 6 members would have to eke out their livelihood from 3-1/2 acres of cultivated land. Besides, as pointed out in the chapter on Geographical Survey, much of the cultivated land is in the hands of 'gompas' or monasteries and therefore the average family holding would in effect not even reach up to 3 acres. This explains the appalling poverty of the people and their low living standards.

Buildings

The buildings in each and every place are typical of and are dependent upon the topography and climate of the place. The scarcity of wood in Ladakh makes wooden materials too costly for building purposes and the high cost of fuel renders fire-burnt bricks uneconomic. The bricks used for building purposes are therefore mostly sun-dried. But luckily for the people of Ladakh the district abounds in rocks and marble sand. These are plentifully used in the foundations of the buildings, steps and staircases and the walls surrounding buildings and yards. The little wood that is used in mainly for windows, doors and roof-beams, and luckily again, the absence of white ants, due to extreme winter cold, accounts for long life for every bit used.

KHAR OR THE PALACE OF THE FORMER RULERS OF LADAKH AS SEEN FROM A STREET NEAR THE BAZAAR.

Even the richest men in Ladakh cannot afford to use lime and sand for the purpose of mortar and white-washing buildings, since these become too expensive on account of the long distances over which they are to be transported right from the sea-shore far down in the South. But the ingenuity of the Ladakhi people has helped them to find cheap substitutes for these and what is called 'Spituk clay' serves well the role of lime. But simple and unostentatious as the people of Ladakh are, their buildings, like their manners and mode of living, are usually not 'white-washed'.

As steel and iron, in a finished form, like all other metals, have to come from the South, the industrial part of India, while communications are not developed the people of Ladakh cannot afford to use them as plentifully as they like and every attempt is made to avoid them except when substitutes cannot be found or when the substitutes are not durable. This explains why the windows, except in modern type buildings, are made in the form of shutters opening upwards and resting on short wooden pegs or cross-cut groves in the sides.

Rest Houses

The houses all over Ladakh are of one and the same pattern. Only the houses in Western Ladakh are bigger and better than those in the Eastern and the Northern areas of the district.

It is also worthwhile noting that for a district like Ladakh which is highly mountainous and devoid of good communication facilities, the State has found the necessity of building rest houses for the convenience of travellers. Men normally cover 15 to 25 miles a day on horse-back and it is but essential that as the day closes the travellers should reach some habitation or other for resting during the night. Where there are villages already in existence the traveller can easily seek refuge for the night; but where there are none the travellers have found the need for some improvised rest-houses. Such a great necessity had forced the State authorities of J&K to build rest-houses along Srinagar – Leh route which has been used for trade purposes from times immemorial. These rest houses though at present in rather neglected state of affairs are of great use to the travellers. The rest-houses are generally one-storeyed and usually consist of 5 to 6 rooms. These rest-houses are to be found at each stage on the Srinagar – Leh route, but on other routes like the Leh to Xinjiang, Leh to Tibet, etc these rest houses are found only rarely and any way those existing are in a reasonably dilapidated condition.

Waterways in Ladakh

The problem of the waterways is as complex as it is uncertain. The following points would bear out the correctness of this statement-

- (a) The waterways of Ladakh are of no use whatsoever as a means of communication. The only waterways in the area are the rivers Indus, Shyok, Suru, Dras, Zanskar and their tributaries.

- (b) None of the waterways are navigable because of the impetuosity of their flow and the presence of huge boulders in their beds.

- (c) The rapidity of the current especially in summer, when the volume of water in the rivers increases enormously on account of the melting snow, is a big obstacle in bridging the rivers. The prevalence of boulders is an additional obstacle in ferry operations.

- (d) While none of the waters is navigable, in summer even the smaller streams (nalas) become swollen with water and it is a dangerous task to ford them. In winter, however, even the major rivers get frozen at many places so that a thick hard icy path is made for people to cross from one bank to the other.

With all these vagaries of water flow and freezing possibilities there is no waterway organization as such in the district and therefore questions regarding control and personnel do not arise. As the waterways are not navigable, questions regarding craft boats also do not arise.

Floods

In spite of the increased flow of water in summer in all the rivers and nalas (streams), floods are rather rare in Ladakh. The Nubra valley, however, suffered serious damage about four decades ago when the natural Shyok dam burst and the huge volume of water thus released deluged not only the basin of the Shyok but also that of the Indus. This is a rare occurrence and may repeat itself once in a generation. In some parts of the district the bridges built by the villagers may be swept away by the increase in the volume of water in summer but it is as much due to the weakness of the bridges as it is due to the increased force of water.

Irrigation

The method of irrigation in Ladakh is peculiar but nonetheless well suited to the country which is mountainous to the extreme. Occasionally as one descends a mountain slope or walks along a river bed, dim in the distance one perceives a thin, green horizontal line, hundreds of feet above the river and extending from one end of the valley to the other. It is nothing but a water canal which brings water from some distant glacier fed stream high up in the mountains. But to the onlooker it seems rather strange how the people of Ladakh could have, with no power houses at their disposal, succeeded in lifting the water of the river that flows beneath to hundreds of feet above where the canal is seen. The only answer could be: Necessity is the mother of inventions; and imagination the father.

While the stream high up in the distant mountain might supply an unending source of water, the ingenuity, the patient labour and the dogged perseverance which make water available to the fields miles away are supplied by the local people. One cannot but marvel at the ingenuity and the natural engineering skill of the people of Ladakh if one sees how even along the most precipitous cliffs, which seem almost inaccessible except to the most skillful among the mountaineers, the cooperative effort of the resourceful farmers has succeeded in building these canals. One of the characteristic features of these canals which make them perceptible even from a distance is the strip of wild vegetation along its banks, vegetation which thrives on the water percolating from the sides of the small canals.

Type of Transport

The district of Ladakh, mountainous as most of the region is, has problem by way of transport facilities.

    (a) **Roads and Vehicles** – Since Ladakh has been connected with Kashmir as well as Himachal Pradesh by roads, Ladakh has all types of vehicles plying on its roads. New roads have been constructed in Ladakh district also which go up to line of actual control with Western Tibet in the East and Xinjiang in the north. However, the roads to Kashmir and Himachal Pradesh get blocked during the winter season due to heavy snowfall on the passes enroute. But, the aircraft from India and Kashmir can fly to Ladakh during the winter season. So Ladakh is not cut off from the rest of India, as was the case in the past.

There are passes in Ladakh which get blocked during the winter season due to heavy snowfall. Then the ponies and the coolies are the only alternatives, as the vehicle cannot be used on these passes.

(b) **Pony** – This is the most important means of travel and transport. People travel from village to village mostly on horseback and rarely by walking. Luggage, merchandise and domestic supplies are also often carried on horses. Ponies therefore become indispensable part of the domestic possessions and every household with some means owns at least one or two ponies. Some local people earn their livelihood by hiring out ponies.

(c) **Coolies** – Even the poor folk of Leh cannot play the role of the beast of burden, as the poor folk in India do, because of the high altitude of the place. It is a common experience of everybody who had been to Leh that even walking bare handed (without a load) on a slightly ascending road makes one rest for breath, on account of the rarified air and the deficiency in oxygen. So carrying heavy loads on one's back, head or shoulders becomes well nigh impossible though the local people, habituated as they are to these conditions and out of sheer necessity, do occasionally carry loads on their back. It is, therefore not strange that one often finds in the bazaar men and women carrying baskets on their back, baskets which are too small to contain anything except a square foot of goods. Secondly, everybody who has a small load on his back to carry over a distance can often be seen to unload it for every furlong or two and halt for a while, out of sheer exhaustion, before resuming the journey for the next furlong.

(d) **Air Service** – During Pakistan's invasion of Ladakh in 1947-1948, an airfield was built on the plains of Spituk in Leh. Ladakh has more than one airfield now. Indian Air Force planes as well as Indian National Airways connect Ladakh with Sri Nagar in J&K and with New Delhi and Chandigarh. This connectivity by air to Ladakh has boosted the tourism to Ladakh. So Ladakh has at present become a tourist paradise with lots of hotels in and around Leh. Because of air connectivity with Delhi and Sri Nagar, many foreign visitors are coming to Ladakh, besides the Indian tourists. The presence of Indian Army units stationed at Kargil and Leh area, have also brought a fresh bloom of prosperity to the people of Ladakh. Many young men of Ladakh have joined the Army and are doing well in the Army too, as they are ideally fit for high altitude warfare. As and when trade with Tibet and Xinjiang opens up once again, it will bring more prosperity to the people of Ladakh.

Fisheries

It is a big mystery why the indigenous population, hard up as it is in food resources, is indifferent to this source of human nutriment. Probably one of the explanations is that the local population being predominantly Buddhist is mainly interested in exploiting the vegetable kingdom, leaving the animal kingdom untouched. It is the Muslims in the local population that find fish a valuable supplement to their meager diet. Though fish is obtained from the rivers and the nalas, it cannot be said that these sources are explored to their fullest extent. The consumption of fish on the whole is quite negligible and one rarely finds fish in the local market. There are no restrictions whatsoever on fishing but it is a pity that there are no markets for fisheries in the district and no organization worth the name to explore and exploit this source of food.

Game Hunting

Game hunting almost suffers the same handicap as the fisheries, though wild animals, good for the pot, are abundant in the hill sides. But in a way this is good since it preserves the wild life of the country from extinction. Some of the local people – here too it is the alien element – do often go on hunting expeditions and though their efforts are often rewarded, the rugged terrain and the lack of communication facilities is a discouraging factor. Among the animals that are easily bagged can be named the following:-

(a) Ibex

(b) Wild goats and sheep

(c) Snow fox

(d) Wolf

(e) Wild horses

Foreign Visitors

Kashmir is called the paradise of visitors and merry-makers. This means much to the Kashmiris. The richer the visitor the more money he leaves behind him in exchange for Kashmir's native products or handicrafts. The same is true of Ladakh. As a matter of fact, the more adventurous among the visitors to Kashmir have always thought their journey to be incomplete unless they travelled up to Leh. And foreign visitors are always welcomed by the Ladakhis since they would not only buy local products but would also engage ponies and vehicles for journeys.

Meanwhile, the Indian Army units stationed at Leh and Kargil have brought a fresh bloom of prosperity to the people of Ladakh. Transporters and ponies are hired in large numbers, servants are engaged, foodstuffs bought and consumed and the bushy haired pups purchased and taken out of Ladakh. More prosperous days would come for Ladakh when Leh is made accessible through a connecting highway for the greater part of the year by a road to Himachal Pradesh.

The Lamaism of Ladakh

Actually, one of the special features of Ladakh's economy is the system of 'lamaism'. Almost every Buddhist family in Ladakh thinks itself blessed if one of the members joins a monastery and becomes a 'lama'. In each and every family, on account of the custom of polyandry (now dying out) and the law of primogeniture, it is usually one of the younger brothers who quits the family and joins the monastery. Though he leaves his family he is not very sorry for it because he is saved from manual labour on the field from dawn to dusk to earn his daily morsel. In the monasteries, however, he is assured of his daily bread without much personal struggle on his part.

But how does this affect the economy of Ladakh. According to some, the proportion of 'lamas' to laymen is so high that 'lamaism' is a drain on the man-power of the area. For a man interested in the economic prosperity of the population, it would seem incredible that fairly large portion of the youth of this land should spend their lives in the cells of the monasteries in an economically unproductive fashion. It is said of one of the Chinese emperors that when Buddhism was holding its full sway over the masses in China and when men and women joined the monasteries in large numbers and became monks and nuns, the emperor saw the economic structure of the

State crumbling and immediately ordered the closure of all the monasteries and forced the monks and nuns to marry and become full partners in the economic and social life of the country.

Not that the 'lamas' and 'chomos' or nuns of Ladakh should be forced to do the same but that something must be done to improve the economy of the area on account of those unemployed or choosing to be unemployed being dependent upon society and the earnings of the poor men. However, the solution adopted by the Chinese emperor is least suited and positively harmful for Ladakh. With the abolition of polyandry, the custom which restricted the size of the families, the growth of population has somewhat accelerated, and if the large number of monks and nuns were to enter upon married life, the population may rise further.

The 'lamas' and 'chomos' (nuns) besides leading a life which is economically unproductive, hinder the economic prosperity of Ladakh in several other ways. Having joined the monastery the 'lamas' and 'chomos' devote much of their time for religious studies and training. Though this education is mostly religious, still, the 'lamas' and 'chomos' occupy the first ranks in the list of literate people. Consequently their influence upon the local masses and the society is considerable. The influence makes people religious and sometimes also quite superstitious. The 'lamas' and 'chomos' are zealous in safeguarding their interests and maintaining their spiritual and intellectual superiority and persistently make the masses believe that their spiritual future is safe so long as the hierarchy of the 'lamas' is intact. In short Lamaism or lamas are likely to continue guiding Buddhists in Ladakh with some reforms in their hierarchy, or working ethics in their monasteries. Thus under the garb of guaranteeing spiritual beatitude the 'lamas' enjoy part of the fruits of the labours of these innocent and credulous working masses. But this is generally true of religious leaders of other religions also.

No doubt the local masses are increasingly becoming aware of the actual nature of 'lamaism' and therefore there is possibility that it may lose its importance or improve its quality which is likely to happen later. But the question is: if 'lamaism' falls into disrepute and releases many young men and women, who would otherwise look after the monastic cells, how is Ladakh going to use this manpower in economic activity? Besides, how would Buddhism survive without lamas propagating this religion?

Of late, the youth of Ladakh has shown great enthusiasm to join the ranks of the Indian Army and a considerable number of the local youth have been already recruited. With the political consciousness of the local masses waxing and with their faith in 'lamaism' waning there is every possibility that the future generations of young men may seek recruitment into the army than into any monastery. Mention has already been made in the first chapter of this book regarding the excellent fighting qualities of these people. What is important to note here is that the local people are so much accustomed and attached to the conditions prevailing here that they refuse stubbornly to venture out of Ladakh, or seek their fortunes in other parts of the world. This is indeed a big handicap for a soldier who is normally expected to serve in any part of the country and sometimes even outside the country. But when one sees how the modern world is changing and changing so fast, one feels confident that the able-bodied youths of Ladakh would by and by overcome their reluctance to leave their region and would be willing to serve elsewhere. When such a day comes Ladakh would be economically enriched and every month the post offices here would receive money orders dispatched by Ladakhi soldiers or other personnel serving elsewhere.

It should be mentioned here that it is not the soldiers only who are reluctant to leave their hearth and home. Even the mercantile community, which should be too willing to go even to the North-pole if only it can conduct some business there and earn a few rupees, is unwilling to shake off its domestic moorings and venture into foreign countries or world markets. That is why so far the trade in Ladakh with its neighbours has been conducted not by Ladakhis but by traders from the neighbouring countries. This is indeed a great handicap to the economic progress of the local masses.

Economic Upliftment of Ladakh

The primary need of Ladakh today is the economic uplift of its people. The appalling poverty of the people is a great danger to India's security especially because Ladakh's neighbours Sinkiang (Xinjiang) and Tibet, have gone Communist. If something is not done to ameliorate the economic lot of these people, communistic seeds scattered over Ladakh by her afore-mentioned neighbours might find a fertile soil here for their germination and growth. It is certainly better that the seeds are not permitted to germinate than to use force in order to weed out full grown plants. Towards this end, the economic uplift of the local people is a sine qua non and that too an urgent one, brooking no delay.

Of course, every economic development plan means some expenses to the Indian Exchequer and the Indian Government, hard-pressed as it is with the development plans in India proper cannot spare much, if it can spare anything, for the development projects of such a remote region as Ladakh.

Of course, while considering the amount of money that the Government of India may have to spend for the development projects in Ladakh, it is to be admitted that Ladakh would not give such a rich harvest for the seeds sown (funds invested) as some other province in India might do. But Ladakh has value of its own – I mean its strategic value. And this is a point which cannot be ignored especially if one recalls what happens across the frontiers, in Tibet and Xinjiang. Secondly, in Ladakh though the fish caught may not be big and the game hunted may not be fat, still, the cost of the bait would never exceed that of the fish and the cost of the game would never exceed that of the bullet.

The economic development plans in Ladakh do not follow any different pattern than elsewhere in India. The need here, as elsewhere, is for better educational facilities, technical schools for training in handicrafts, dams for irrigation, bridges for better communications, and development of electricity producing projects etc. This list can be considerably enlarged, but the best thing is to appoint a special Economic and Industrial Survey Commission which can study these items on the spot and draft plans as to which is more important and which is less, which scheme should have priority over other schemes.

Chapter VI

RELIGION

I was Army Head Quarters based officer in Ladakh and I stayed in Ladakh for over two years and often met the Christian, Muslim and Buddhist leaders in Ladakh. I had good relations with all of them and so they expressed their views quite frankly. I moved in various parts of Ladakh, on horse/mule or on foot (1952) depending upon terrain and the weather, as I had to send a monthly secret report to the Military Intelligence Department at Army Head Quarters.

The people of Ladakh, comparatively backward by our standards as they are, are a highly religious minded people. Religious affinities and affiliations are dominant factors in the activities and relationships of the local people. Consequently the political scenes, as stated in the next chapter, are completely dominated by the religious leaders and religious organizations of the locality. While Buddhists form the majority among the local population, the Muslims come a close second, Hindus and Christians are comparatively just a handful.

Buddhists

The Buddhists are unsurpassed for their broad-mindedness, generosity, straightforwardness and good nature. Cosmopolitan in general outlook as they are, and equally tolerant towards other religions, they observe no taboos with regard to interdining, intermarriage or with regard to eating the meat of particular animals. Because of the custom of polyandry, which was outlawed recently, there has been a surplus of marriageable girls among them and these girls have been most of the time married to the Muslims. The temples and rest houses for travellers maintained by Buddhists have always been open to men of all nationalities and religions without the least distinction.

One of the biggest drawbacks of the Buddhist community is their inordinate addiction to the drinking of 'chheng', a beer like drink, and the habit has done great harm to the community in several ways. Even some of 'lamas' are not immune from this vice, though religious discipline demands that they should abstain from it. The habit is both the cause of and result of the low economic standard of the people. Living in a comparatively barren land, semi-starved and without much of an occupation, a pot or two of 'chheng' is more than welcome to them and the subsequent stupor makes them take to life in an easy fashion.

The Buddhist community depends largely upon agriculture to sustain them. Trade and commerce, both local and foreign, are largely the monopoly of other communities.

A good proportion among the Buddhist population have no lands to cultivate and they earn their livelihood by menial labour and sometimes by daily wages. The gross illiteracy of community has, alas, deprived them of their due share in the public services. Thus, their interests are always neglected both by the local as well as by the Central Administration, and it is only recently that they have, under the inspiring leadership of Kushak Bakula, the Ex Head Lama, as well as other Lamas started voicing their grievances in many ways and seeking constitutional redress of them.

Though polyandry is abolished by law and monogamous marriages are becoming more popular, but the custom of monogamy will attain universality only when the resources of the land are developed and the economic conditions improve substantially.

The Buddhists look upon India as a holy land where the Buddhist religion and the founder of the religion were born, and where all the spots and monuments of their religion are. Their veneration for the land is beyond words and their love for the Indians is genuine.

Muslims

At Leh the Sunis have an organization called the Anjuman Mamin-ul-Islam of which Syed Mohd Syed was the Ex President (1952). The Juma Mosque is the pivot of their religious life. The parallel Shia organization is called the Anjuman Imamia.

For the Sunis mosque is, in general, the centre of religious life, while for the Shias it is the Matam Sarai or House of Mourning where ceremonial mournings, over the death of the martyrs of Karbala, are regularly conducted as the most important function. The Shias hold the Aghas – religious leaders believed to be descended from the prophet and Sheikhs – men, well versed in religious lore, in great reverence. Every village has got its religious seminary where the local 'mullah' teaches the scripture and the practice of religion. The Shias will never bear witness against one another when the other party happens to belong to another faith.

Shias

A Shia barber will never shave non Muslims in Ladakh. They are perfect teetotalers, because drink is forbidden by Islam, but some of them freely practice usury though it is equally condemned by their religion. They are austere in their ways and look upon ceremonial mournings as an essential part of their religion. The custom of temporary marriages contracted for definite periods is sanctioned by their religion and prevails among them. They look upon Lucknow as their cultural stronghold in India.

Sunis

They are more liberal than the Shias. They abstain from drink like the Shias, but some of them are not averse to dubious ways of conducting business which may be regarded as a substitute for usury. Temporary marriages do not prevail among them.

Doctrinal differences stand in the way of the two sects coming together; but against non Muslims and in the general interests of Islam, they will always present a united front.

Christians

The local branch of the Moravian Mission, of which mention has been made in the next chapter, is the main organization which regulates the religious life of the Christian community of the District. There is a church of the mission in town where Christians go and offer prayers on Sundays.

The Christians are a microscopic minority, concentrated in about a dozen families, generally prosperous and better educated. The number of Christian families being small and each of them being the victim of a superiority complex, the Christians are generally averse to intermarrying between themselves and seek brides for their young men from the Buddhists. Some of their girls at times find their husbands among other communities and a good number remain unmarried for long after they have reached the age of puberty.

Notwithstanding the superiority complex of the different families, the Christians, under the leadership of Rev. Driver, the past Superintendent of the local branch of the Moravian Mission, who was ably assisted by his wife and Dr. and Mrs. Vittoz, are a closely knit organisation and each of the Christians is willing to take infinite trouble to help another Christian in order to further the cause and prosperity of the community. Though of late the work of conversion has suffered a big set-back on account of the political consciousness of the local people and also on account of Indo-Pak and Buddhist-Muslim problems looming large in the minds of the people, the dogged perseverance of the Christian missionaries, who draw financial assistance from abroad, is showing no sign of abatement. The Rev. and Mrs. Driver as well as other Missionaries have been staying here for more than 19 years and their activities extend beyond the bounds of religious work also. The other, Christian members of the church have also been doing good work since then.

Monasteries of Ladakh

The people of Ladakh who live so close to nature and strenuously strive to wrest their daily morsel, who suffer the rigours of the severe winter cold and uncertain snowfall, who during their literal as well as metaphorical mountainous journey in life expose themselves to the vagaries of nature, sometimes kind sometimes hostile, cannot but have faith in and seek solace from religion.

During the early part of the Christian era when Buddhist monks, imbued with the zeal of the new religion, traversed the long trek of mountainous terrain from India to China, the villages in Ladakh became inns for these emissaries of the enlightened one. The messages of peace that these emissaries brought, the simple, holy and saintly atmosphere that these monks created wherever they went, could not but touch the feeling faculty and hearts of the people of Ladakh and appealed to their imagination. Ladakh slowly but surely underwent the metamorphosis of Buddhist creed and the sacred serenity of this religion was in perfect tune with the general peace loving nature of the people of Ladakh. But when the centuries rolled on, when the age of philosophical renaissance came to an end in India, when Hinduism again managed a grip over the minds of the Indians and when Tibet became the repository of Buddhist scriptures, Ladakh; which was so far the highway of religious traffic between India and China changed her position too and became the backyard of Tibetan Buddhism. The Buddhists of Ladakh started drawing inspiration from the sanctum sanctorium of Tibet and the 'lamas' of Ladakh made holy pilgrimages to that roof of the world for religious benediction and scriptural training.

With the advent of Buddhism there came a change all over Ladakh. Monasteries began to rise in every village and in every cluster of human habitation. Imposing structures with several storeys were built on hill tops or on hill slopes overlooking the valleys where the Buddhists had their habitations. Strewn over the entire length and breadth of Ladakh wherever there is a handful of Buddhist population, these monasteries not only used to cater to the religious needs of the people but also serve the purpose of landmarks and inns to the young 'lamas'. The importance and influence of these monasteries over the religious, cultural, economic and even the political life of the people is so great that it is comparable to that of the churches in medieval Europe. These monasteries are, as a matter of fact, centres of all local organizations and they are themselves closely knit into another huge apex organization. Religious minded as all the people are, the interests of the people rarely clash with the interests of the monasteries. Thus, so long as there is no extraneous interest or influence at work, the monasteries and the local population live in mutual cooperation and harmony.

The religious life of the Buddhists revolves round the 'gompas' or monasteries which house, feed, clothe and educate the 'lamas', who in some cases number up to 500. The order of monks is an essential feature of Buddhism. It is considered to be one of the three jewels of Buddhism. The monks who are admitted to the monasteries in very early life have to live lives of celibacy and self control according to a prescribed code of discipline. The 'gompas' are the preservers of the Buddhist culture, veritable spiritual light houses, while the 'lamas' are the torch bearers of the Dharma.

The 'gompas' are administered according to strict democratic principles and as none of their inmates, from Kushak Bakula well known Ex Head Lama of Ladakh down to the lowest functionary, can enter into married life, so too they cannot, as individual persons, own property of any kind.

Some women also enter into monastic life and such women are called 'chomos'. Besides their religious duties, these nuns do a lot of manual labour and are therefore assets to the monasteries to which they are attached. There are instances when even girls of 5 years age are 'donated' to the monasteries to become 'chomos'. These 'chomos' are distinguished easily from rest of the folk on account of their yellow coloured head wear.

'Gompa' Association

The different 'gompas' have formed an association called the 'Gompa' Association to safeguard the interests of the 'gompas'; to eradicate social evils and to propagate practical Dharma in an organized manner. When recently the Jammu and Kashmir Government enacted a law, delimiting land holdings to 82 kanals per landlord the 'Gompa' Association made a concerted attempt to exempt the 'gompas', which hold large tracts of farms and land, from the purview of this enactment, since it would be impossible for the 'gompas' to feed the large number of 'lamas' and 'chomos' if the 'gompas' were to lose their main resources.

Other Buddhist Organisations

The Buddhist Association and the Kashmir Raj Bodhi Mahasabha are other Buddhist organizations which are concerned with the general welfare of the Buddhist community in all the departments of life. Besides being the President of the Leh Tehsil National Conference, Kushak Bakula has been a successful President of the 'Gompa' Association and the Kashmir Raj Bodhi Mahasabha and did good work for Ladakhis.

These organizations are chiefly religious organizations. However, Kushak Bakula being the President of most of the religious organizations, he was making use of them for political purposes also. These organizations are now a days trying to get help from Maha Bodhi Society of India also to safeguard and strengthen the interests of the Buddhists of Ladakh.

Relics of Buddha and His Two Chief Disciples

One of the recent events of rejoicing to the Buddhists of Ladakh was the worship of the Sacred Relics brought to the district by a delegation of the Maha Bodhi Society. The Sacred Relics of Buddha and his two Chief Disciples remained in Ladakh for exactly three months from June 1951 to August 1951. Almost the entire Buddhist community of Ladakh paid their homage to the Sacred Relics.

Festivals

In a lonely and sequestered place like Ladakh where life is monotonously smooth, dull and uneventful, there is a great need for social functions and festivals to add some spice of variety to the hum-drum life of the people. Modern means of entertainment such as Cinema halls, Drama Theatres, were unheard of in the remote and mountainous regions of Ladakh. In the past the local people therefore have evolved their own means and methods of entertainment to drive away the monotony of life and to get some social stimuli.

The local people being highly religious and the monasteries being centres of all social activity, most of the entertainment and social functions of the Ladakhis are associated with religious festivals celebrated in some monastery or other. The monasteries scattered all over Ladakh have some fixed days when a 'mela'(fair) is held and the people from all the surrounding villages take a day or two off from their routine work and make a trip to the respective monastery both to entertain themselves and to recharge their religious faith. These 'melas' or festivals usually last for two or three days – sometimes even four or five – and the inmates of the house take their turn to attend it on the first day or any subsequent day as it suits their convenience. The following table gives a list of the famous among the local festivals and the approximate time when they are celebrated each year.

	Name of the festival	Week and month of the year
(a)	Mela Losar	3rd week of December
(b)	Mela Spituk 'Gompa'	3rd week of January
(c)	Mela Trikse 'Gompa'	1st week of February
(d)	Mela Dosmochey	3rd week of February
(e)	Mela Phiang 'Gompa'	3rd week of February
(f)	Mela Mashro 'Gompa'	1st week of March
(g)	Mela Chimrrey 'Gompa'	1st week of November

	Name of the festival	Week and month of the year
(h)	Mela Hemis 'Gompa'	Later half of June to first half of July
(i)	Mela She Shubla	1st week of August
(j)	Puja Kagyur Stangyur	Sometime between the middle of February and middle of May

The time when each of the festivals is celebrated shows that most of them come off in the winter season when people are not busy on the farms and the fields and when they badly need some entertainment to brighten their idle days.

Mela Losar

This festival is actually the New Year Festival (Losar means New Year), though it is celebrated in the 10th month of the Tibetan calendar. This comes off somewhere in the month of December. The farmers would have, by November, harvested their crops and those that tend goats and sheep would have found their flocks fat and well grown. Thus, everything is bountiful and people need the rewards of merriment for their season's long labours and therefore without waiting for the end of the actual year they celebrate the New Year festival two months earlier.

As far as the celebrations as such are concerned they resemble the Diwali festival of the Hindus, because, starting from the 25th day of the tenth month to the 30th, the local people illuminate their houses with candles and oil lamps to the best of their economic means. The 30th is the day of the highest rejoicings. The remnant of the former Royal grandeur was manifested on this day when the descendant of the former Raja of Ladakh used to entertain the elite of the town, particularly the descendants of the former ministers and other notable officials, and a grand feast was held. Next morning, the guests who were entertained by the Raja the previous day pay their homage to the host by placing 'khatak' (ceremonial scarf) around the neck of the Raja and then bowing in obeisance in the local fashion. After his ceremony all the guests used to move to the open yard in front of the Royal Durbar Hall and here a grand dance was held to entertain the descendants of the former ministers and other officials. A special band of 'dam damwalas' maintained by the royal family used to sing while the best dancing girls in the most gorgeous costumes used to entertain the guests. This Mela is not held now a days.

The next day, the Raja wearing crown and in his royal robes used to visit most of the 'Mana' walls in the town accompanied by some of the elite of the town. This was followed by horse race for three days. The horse race over, the Raja was taken in a procession from the town to his palace on the hill. There again the 'takchos' (dancing girls) used to give dancing performances for ten days to entertain the local people. This festival was celebrated till 1952.

Mela Spituk 'Gompa'

This is held in the Spituk monastery situated five miles away from the Leh town. The 'lamas' offer pujas (prayers) and one of the peculiar features of this puja is the dance part of it. The dancers (all 'lamas') wear grotesque masks and dance in the yard of the monastery. These dances have a significance of their own. They are an essential part of the religious rites. A mythical devil called 'Drud' is supposed to have the evil intentions towards the monastery and the local people and therefore an effigy of that devil is made with flour and after the dances are over, the effigy is burnt and the devil is supposed to be subdued. Though all this is based on mythical stories, the weird faces and the grotesque masks, the odd dress and the queer dance entertain the masses who throng the temple yard. Occasionally a dancer with delicate sense of humour will pull the cap of some onlooker and throw it into the open court thereby making the victim run after it and the whole audience will be bursting into a peel of laughter.

Mela Trikse 'Gompa'

This mela is celebrated very much in the fashion of the Spituk Mela but the masks worn by the dancers are of a different pattern. The most interesting and special feature of the dancing programme is what is known as the Skeleton Dance. In this, the dancer wears a dress resembling bones and to the onlooker it gives the appearance that a skeleton is dancing. Another important feature of the dance is the costly costumes worn by the dancers; probably the costumes worn at Trikse are the costliest as compared to any other monastery.

Mela Dosmochey

This mela is named after the devil Dosmochey whose effigy forms the central figure around which all the ceremonies take place. The 'lamas' of Phyang and Mashro 'Gompa' officiate during these ceremonies. The festival starts with pujas and dances in the old palace of the ruler of Ladakh. Then, a procession headed by the descendents of the Raja would move down to the open space near the PWD Rest House where a big effigy of the devil Dosmochey stands tied by with strings fastened to some pegs in the ground. Around this effigy several pyres are arranged and the ceremony starts with puja and dance by the 'lamas'. The 'lamas' then place effigies of various devils inside these pyres and they are subsequently burnt to ashes. This done, the turn of the devil Dosmochey comes and with the musicians playing funeral tunes, the strings with which the effigy was tied to the ground are cut asunder. No sooner does the effigy fall to the ground than the audience rushes to the scene and there is a scramble to tear off some portion or other of the devil's body and keep it as a trophy of victory. It is the common belief among the local people here that if these mementos are kept in their granaries it would add to the wealth of the family. Horse racing concludes this festival. This festival is almost dying out.

Mela Phyang 'Gompa'

This is on the same pattern as the melas at Spituk and Trikse but with slight variations in the dances and the costumes. One notable feature of this 'Gompa' is that it belongs to the red sect who believe that this world is a place "to eat, drink and make merry".

Mela Mashro 'Gompa'

The one peculiarity or special feature of this mela is that two monks after undergoing rigorous austerities for 30 days appear before the public dressed as two gods called 'Lha' and then parents bring their children for the naming ceremony. The names are given depending upon some astronomical calculations and children thus named are supposed to derive great benefit in their life.

Mela Chimrrey 'Gompa'

This mela is held alternately at Hemis and Chimrrey villages. The specialty about this mela is that dances are held in the night. While dances after sunset are never held in other 'gompas', during the Chimrrey Mela the 'lamas' dance without any mask in the day time and after sunset they dance in gorgeous costumes.

Mela Hemis 'Gompa'

This mela is the acme of all other melas in as much as there are scores of dances and people never fail to attend it. The Hemis 'Gompa' is one of the oldest and richest. Elaborate arrangements are made by the 'lamas' for the reception, stay and entertainment of distinguished guests, particularly strangers to this place. Another important feature of this mela is that it comes in summer while all other melas are held in winter.

The Hemis 'Gompa' is the biggest in Ladakh and is about 25 miles away from Leh proper. Though the mela is held in honour of the birthday of Padma Sambhava, but on account of the numerous dances it almost looks like a festival whose chief purpose is the annihilation of the demons and other evil spirits who are a menace to the peace and prosperity of the local people. The two days of the festival are the busiest for the 'lamas' and the most tiresome too since the dances in which they have to participate are too many and too complicated. They have to scrupulously adhere to the minutest detail of gesture and action and a slight flaw during the dance would mean punishment at the hands of the Master of the Ceremonies the next day. Months are spent in learning and rehearsing the dances and every minutest point is remembered and adhered to. All the groups of dancers come in strange masks and portray either some devils or some well disposed gods.

A side attraction during this mela is the unfurling of two gigantic silk curtains, hung on two consecutive days, one containing the portrait of Drukpa Rinpochey, the Head of this Buddhist sect, and the other containing an image of Skushok Gial Sras, who rebuilt the Hemis monastery. These images are elaborately embroidered on silk and the curtains when hung can be seen from a great distance on account of their vast size.

One of the special features of the Hemis mela is that towards the end of the dances a huge fat figure with an abnormally big head comes upon the scene surrounded by half a dozen brats in masks. This fat creature, Hashang Gyapo as he is called, lends a comic element to the sober and systematic dances that have preceded it. With a stick in hand, this fat, funny, figure goes about beating the imps surrounding him and occasionally beating a fellow or two among the audience. Since the kind of beating that he administers does not hurt, every blow evokes a burst of laughter from the audience.

Mela Sheh Shubla

This festival is named after the village Sheh since the festival is held in that village. It is about 8 miles from Leh. Formerly there was no 'Gompa' there but when one of the concubines of the ruler of Leh, who had a huge building in that village, died, her palace was converted into a 'Gompa'. In one of the chambers of that building there is a huge idol of Dorjey Chemmo. All the zamindars (farmers owning land, normally much above the average) are expected to offer the first ear of their corn to this god and it is this ceremony which constitutes the festival. It is presumed that unless a farmer has offered the first ear of the corn grown in his fields to this god, he should not harvest his crops and if he does he is destined to ruin soon. So the festival takes the shape of a thanks giving ceremony for the harvest of the year.

One peculiar feature of the festivals is that no 'lamas' take part in the dance and it is the male and female folk who dance together in their brightest robes and ornaments. These people eat, drink and enjoy in their green fields and at appointed hours participate in the dance in their gayest moods.

Puja Kagyur Stangyur

This festival is known after 308 religious books which are recited by the monks during the four days of the ceremony. Two hundred of these books go by the name of Stangyur and the remaining hundred and eight, by the name of Kagyur. Monks from almost all the monasteries, except those that are cut off by snowfall, gather together and complete the recitation of the 308 books or 'pothis' within four days. There would be a congregation of about 400 monks and they are led by the Skushok of the Phyang monasteries. It is a laborious recitation ceremony, since each of the books runs to about 500 and odd pages. But the festival has its entertaining side too. Two effigies of the devils Marchin Storma and Storlok are made and are carried to the open ground near the PWD Rest House in a grand procession. There, in the presence of the elite of the town and the onlookers who have assembled from far and near the effigy of Marchin Storma is first set on fire. That over, a horn filled with blood and hanging from a thread tied to two vertical poles becomes the target of all marksmen. The gunners fire at this horn from a distance until the horn is broken and blood oozes out of it. Next comes the turn of the effigy of Storlok, made in human form, and he is made the target by the musketeers until he falls prostrate on the ground. Thus, the devils and evil spirits supposed to be the cause of devastation in the country are disposed of.

General

While all these festivals are celebrated by the Buddhists, the Muslim and Christian population of the district celebrate their own festivals and since they are not very much different from those celebrated by the Muslims and Christians elsewhere in India, no special mention of them is called for here. But one thing that is noteworthy is the fact that the Muslims and Christians are not debarred from going to the Buddhist monasteries and though they cannot participate in the religious functions as such, nothing stops them from joining the audience and deriving entertainment from those festivals.

Prayers

The Buddhists of Ladakh have different ways of offering prayers. Whatever their original significance might have been, today some of the prayers have taken more a mechanical form than religious utterance or spiritual communion.

First and foremost among these mechanical methods of prayer is what is known as the "Prayer-wheel". It is a small brass or copper cylinder two or three inches in diameter and almost the same in height. This cylinder is mounted on a rod, which forms the handle of the "Prayer-wheel" and on which it can be rotated through pivotal action. Inside the cylinder there is a piece of paper or cloth on which are written the characters "Om Mani Padmi Om". This is one of the most popular, simplest and yet the highest prayer of the Buddhists in this part of the globe and its literal translation is: "O. thou, jewel in the lotus, O:" the repetition of these words is supposed to cut short the cycle of birth and death and every devout Buddhist deems it his religious duty to utter these prayers as many times in his life as possible. The prayer wheel is a good substitution to this verbal prayer and Buddhists with abundant faith in the efficacy of this prayer carry one along with them wherever they go and they continuously rotate the cylinder containing the holy prayer by giving a slight jerk to it. This they do even while walking along the road, witnessing the dance performance in the 'gompa' or bargaining the cabbage in the bazaar. Though their attention is diverted from the divine to the mundane world and their mouth is busy in idle rigmaroles or practical business of life, they believe that every circle the prayer-wheel taken would cut short the cycle of recurring birth and death.

A bigger size prayer-wheel can also be seen at the entrance of the 'gompas'. In a grove in the wall a big cylindrical prayer-wheel is fixed on hinges and every devout Buddhist visitor to the temple deems his pilgrimage to be incomplete unless he has given a jerk to the big prayer-wheel and has set it rotating on its hinges.

Chortens

These are religious structures very much resembling the Pagodas but stunted, so to say, in size. They are usually seen at the entrance or end of a village. The height of these structures may vary anywhere from 20 feet to 40 feet or so. The base is a cube-like structure and the top or the roof is pyramidal in shape. Inside these religious buildings are kept some books and manuscripts containing some holy prayers. At the base of the building sometimes there would be a tunnel and any person who enters this tunnel from one end and passes out through the other is supposed to get all the blessings of the sacred script placed above.

Mana Walls

In ancient times when some ruler died long stone walls were built to commemorate the royal personage. This custom became more popular subsequently and when any rich man died his sons thought it fit to honour him by building similar stone walls. These walls, in due course of time acquired some religious significance and some practical value too.

The monks and other devout laymen thought it to be a great religious merit if they could carve or etch the sacred words "Om Mani Padmi Om" on as many stones and rocks constituting these walls. Thus every wall contains innumerable stones and rocks with the sacred prayer carved on them and it was the belief of all the carvers that every prayer thus etched reduced bit by bit the miseries of this life and the lives after. This is the religious significance of these 'mana walls'.

The 'mana walls' have their practical value too. Ladakh is such a place that a traveller is often liable to lose his way and find himself in a barren land where the nearest human habitation may be miles away. There are no hand-posts in this area showing directions or distances. The 'mana-walls' are so built that they are the safest guild to the stray traveller who is on his way from one village to another. As a matter of fact the track from village to village always passes beside these walls. As soon as the pathway approaches a wall it bifurcates itself into two, one passing by the left of the wall and the other on the right, but both meeting again at the end of the wall. The traveller always passes by the pathway on the left of the wall leaving the wall towards his right. Anybody who transgresses this rule and passed by the right is supposed to lose all the religious merit which he would otherwise gain if he adheres to the acknowledged convention. So all travellers make it a point to follow the age long tradition and always ride by the left side path. Even the ponies and beasts of burden are so much accustomed to this rule that when given a free rein they always, though unconscious of the religious significance, turn to the left when they encounter a 'mana walls'. So too, on leaving a wall behind, the ponies and the beasts of burden seek such a track which leads them to the next 'mana walls'.

The 'mana walls', some of which are in a dilapidated condition now, are usually as high as six feet and as broad too. The longest 'mana walls' in Leh is about a mile away from the bazaar and runs for about 3 furlongs.

The traveller as he rides or trots along these walls cannot help giving a glance at these prayers inscribed on stone. To a man of faith these prayers become a sort of beacon light brightening his path in the dark and dry desert land of life. The inclemency of weather, the long distances from human habitation, the immobile and impervious mountains and the deadening silence of the dry land – all these bring to the mind of the stray traveller the futility and evanescence of this life and the words "Om Mani Padmi Om" find a real echo in his heart.

Chapter VII

POLITICAL SCENARIO

Political Parties

The political parties in Ladakh may be termed as "Religious Parties" because the only political organizations here are the religious ones. In most of the undeveloped regions of the world, and Ladakh is certainly one of the foremost among them, the first organization to come into being is the religious one. When these religious organizations are built up, and subsequently people become more and more enlightened and politically conscious and they seek to assert their political rights, instead of building up new organizations on a political basis, they often tend to merge these political grouping with the already existing religious organizations. Or, in other words, they seek the easy way of making the already existing religious bodies as the mouthpiece of their political grievances and aspirations. After all, politics draws its sap of life from organizations and not from individuals, no matter how important the latter are. And the people in almost all the backward areas of the world, until they get revolutionary enlightenment and realize the dominant part that politics plays in this modern age, are always liable to seek their political ambitions through long established religious parties and organizations.

Secondly, politics everywhere, during its infancy, seeks to thrive as a hand maid of religion. In Ladakh too this history is being repeated. Intensely religious as the local people are, their lives and activities are inextricably woven with some religious organization or other. Secondly, the monasteries, which own the bulk of the land here, have always held the reins of economic life. Thus when these religious organizations control not only the religious, social and cultural life of the people but also their economic life, it is but natural that the new portfolio of politics must also inevitably come under the control of religious organizations. The latest events which have tightened the grip of these religious organizations over the local politics are the partition of India and the wrangle over Kashmir's accession, both of which are related to, though not strictly based on, religious differences. Political parties of Ladakh are, therefore, determined by religious affiliations and the political organizations are not separate from the religious ones.

Buddhists

They form about 90% of the population of Leh District and about 55% of the whole Ladakh including Kargil. The Buddhist Association, Leh is their representative organization which aims at uplifting the Buddhist community, socially, economically, politically and culturally, raising it to a position of equality with the other communities and securing for it just rights. It stands solidly behind Kashmir's accession to India, but does not stop there, for, its ultimate aim is the direct merger of Ladakh and the adjoining Buddhist areas with India. The Government of Jammu and Kashmir initially did not take any representative of this Community into the ministry nor did it take any steps to give this community its due share in the administration. Consequently the Buddhist community was unhappy over their grievances and it may well happen that one day they may seek a separate Constituent Assembly for Ladakh. In this District this is the main community on whose loyalty India can count with absolute certainty.

The financial resources of the Buddhist Association are exclusively drawn from within the community. The activities of this body embrace the entire Tehsil of Leh and those parts of Kargil which contain Buddhist population. Among the past prominent personalities in the community, who largely influenced its plans and programmes may be mentioned, the following Leaders:-

(a) Kushak Bakula, the Past Head Lama of Ladakh.

(b) Kalon Chhewang Rigzin, a local landlord.

(c) Pandit Shridhar Kaul, an eminent educationist of Kashmir.

The Buddhist Association was formed more than fifty year ago. The association is also known by the name "Young Men's Buddhist Association" or briefly YMBA. Though for a time it was slack in its activities, with the problem of Kashmir's accession looming large, and with the people becoming more and more politically conscious, it has become a powerful body wielding influence on almost all the spheres of local activities and taking proper stand on political matters. The Buddhist leaders having fully realized the need of the hour, had come out of the religious seclusion and had taken over dynamic leadership of their people with a view to achieving their social progress, economic uplift and political betterment. They not only conducted tours from village to village and educated the masses through inspiring lectures but also made many trips to Delhi and Srinagar to acquaint the prominent personalities there with the problems of the Ladakhis in order to seek the best solutions to them. With his good fortunes Kushak Bakula was dependent upon none and engaged himself in ceaseless activity, not for any self aggrandizement but for the amelioration of the masses.

Muslims

In the past, The Shias were initially politically led by Akhon Abdul Hussain in the past, his son G.H. Mohammed, Haji Taqi and the Sunis by Syed Mohd Syed Mirwaiz, Khan Abdulla Shah, Munshi Ghulam Mohiuddin and Abdul Sattar. Syed Mohd Syed, as his title Mir-Waiz indicates, was also the religious head of the Sunis in 1952. He was employed in Leh high school as the Persian teacher. The Mir-Waiz of Chushot was the religious head of the Shias in 1952. Most of the Muslim leaders are financially well placed as a class as compared to Buddhists. At the moment, they are interested in looking after their interests like the Buddhists are doing. However, whenever the emergency arises, India can depend more on Buddhists. This was proved when Ladakhis joined the Indian forces to fight against Pak forces in 1947-48 Indo Pak War where they suffered many casualties and won many decorations also. This was proved beyond doubt by their active assistance in addition to the fighting during the 1947-48 Indo Pak war.

Christians

Among the earliest Christian personalities in 1952/53 may be mentioned Mr. and Mrs. Driver, Superintendent of the local branch of the Moravian Mission, Mr. and Mrs. Vittoz, associates of Mr. Driver of the Moravian Mission, S Gergon, Forest Officer, son of the late Rev: Joseph Gergon, the first Buddhist in Ladakh to be converted to Christianity, Mr. Chetan Phunchok, formerly information officer but now doing active missionary work for the Moravian Mission, Elize R Jordan B.A., Assistant Head Master at the local high school, Babu Durje SDO and Mr. Dachan (1952) Deputy Commissioner of Ladakh.

The Christians are a microscopic minority numbering about 300 or so. They form the intelligentsia of Ladakh. The community as a whole tries to be on good terms with other communities. Generally speaking, the community abstains from taking part in politics. The conversion work of the local mission is however almost at a standstill. Inspite of the best efforts, there have been hardly three dozen conversions in the last few decades. The Moravian Mission is generally not liked by all Lamas as well as other Buddhists for their conversion work.

The above mentioned religious organisations of Muslim, Christians and Buddhists have been functioning in Leh since early 1950 and are contuing to function quite well even in 2015. Shri Sewang Thinles is the President of the 'Ladakhi Buddhists'. Shri Sonam thinles is the President of the 'Christian Association of Leh'. Shri Ashraf Ali is the President of the Muslim organization known as 'An Human Imami Leh', while Shri Saifudin is the President of another Muslim organization known as 'Moin Ul Islam Leh'.

The National Conference

Two branches of the All Jammu and Kashmir National Conference have been established in the District, one for Leh and the other for Kargil with their Headquarters at Leh and Kargil towns respectively. Because Kargil Tehsil has limited Buddhist population, the Tehsil Conference did not contain a single Buddhist member initially. The Leh branch, on the contrary, has naturally a large number of Buddhist members. But the Buddhists as a community are not really convinced of the national character of the organization and its commitment.

The Functions and objects of the National Conference are as under:-

(a) To settle minor disputes relating to marriage, divorce and land.

(b) The Conference is basically the political organ of the people of the District. Its main objective is to carry out the programme of the All Jammu and Kashmir National Conference as laid down in the New Kashmir Theory. The programme envisages a better future for the inhabitants of the whole state. Its activities are mainly concerned with the following reforms:-

i) Economic Reforms

ii) Land Reforms

iii) Social Reforms

Mohalla Committees

Every Mohalla and village has a committee to keep watch over the developments and activities that may take place. The total strength of ordinary members in the District is about 8,000. In order to become a permanent member one has to pass through several stages. The period of ordinary membership is one year. On completion of the first stage, the member automatically becomes permanent and enjoys certain privileges. The rights and privileges of these members increase with the length of their membership. For instance, a member can be selected as a delegate to the annual session of the All J&K National Conference and can hope to become a member of the General Council subsequently.

The resolutions passed by the Tehsil National Conference are forwarded to the All J&K National Conference from time to time for information and necessary action.

Kargil

The religious leaders of the Shias and Sunis are also their political leaders. They wield tremendous amount of influence over the masses. The people of Kargil have personally experienced the difference between India and Pakistan and the Indian Army has helped the local population in all respects. The main aim of local Muslims seems to be to root out Buddhism from the District so that Kargil area becomes predominantly Muslim area. The recent migration of some Buddhists from Zanskar to Kulu valley as well as to Leh area is an instance in point. Their financial resources are derived from the local population which is normally less than 50% of the total resources raised in the District.

Present Political Conditions

The strategic importance of Ladakh is also responsible for bringing it into the lime light of politics. China and Pakistan are both interested in Ladakh region. The Ladakhis do not like communist control over Tibet. But so long as Kashmir's accession to India is not finalized, the Ladakhis as a whole have not got much to choose. The majority of the Ladakhis being the Buddhists, they want Kashmir's accession to India to be final as soon as possible, so that they don't have to come under Pakistan under any circumstances. The Muslims are also not happy because Kashmir has tentatively acceded to India. So there is definitely certain amount of discontentment among the people. And it does not need a prophet to pronounce that discontentment is always strewn with dangerous possibilities. The Communists are sitting just on the other side of the border. So the situation in Ladakh has to be tackled with great caution. The discontentment of the Buddhists and Muslims in Ladakh is further enhanced by several other factors. The people of Ladakh being highly religious, their love and loyalty are mostly determined by the religion they possess. The Buddhists while rejoicing over Kashmir's accession to India, even though tentative as it is, are not really happy under the Kashmir Government administration.

The problem of the people of Ladakh is the same as that of the people of Kashmir but with further complications. Ladakh has always felt that Kashmir has been consistently meeting step-motherly treatment to it and therefore Ladakh has time and again, but secretly, told India that she would prefer to come under the direct control of India and not under the joint care of India and Kashmir. Many years ago, Kushak Bakula, the most popular and powerful figure in Ladakh in the past, made a representation in the United Nations to the effect that in the event of a separation between India and Kashmir, if Ladakh cannot come under the custody of India, she would rather go with an alien, to name Tibet, than come under the roof of Kashmir when it is under the control of Pakistan. Of course Kushak Bakula was in his statement, just voicing the feelings of the local Buddhists only and the last part of his statement might have been nothing but a time bomb exploded at the time when the Security Council was discussing Kashmir. But nonetheless it gives us an idea of how complicated problems here are. Discontented as the people are, they are becoming opportunist to make the best of everything that they can. The tragedy of the situation is that opportunism, like corruption, is born in discontentment and nurtured in political chaos. Worse still, opportunism, like its twin, corruption, breeds like bed bugs and migrates from place to place enveloping the entire area in a vicious pest. The clamour for opportunity to grab a job or make some other profit is leading the population towards communalism. In Ladakh both the Muslims as well as the Buddhists have been living peacefully and happily for the past many centuries. Even inter marriages used to take place between the Buddhist and the Muslims in the not too distant past. However, the present trend towards communalism is strewn with dangerous consequences.

There are many reasons for the growth of communalism in Ladakh. The accession of Kashmir to India gave the Buddhists some hopes of getting their demands fulfilled which include Regional Autonomy, more representation in Parliament and Administrative posts. The Buddhists are now hugging the hope that once Kashmir's accession to India is final, they may be able to get their demands fulfilled. But the sands of time are running fast and so is the patience of the Buddhists. With the discontentment raging and opportunism slowly tightening its grip over their minds, new ideas are taking roots and the proof of this is seen in the statement of Kushak Bakula to the United Nations (1952). Of course, Kushak Bakula knows it, and knows it well, that nothing is better for Ladakh's peace and prosperity than merger with India. But in the alternative between Pakistan and Tibet, Ladakh cannot help choosing the lesser evil. While the Buddhists have the ideas as enumerated above, the Muslims of Ladakh have different ideas. They want Ladakh to remain within Kashmir under all circumstances irrespective of the fact whether it opts for India or Pakistan. The Kashmir Government naturally prefers the ideas of the Muslims and consequently takes them into their confidence rather than the Buddhists. The divergent views of the Muslims coupled with the preferential treatment of the Kashmir Government to these views are an important factor which is leading to the growth of communalism in Ladakh. The Kashmiri officials posted in Ladakh consequently tend to side with the Muslims and distrust the Buddhist Leaders which in turn widen the gap between the Muslims and the Buddhists.

The people who are optimistic about the ultimate triumph of democracy over communism often put forward the argument that so long as religion has its hold on masses, communism cannot thrive. Their argument is that since communism; though not in theory at least in its practical working, wrecks the very foundations of religion, religious minded people would never allow communistic doctrines to infiltrate into their ranks. But the historic strides which the communism has taken so far go to prove that this argument is not very logical. The people of Ladakh, who have donated much of their hard earned money to the building of monasteries and the feeding of Lamas, are slowly awakening to the fact that the religious edifices are nothing but monuments of their past ideas. When these toiling masses get a little more education, a little more enlightenment they might realize that their own tiny huts and homes should be as dear and important to them as those majestic monasteries. Of course it will take time, but the march of time cannot really be stopped and consequently it will not be very long before the religion in Ladakh also loses some of its power.

Political Future of Ladakh

The political future of Ladakh is irrevocably connected with the future of Kashmir. But there seems to be no immediate solution of the Kashmir issue. This fact, however, should not be allowed to keep the Ladakh problem in cold storage. People of Ladakh being extremely poor, economically very backward, politically perturbed and discontented, their problem needs immediate and sound solution. It is in the interest of India that a border area like Ladakh is not kept long in its present perturbed condition. Best interests of India can be served if Ladakh is first brought within her economic and cultural sphere.

Ladakh, as we know is really a backward area. Development in almost all spheres is needed. Therefore a technical committee should be appointed which should go into the detail as to which sphere needs immediate development and consequently draft the development plans for the area. Community projects should also be sanctioned. Though it is the primary responsibility of J&K Government to finance the various development schemes of Ladakh, it is in the interest of India that Kashmir Government is helped in financing the projects in Ladakh. The people of Ladakh who are already looking towards India for guidance will feel all the more obliged towards India after this economic aid. Along with the economic aid, attempts should be made to bring Ladakh within the influence of Indian culture. Regarding this cultural conversion some leeway has already been made by the Indian Army units in Ladakh. Particularly, the secular nature of the Indian Government and the Indian army has been brought home to the minds of the people of Ladakh. The Indian army personnel from the sepoy to the senior most Commander have shown complete impartiality in communal matters. Secondly, the sorties made by IAF planes in the winter season have conferred many a boon upon the people of Ladakh who would have been, otherwise, completely cut off from the rest of the world for full three or four months in a year. Thirdly, the stationing of troops in places like Leh and Kargil has considerably added to the economic prosperity of the local people. Fourthly, modern amenities of life such as for instance tooth brush and tooth paste, Pond's cream and Polson's butter, radio and typewriter, camera and bicycle, and beyond all jeep and aeroplane, are slowly being introduced to the local people. But the most important thing of all is the new enlightenment that the local people are getting on account of the Indian Army personnel who have come from distant parts of India bearing the stamp of different habits, customs, manners and diet. In a word, new aqueducts have started pouring fresh water into the stagnant pool of Ladakhi culture. The economic development plans, when implemented, would bring another stream of Indians to this remote region, as technicians, and there would be further cultural stimulus. But all this cultural stimulus is not far reaching in its effects in as much as it comes indirectly through men who are not in any sense cultural emissaries. For effective cultural conversion what is needed is that the future generations of Ladakh should be imbued with the Indian ideals. Towards this end, boys and girls of Ladakh should get their education in Indian universities and the newly recruited monks of Ladakh should be able to foster ties with the Maha Bodhi Society of India.

Political Accession

According to some experts of Ladakh, the permanent cure for Ladakh's malady would be to come under the administrative control of Govt. of India. This political adoption can be expected to take care of the following three forms:-

(a) Firstly, Ladakh can be classified as a tribal area and put under the charge of a commissioner appointed by Govt. of India in consultation with J&K Govt. Then Ladakh would come under the category of centrally administered area like some of the hill-tribes in Assam.

(b) Secondly, Ladakh can continue to be District of Kashmir provided Ladakh gets a fair amount of autonomy and also provided India's control over Kashmir is complete, secure and irrevocable. In other words, the Ladakhis must feel secure in Kashmir's hands and the Government of India must feel convinced that Kashmir would always honour and implement the counsels of India on each and every matter concerning Ladakh.

It is superfluous to discuss which, out of the two ways enumerated above is best suited in fortifying India's border defences in Ladakh and in preserving her territorial integrity. India must wait until the Kashmir issue is settled and the circumstances prevailing then will have to be studied before a decision is taken as to what form Ladakhi's accession to India should take. But one thing is certain and that is: having taken the fullest cognizance of Ladakh's strategic position and having known the danger of allowing infant Ladakh to be influenced by her vicious neighbours, the Indian Government should take early and concrete steps to see that Ladakh does not become a spoilt child nor does it break off from its territorial bounds.

Ladakh is strategically important for India as China and Pakistan are keen to capture it. China's Line of Actual Control keeps on moving forward in Ladakh.

China had already captured about one fourth of Ladakh before 1962 India – China war and some more territory after 1962 war by moving forward it's Actual Line of Control. China has made excellent roads in Western Tibet and Xinjiang in the north.

Chapter VIII

MILITARY IMPORTANCE*

Topography

The topography of a region determines the course of its wars and a previous topographical knowledge of the land helps to interpret the influence on strategy of the region's main topographical features. It is, therefore, essential that the topography of Ladakh should be studied in detail in order to find its true importance.

Ladakh is probably one of the most mountainous areas of the world. How high these mountains are can be easily imagined when one remembers that the average height of this area is 10,500 feet above the sea level. The mighty Himalayas which constitute by far the greatest portion of the area are interspersed with rivers and streams; famous among them are the Indus, the Shyok, and the Nubra. The whole area is for the most part a mountain desert composed of rocks and hills, granite dust and boulders. Interspersed between the mountain ranges are a few tablelands of high elevation. These tablelands are at an average height of 10,500 to 13,000 feet. Due to the high altitude and lack of moisture all the mountain ranges are completely bereft of any forests or pastures, except for very few places where one can find small groves of poplars or tiny meadows. Ladakh, it seems, is one of the highest inhabited places in the world, though it can equally be called one of the most desolate portions of the inhabited world.

The exact extent of the area designated by the name Ladakh has varied at different periods. In the middle ages, it included Western Tibet on the East, while Kargil and Skardu and Gilgit area formed its Western boundaries.

---
* With some updations on roads.

Military Importance

Just before the J&K Operations in 1947-1948, the boundary on the East ran along the Aksai Chin, while in the West it included Kargil and Skardu. However, during the J&K Operations, the Pakistanis over-ran Skardu and consequently now the Western boundary of Ladakh runs just North of Kargil. While describing the topography in detail, only the present boundary of Ladakh will be taken into consideration. Ladakh's Eastern boundary can also be described including Aksai Chin Range Mountains of Western Tibet (which is now in Chinese possession) and Sia Chin Glacier in the West. Both the borders are not quite defined on the ground according to the Chinese and the Pakistani Governments but the Indian Govt. is correctly sure of Ladakh's boundaries with Tibet (China) and Pakistan based on the historical maps of these high mountainous ranges and historical reasons based on treaties. The Chinese as is their mode have decided after occupying in the East the Aksai Chin Area in the 1950's (say 1953-56) that only their version is correct while the Pakistanis are very keen to annex SiaChin in the West.

Ladakh at present occupies a strategically important position as it is situated between Tibet, Sinkiang (Xinjiang) and Pakistan. From Leh run the routes to Tibet in the East, Sinkiang (Xinjiang) in the North and Skardu (Pakistan) in the North-West. Through Leh also passes the ancient route to Kashgar (Sinkiang) or Xinjiang from India. Along this route the tides of thought, trade and war have flowed between Ladakh and Sinkiang ever since the dawn of history. Almost every name studded along this route awakens a memory of some famous chieftain or of some noted deed of a caravan leader.

In order to study the whole area in detail, Ladakh area can be divided into three parts:-

(a) The Indus Valley

(b) The Shyok – Nubra Valley

(c) The Eastern Tablelands and Aksai Chin

The Indus Valley

The River Indus flows right across Ladakh from East to West. The only route from Western end of Ladakh to the Eastern end runs along its banks. This valley is very small in breadth and never exceeds more than few miles. At places the River Indus flows in very rocky ranges and through gorges like near

Khalatse. The track along the river at such places runs along the dangerous rocks and is narrow. On both sides of the river are high ranges of mountains which reach up to 18,000 feet. The river valley in the Eastern half of Ladakh and up to Leh is broader comparatively, but in the Western half it becomes narrow and at places it almost disappears as the river passes through deep gorges. The river is itself not fit for navigation for most of its course. However, most of the important towns and villages in Ladakh are situated along the Indus Valley. Looking at the map from East to West one finds the towns of Chumatang, Kumdok, Likche, Upshi, Hemis, Tikshe, Stak, Leh, Nimu, Saspul and Khalatsi (Khalsi) in the valley. The important trade route from Kashmir also runs along this valley before branching off to North from Leh for Xinjiang. Numerous small and big tributaries join the Indus River in this valley like Shyok and Nubra.

This valley, as we have already seen in Chapter I – Historical Background, forms the natural and historical route for all foreign invaders on Ladakh. The river throughout its course is rapid and seldom exceeds 120 feet in breadth in winter. It has many fords in winter and yet another important point in this connection is that in winter the river is frozen for a considerable length of its course and consequently infantry with fully loaded mules and camels can cross the river at will. It is not, therefore, in itself a particularly formidable obstacle in winter. However, during the summer due to the melting snows the current increases manifold, the banks are often overgrown and it is impossible to ford the river at any point. There are no boats available in the countryside either. Consequently, the communications are strictly limited on both sides of the river as the important bridges exist only at the following places:-

(a) Khalatsi in the West

(b) Saspul in the Centre

(c) Leh and Hemis in the East

But for these bridges, it is very difficult to cross the river in summer.

The mountain ranges on both sides of the river are very high with hardly any tracks running from South to the North in this valley. The steepness of the descent from and ascent to the mountains on either side, the lack of communications, and the intense cold of the deep valley coupled with the fast current of the river have combined to restrict intercourse between the inhabitants living on both sides of the river. There have been few attacks across the river valley ever since the dawn of civilization in Ladakh. For military operations the holding of the track running along this valley from West to East is of vital importance as any reinforcement into Ladakh can only be sent along this route.

The Shyok – Nubra Valley

The River Shyok flows from East to West like the Indus approximately 60 to 80 miles north of it. It meets the River Indus approximately 25 miles East of Skardu. The Shyok River has got an important tributary known as the Nubra River. Both these rivers form important valleys in the Northern half of Ladakh. Through the valleys of Shyok and Nubra also go the routes to Pakistan and Xinjiang. Like the Indus valley, the Shyok valley is also broader in the Eastern part of Ladakh and becomes narrower in the Western part. However, it is broader than the Indus Valley comparatively. A mule track runs all along the Shyok valley from Tibet in the East to Pakistan in the West. The Chinese have converted this track into a road in the North East Ladakh area.

There are high ranges of mountains on both sides of the Shyok River and consequently there are no tracks which run North and South except in the river valleys. The important towns and villages along the river running from East to West are Chang Chenmo, Shokpa Kanzag, Shyok, Khalsar, Unmaru and Biagdangdo. After Biagdangdo the Shyok River enters Pakistan territory. The river Nubra joins Shyok River near Tiggur. River Nubra gets its perennial water from Sia Chin Glacier and flows South-East before joining the river Shyok. Along the Nubra valley runs the route to Sinkiang. This route is followed in winter as well as in summer. The important villages and towns along this river are Henache, Panamik and Nubra.

Both the rivers Shyok and Nubra have got more or less the same amount of water. In winter both of them get frozen and infantry with loaded mules and camels can easily go across the rivers at any point. However, in summer the rivers get swollen due to the melting snows and it is very difficult to cross them except at few selected places. There are no bridges on these rivers and consequently no large movement of troops can take place in this area in summer unless arrangements are made for bridging or boats and rafts are available. The locals do not use any boats or rafts to go across and consequently all arrangements to go across these rivers must be made in advance if any large movement of troops has to be made. The mule tracks from Leh to Sinkiang

(Xinjiang) run along the Rivers Shyok and Nubra and have been in use ever since the dawn of civilization in Ladakh area.

The Eastern Table-lands

These table-lands are situated at an average altitude of 11,500 to 14,000 feet and stretch from Tangtse about 50 miles East of Leh to the Tibetan border. These high altitude table lands stretch about 60 to 80 miles in length but in breadth these are very narrow. These are usually to be found in between the various mountain ranges. These mountain ranges run East and West and these high table-lands consequently also run East and West in length. As these table-lands are situated at a high altitude, there is very little population in these table-lands. The Lake Pyong Gong Tso is situated to the North while the Spanggur Lake is situated to the North-East of these table-lands. Movement in these plains is easy as there are no passes to overcome. Before one reaches these table-lands from Leh, one has to cross the Changla Pass which is 18,300 feet high. After crossing Changla Pass, one reaches Pyong Gong Lake area. The track going northwards has to cross the Marksmik La Pass (18,300 feet) before reaching the Shyok River and its Eastern Tributary, the Chang Chenmo River. Thereafter the route moves along the mule track to Lanak La which is located along India-Tibet border. The winter mule track to Sinkiang (Xinjiang) from Leh used to go north of track to Lanak La along high mountain peaks as well as high table-lands in area generally known as Aksai Chin. But for this pass, there is no other pass which one has to cross till one reaches Tibet. The important villages and towns in this sector are Koyul, Chushul and Hanle.

Communications

General

If there are any areas in the world where the communications are so very difficult, Ladakh is undoubtedly one of them. But many roads have now been constructed in Ladakh. But high passes over 17000 feet in height in Ladakh block the roads in winter. The roads from SriNagar in J&K and from Manali in Himachal Pradesh go to Ladakh but are closed in winter due to heavy snowfall. The area can only boast of mule tracks which are also at places dangerous. The whole area being very mountainous, the tracks run along the high mountain ranges and one wrong step on the narrow, steep, winding mountain path may mean instantaneous death. As the population in the area is very scarce, one finds that there are not very many villages along these tracks either. The current of the rivers and streams in the area being very fast, traffic in the rivers is also unheard of. The means of communication are equally poor. Besides the vehicles, the following animals are also source of communication in the area.

(a) Yaks

(b) Camels

(c) Ponies

(d) Donkeys

The yaks and camels are used mostly for communication on the tracks leading to Xinjiang and Tibet which run at very high altitude and where one has to cross very high and dangerous passes. The ponies and donkeys are usually used inside Ladakh area or for trade purposes on the tracks leading to Kashmir or India, when roads are blocked due to heavy snow on the passes.

Leh, the principle town of Ladakh area is situated at a very central place. From Leh tracks lead to Tibet in the East, Sinkiang in the North, Pakistan in the North-West, Kashmir in the West and India in the South. We shall study each of these routes in some detail.

Leh to Sinkiang (Xinjiang)

There are two routes leading to Sinkiang (Xinjiang) from Leh, the Winter Route and the Summer Route. There are no direct roads from Leh to Sinkiang even at present. But there are few mule tracks, these mule tracks are not being used at present (1953). The information regarding one such mule track is given for information only.

WINTER ROUTE FROM LEH (LADAKH) TO Xinjiang IN THE NORTH (1953)

Abbreviations - P.O. - Post office, T.O. - Transport office, S – Supplies, W – Water, T – Transport, F – Fuel, Fodder, Food, G – Grass.

Name of Stage	Map reference	Inter miles / total miles	Height above sea level in feet	Remarks
Leh	52F		11,500	Large town, District, fort, bazaar, Post Office, TO, Dispensary, Moravian Mission, Supplies, transport, Fuel, Grass, Water- fairly abundant
Digar Polu	52F	13/13 ascent to Digar La 17,900 ft, steep and rough. Descent along snow covered slope. Track boggy below snow line.		Huts STFG Nil W – available
Digar	52F	14/27 Descend Lung-Thung Lumba	13,080	Small village. STF Nil GW – plentiful
Agham	52F	8/35 Track fair Eastwards up Shyok valley	10,500	Small village. ST - scanty FGW - plentiful

Name of Stage	Map reference	Inter miles / total miles	Height above sea level in feet	Remarks
Pakra	52J	12/47 Track fair Eastwards up Shyok valley bottom	11,000	ST Nil FGW plentiful
Chim Chak	52J	10/57 Track fair Eastwards up Shyok valley bottom	11,600	ST Nil, FGW plentiful
Shyok	52J	8/65 Cross where bed is sandy or gravelly with guide from village. Above this point river is frozen for 4 months, and route generally lies over the ice. Valley bends N at mile 8.	12,140	Village S available T Nil, FGW ample.
Chong Jangal	52J	18/83	11,950	Grazing ground, uninhabited in winter. ST Nil, FW ample, G fair, Pass Chang Chenmo confluence mile 4, track as before over river ice.
Dang Yailak	52J	18/101	12,230	ST Nil, FW plentiful track as before.

Name of Stage	Map reference	Inter miles / total miles	Height above sea level in feet	Remarks
Yargulak	52J	20/121	12,950	ST Nil, FGW plentiful. Track as before. Pass Shivolung, E, at mouth of Galwan R, mile 8.
Kataklik	52J 52I	18/139	13,900	ST Nil, F scanty, G fair track as before. Pass the snouts of several large glaciers descending from the Nubra watershed. The passage of these may be difficult and dangerous.
Sultan Chuskum	52E	15/154	14,200	ST Nil, F scanty, G fair Pass Saser Brangsa, mile 10. Track as before.
Kumdun	52E	18/172	15,000	ST Nil, F scanty, G fair track as before.
Ishak-Art- Aghzi (Khalastan)	51G	20/380	8,350	ST Nil, FGW plentiful. Continue down streams for about 2 miles, then strike up side stream on r. bank, by narrow gorge. Track rough and steep, then fair to Ak-Koram-Dawan, or Topa Dawan 10,750 ft, descent easier.

Name of Stage	Map reference	Inter miles / total miles	Height above sea level in feet	Remarks
Ak-Masjid	51G	15/395	8,490	Small scattered village. ST procurable with difficult FGW plentiful. Track follows centre of large grassy valley, Yaghaile-Jilga, and drops steeply to the plains. Track fair. Pass small village of Pussa, mile 12.
Kokyar	51G	17/412	6,440	Small town, bazaar, STFGW available. Road crosses sandy tract of low barren undulating country.
Beshterek	51G	24/436	5,890	Oasis with hamlets. S scanty, T Nil, FGW available Road across barren sandy country to within 5 miles of Karghalik, where begins extensive cultivation.
Karghalik	51G	20/456	4,430	Large town, important bazaar, STFGW plentiful.
Yarkand	51F 51B	40/496	4,430	Large town and trade centre. STFGW abundant.

Name of Stage	Map reference	Inter miles / total miles	Height above sea level in feet	Remarks
Kashgar	51A	132/628	4,380	The intermediary stages between Yarkand and Kashgar are Kok-Rabat, Kizil Bazar, Yangi Hissar and Yapchan

Staging Camps

The various stages as mentioned in the above routes do not generally possess staging camps at all. Most of the villages consist of only a few houses and at the most one platoon may be able to squeeze itself in these tiny houses. The routes can boast of a few villages only. Quite a few villages on the map as well as on the route exist only in name. Consequently any movement of troops above one platoon in strength will have to be catered for in advance and it is essential that tentage should be carried especially in winter season.

From Kumdun on the Indian border till Kirghiz - Jangal in Sinkiang (Xinjiang), there is no habitation at all and consequently there is neither any village nor any houses to take shelter.

PYONG GONG LAKE IN EASTERN LADAKH

Fuel

All along the route, wood is available in limited supply except for the distance in between Kumdun and Kirghiz Jangal which is approximately 150 miles long. Between Kumdun and Kirghiz-Jangal there is neither any habitation nor any vegetation. The mountains are bereft of any vegetation whatsoever and the caravans have to carry even the grass for the camels and yaks. However, as stated above, the fuel is available only in limited quantity. If a force even upto two company strength has to move along this route, arrangements in advance must be made to store and collect wood for burning purposes.

Food

Food is available in very limited quantity upto Kumdun on Indian side. However, since the locals can live upon barley and little rice, there is nothing else which army personnel can obtain from villages. However, one section to two sections is the maximum that can live upon the land along this barren route. Moreover, for any force going over this route, it has to be 100 percent self-sufficient in food.

Seasonal Variations

The routes to Sinkiang (Xinjiang) from Leh are open both in summer as well as winter. The track though runs over such high mountains and at an average height of 14,000 to 15,000 feet for over 150 miles. Here not much snow is to be met along the route due to the very dry climate and lack of moisture. The only time when it is dangerous to go along this track is during March and April as avalanches and snow slides are likely to occur during these months. As there is no rainy season in this part of the world, there are no seasonal variations.

Type of Route

The route to Sinkiang (Xinjiang) from Leh is probably one of the most difficult mountainous route in the world. However, this route as existing at present can be improved and broadened wherever it runs in the valleys. But whenever the track runs along the high mountains, it is difficult to widen it and it can be improved only at high cost. The route passes through one of the most barren mountains in the world and for over 150 miles there is neither any habitation nor any vegetation. The route has to cross over the Karakoram Pass which is about 18,300 feet high. Besides, this route goes at an average height of 14,000 feet to 15,000 feet for over 200 miles. With the route running through altitudes as high as 14,000 feet, the mountains completely bereft of any vegetation, the population conspicuous by its absence, large scale movement of troops is difficult unless all supplies are carried by troops or proper road is constructed which will take lot of time and money. The Chinese are reported to have developed roads in this area after great efforts.

Waterways

Importance

There are only three big rivers in Ladakh and these are the Indus, the Shyok, and the Nubra. All of them flow through high mountain ranges where the current is fast. At many places the rivers make small falls from where electric power can be generated.

Navigation

The rivers, generally speaking, are not navigable. The River Indus is navigable between Leh and Khalsi (about 51 miles) in summer season only. The rivers Shyok and Nubra do not provide much facility for navigation. In winter navigation is not possible at all as the surface of all the rivers get frozen.

Water Organisation

As the rivers do not provide much facility for navigation, there is no water organisation in existence in this area.

Crafts

The people of Ladakh are quite ignorant about the construction or the use of the water crafts. One seldom comes across any country-made craft being used. The people are quite content with the land communications and pay no attention to the rivers as source of communication. Consequently no water crafts are constructed by the Ladakhis nor are these used.

Rivers as Obstacle

In summer when the rivers like Indus, Shyok and Nubra are full of water, they are a formidable obstacle. It is difficult to ford them and one has to cross them either via bridges or at few selected places where these can be forded. However, in winter these rivers get frozen on the surface and can be crossed at any place.

The rivers provide little difficulty by way of bridging them. The course of the rivers is through high mountain ranges and rocks and consequently the width is not more than 100 to 120 feet. The current is fast and strong but since the width is small, there is no need to construct any piers. The stones to construct the foundations of the bridges on the sides are available in plenty. However, no other material for the construction of the bridges is available. Even wood is scarce in this area.

Moreover, it is not difficult at all to ferry across troops over the rivers in summer season as ordinary assault boats can serve the purpose.

Landing Grounds

Importance

The importance of landing grounds or dropping zones in a country like this cannot be over-emphasised. The country being highly mountainous, it takes very long time to traverse even small distances. For example, it takes, over six hours to reach Leh from Srinagar by road while the same distance is covered by air within one hour.

Location of Areas fit for Landing Grounds

The following areas are fit for the construction of landing grounds:-

Leh:

(a) Plain near Ranbirpura (MR 7823 Map No. 52F) 3 miles in length and 2 miles in breadth.

(b) Plain near Stok (MR 6734 Map No 52F) 4 miles in length and 3 miles in breadth.

(c) Plain between Spituk and Leh (MR 6745 Map No 52F) An airstrip already exists.

(d) Plain about 7 miles from Hemis (MR 7823 Map No 52G) 3 miles in length and 2 miles in breadth.

Kargil:

(a) Plain near Kurbathang (MR 1289 Map No 52B) 4 miles in length and about 2 miles in breadth.

(b) Plain near Padam in Zanskar (MR 9056 Map No 52C) 3 miles in length and about 1-1/2 miles in breadth.

Chushul:

(a) Plain near Chushul (MR 8990 Map No 52K) About 2-1/2 miles in length and about ½ mile in breadth.

Shyok:

(a) Plain near Khalsar (MR 7889 Map No 52F) About 2-1/2 miles in length and ½ mile in breadth.

(b) Plain near Khuru (MR 2301 Map No 52F) About 3 miles in length and ½ mile in breadth.

Type of Ground and Surrounding Features

The areas mentioned above can also be used easily for dropping zones. These areas as mentioned above can be converted into air strips as these are all almost level plains and with little effort these areas can be levelled into a smooth surface. The areas are neither rocky nor very sandy. As all these plains are situated in between the two mountain ranges which run parallel for miles on, there is enough place for the plane to land and take off. The wind in all the valleys as well as between the mountain ranges becomes fast as the day lingers on. Consequently it is easy for the plane to land and take off till one O'clock in the day time. After this time, the wind will usually have to be taken into account while landing as well as taking off.

Material for Construction of Air Strips

The stones are available in plenty near the suggested places for airstrips. Some wood is also available for the construction of barracks. However, for construction of a cemented airstrip, lot of material will have to be brought from outside as nothing more than stones, wood or labour is available in the surrounding areas.

Special features affecting Air Force

The two main features of Ladakh must be kept in mind while studying the possible effects on Air Force. These are:-

- Height of Air Strips

- Extreme Cold Climate

(a) Height of Air Strips: Almost all the places suggested above are situated between 10,000 and 12,000 feet except Chushul which is situated at a height of 14,320 feet. The velocity of wind due to lack of any vegetation is fast. The air due to the great height is rarefied as compared to the plains, and the aircraft will not be able to take its full load while taking off due to the rarefied atmosphere. How this height is liable to affect various types of planes is a technical matter for Air Force authorities to consider in detail.

(b) Extreme Cold Climate: The climate of Ladakh in winter is very cold and temperature often goes below -5 degree to -10 degree Fahrenheit (i.e. -37 degree to 42 degree below freezing point). Sometimes there is snowfall also which can block the air strip unless it is cleared. However, the snowfall is surprisingly little and the snow easily evaporates (snow evaporates due to extreme dryness of the atmosphere and does not melt). So snowfall in itself is not a great problem. However, the weather remains cloudy in winter season and it can be hazardous to fly sorties in cloudy weather. Besides what effect the extreme cold can have on the working of the aircraft engines is a technical matter for the Air Force authorities.

Likely Lines of Advance into Ladakh (updated on roads)

After studying topography, communications and routes connecting Ladakh with the surrounding countries, it becomes essential to appreciate, as best as can be done, the likely lines of advance into Ladakh from other countries.

It is clear that the likely enemy lines of advance into Ladakh can be the following:-

(a) From Xinjiang to Leh

(b) From Tibet into Eastern Ladakh

(c) From Pakistan held Kashmir into Western Ladakh.

(a) **From Xinjiang to Leh:**

While I was there this was a track only but by 1956 China had constructed a road through Lanak La Pass. It has reportedly constructed a road from Xinjiang toward Leh as well as the Eastern and Western parts of Ladakh. China has also constructed roads from the Aksai Chin Highway towards North Eastern Ladakh. (The Aksai Chin region was once a part of Ladakh, the Chinese occupation though continues because of its military strength and obduracy. When I was there we considered the Aksai Chin area very much Indian territory). It connects Xinjiang with Western Tibet and can be used for attacking North Eastern Ladakh.

China has now developed roads from Western Lhasa towards the Indian border in Ladakh. From Western Tibet to the Northern part of Himachal Pradesh there is a good road from Western Tibet. The Chinese advance along this road to Himachal Pradesh can adversely affect the communications to Ladakh - Himachal Pradesh by cutting off the road from Himachal Pradesh to Ladakh.

(b) **From Tibet into Eastern Ladakh:** From Western Tibet there are two important routes:-

i) From Rudok to Leh via Chushul

ii) From Gartok to Leh via Indus Valley

Of these two routes, the second route – From Gartok to Leh via Indus Valley – is better for the enemy to advance and difficult for us to defend. All along this route there is not a single pass which is formidable in climbing or which offers any special advantage for defence. The River Indus itself is no formidable obstacle at all. In winter the surface of the river is frozen and infantry along with loaded ponies can cross it at will. In summer also there is not very much current in the Indus when it flows in Eastern Ladakh as no tributaries with any great amount of current join it. The river grows stronger in current as it moves westwards as more tributaries join it. However, taking into consideration the heavy melting of snow on the mountains in summer, it can be considered that the River Indus will be very difficult to cross for 3 months, June, July and August. But for the rest of the nine months the river Indus itself provides no formidable obstacle at all in Eastern Ladakh. Hence this route does not offer the enemy with any great problem of communication which is of vital importance in mountain warfare. The Chinese tanks and Artillery along with mechanized forces can also use it for quick advance.

The first route – From Rudok to Leh via Chushul – though less advantageous than the above mentioned route can also be selected as line of advance by enemy into Ladakh. From Rudok in Tibet till the Changla Pass (18,300 feet) the ground offers no formidable obstacle worth the name. The route passes over the High Eastern Tablelands where passage is fairly easy. However, the Changla Pass is a formidable obstacle if it is properly defended. Consequently this route is easier to defend as compared to the other route and therefore enemy is less likely to adopt this route.

Another route available to the Chinese is to advance along Chang Chenmo River which later joins Shyok River in North Eastern Ladakh. River Shyok later runs through central part of Ladakh from east to west and later joins Indus River in north western Ladakh.

(c) **From Pakistan held Kashmir into Western Ladakh:**

From Pakistan held Kashmir, there are two routes which can be used effectively to advance into Western Ladakh.

(i) From Skardu to Leh via Biagdangdo

(ii) From Skardu to Leh via Kargil

From Skardu to Leh via Biagdangdo: This route was followed by the Pakistanis during J&K Operations when their forces advanced within 20 miles to Leh in 1948. This route compared to second one is shorter. However it has several disadvantages for over-running Western Ladakh due to highly mountainous terrain.

From Skardu to Leh via Kargil: This route is longer than the first route but is more dangerous to our side. Kargil is situated right on the border and once it is captured the line of communication between Leh and Srinagar by road is cut off. The enemy forces after capturing Kargil can not only advance towards Leh but can also advance towards Srinagar. In other words, advance on this route means splitting of the Indian defence line and is consequently more important to us from strategic point of view.

Vulnerable Places

The following areas in Ladakh are vulnerable at present:-

(a) **Kargil Area**

Kargil is a vulnerable point as it is situated right on the front line. Round about Kargil, the Pakistani forces are occupying few commanding heights from where they can attack the Indian defenses. Besides, Kargil is situated in a very strategic area, the capture of which will split the Indian front in Ladakh into two parts. Gurgurdu and Chorbatla are included in this area.

(b) **Biogdangdo Area**

In summer, the River Shyok provides a fairly big obstacle for Pakistanis to attack the Indian defences. However, in winter the river's surface gets frozen and attack on Indian defences is comparatively easy. The Indian forces near Biagdangdo are occupying commanding positions. Still this is a vulnerable point as its capture will enable the enemy to advance towards Leh. After capture of Biagdangdo, the track forks and one route goes to Khalsi, the capture of which will cut the line of communication with Kargil. Besides, the capture of Biagdangdo will endanger the whole Shyok valley.

(c) **Eastern Ladakh (Koyul – Demchok Area)**

Whenever an attack does take place from Tibet, the road coming from Rudok via Chushul and the road from Gartok along the River Indus are the main routes along which the invading forces can easily advance. Consequently, the area between Chushul and Demchok which is situated along these routes is the vulnerable area.

(d) Tangtse

Tangtse is situated just east of the Changla Pass and consequently occupies a very important position as regards the defence of Eastern Ladakh. Besides, two routes – one coming from Xinjiang (Winter Route) and the other from Tibet – meet at Tangtse.

In this connection, it should be noted that Northern area of Ladakh bordering Sinkiang (Xinjiang) is also considered a vulnerable area. However, the threat from Sinkiang (Xinjiang) to Ladakh is comparatively less because of the long and hazardous route. Though forces can always operate along this route but any large scale attack by a modern type army with all its supply and administrative problems would cause more problems.

Special Characteristics of Ladakh

Before we start analyzing the defence problems of this area and see how best the defence of this area can be organized, it is only essential that thorough study be made of the special characteristics of this area which can play a prominent part in the actual operations.

To any commander of the army of defending Ladakh studying the character of the country he had to traverse and operate upon, the most striking features would appear to be the high altitude of the area, extreme cold, lack of accommodation especially in winter, paucity of supplies from within the region and lack of proper communications. Let us discuss these characteristics in some detail.

High altitude

The area of Ladakh is one of the most mountainous regions in the world. The mountains also being very high, the average altitude of the area ranges from 10,500 feet to 12,500 feet. The area in the Western part of Ladakh, i.e. Kargil and its surroundings, is comparatively lower as compared to Eastern and Northern parts of Ladakh. The average altitude of the area being so high, the height of the commanding features where picquets have to be established for defence purposes run from 12,500 to 16,000 feet. The personnel from the plains who are not accustomed to the high altitude find it difficult and at any rate take some time to get acclimatized to the high altitude. The air starts becoming rarefied as one goes higher up and one starts feeling little difficulty in breathing when one is over 11,000 feet above sea level. The breathing becomes more difficult as one goes still higher up. Consequently, one gets tired after little exertion at these high altitudes. This is an important point as it affects the mobility of the forces. The area being highly mountainous, the only means of communication are ponies, camels, or vehicles where the roads are available. As one gets tired after little exertion, one can neither go very fast nor can one carry on riding or walking for a long period. The power of exertion declines appreciably when one has to climb at these altitudes. Hence it is difficult for forces to possess any great amount of mobility in these areas. The infantry covering the distance on foot can hardly do more than 15 miles a day while on ponies the distance travelled can hardly exceed 20 miles a day. Thus the altitude limits the mobility of the forces, till proper roads are constructed at most places, which the Chinese have done and continue to do so. However, we are also constructing more roads now.

Another aspect though minor one of the high altitude is that the personnel from plains are liable to contract minor ailments like bad throat, indigestion and giddiness. However, these diseases are not permanent and after a stay of a few weeks, one usually gets acclimatized. The cooking of foodstuffs like meat and 'dals' also take more time at high altitudes.

Extreme cold

As the average height of the area is so high, it is extremely cold in winter season. The cold in this area can be favourably compared to the Arctic cold. The temperature goes as far as -20 degrees Fahrenheit (i.e. 52 degrees below freezing point) and consequently all the streams and the rivers get frozen. Though the snowfall is not very much due to the extremely dry atmosphere, the passes usually get blocked in winter and remain closed for weeks.

The personnel who are not used to this cold are liable to get diseases like Frostbite and Chilblain. Besides, the personnel from the plains often get their hands and feet also swollen due to the extreme cold. Consequently, unless the troops are used to the climate or are at least acclimatized, they cannot put up any fight worth the name in winter season.

Even the vehicles which have to be used in this area require 'anti-freezing mixture'. However, the effect of cold on automatic weapons like MMG, LMG and sten gun is not so bad and these weapons can normally give automatic fire. However, in higher picquets at heights of 14,500 feet or above, in winter some of these automatic weapons may not be able to give automatic fire and consequently supply of 'anti-freezing mixture' has to be catered for.

Another problem to tackle in the extreme cold is the provision of winter clothing. The administrative arrangements have to be made in advance for the provision of winter and snow clothing for all the forces operating in this area.

Consequently, it becomes imperative that the troops who have to fight in this area should be sent before the advent of winter so that they can become acclimatized before winter sets in. Besides, it is also true that winter is not the season when any large scale operations can take place in this area. That phrase in the Bible "The time of the year when kings go forth to battle" need puzzle no one who has to live in Ladakh in winter season. It is then impossible for kings (of the past) or comers of today to go forth to battle with any comfort or profit in the winter season.

Non-availability of Supplies

The third important characteristic of Ladakh is that this area is completely devoid of any supplies on which an army can exist. The country being a mountain desert, the inhabitants can hardly grow enough for their own existence. Consequently, the troops will have to depend on outside help for all their supplies. The only commodity that this area can supply is wood but unfortunately that also is fast disappearing. The growth of new trees being very difficult while the existing ones are mercilessly being cut can only result in wood famine in this area before long. The non availability of supplies in the local area means that troops will have to be supplied for every item all the way from Srinagar or Himachal Pradesh. This will result in making exhaustive administrative arrangements for the troops compatible with operational necessity.

Whenever any force moves from one area of Ladakh to another even after the construction of road, it has to be self sufficient by way of supplies, till big depots are constructed in Ladakh region.

Lack of accommodation and communication

The whole area of Ladakh being so sparsely populated due to the difficult mountainous terrain, the problem of accommodation is acute. Any large force will have to make its own arrangements for accommodation in this area. Proper accommodation has to be built in Kargil, Ladakh and in other forward areas to accommodate more troops properly. At the same time proper depots have to be made in Leh, Kargil and other areas for stores and supplies. Proper roads from Himachal Pradesh and J&K must be made including tunnels to maintain troops in Kargil and Leh area. The air force can also ferry stores but it is much more expensive. Besides, the air force can give effective air support, but it may need more airfields in Ladakh-Kargil region particularly for reconnaissance of forward areas which are quite large. The helicopters can also play an important role for reconnaissance as well as for ferrying troops to forward areas, which is so vast. The roads to Ladakh both from Kashmir and Himachal Pradesh which is nearer need proper maintenance at all times for obvious reasons.

Defence of Ladakh

It is said that "The Frontiers of States can be great rivers, or chains of mountains or a desert. Of all these obstacles opposing the progress of an army the most difficult to surmount is the desert, next come the mountains and third only, the large rivers."

Introduction

Ladakh as we know is a "mountain desert". Though the area of Ladakh is extremely mountainous yet the climate conditions, the arid and rugged mountains, the little produce of the sandy and stony fields and the complete absence of forests or vegetation give it the appearance of a "mountain desert". In view of the above quoted "Military Maxim of Napoleon", the attempt to capture Ladakh by a foreign invader will present him with manifold problems. It, therefore, follows that Ladakh can hold out against any invader provided its defences are properly organized. The difficulties and the special characteristics of Ladakh, viz, high altitude, extreme cold, and paucity of supplies and lack of communications as described earlier, not only hinder the proper and planned defence of Ladakh but also equally hinder the progress of any foreign army into Ladakh. It, therefore, is logical to assume that aided by nature itself, Ladakh if properly defended by the ingenuity of man can be an impregnable stronghold.

Principle of Defence

The area of Ladakh is so vast that it is neither logical nor practicable to defend it from all the sides. It, therefore, follows that outer defence positions should be established only at the important and vulnerable points. Mobile reserves should be kept at strategic points from where these can be rushed to any threatened area. The landing grounds and the dropping zones should be developed at the proper places so that immediate aid can be rushed to any place. Lastly, large stocks of ammunition and supplies should be stocked in central and important points in Ladakh so that when the troops come as reinforcements to Ladakh they do not find any difficulty from administrative side. In other words, there is need to station adequate forces in Ladakh, but means and ways should also be improved by which large forces can easily come into Ladakh and can go into action straight away without facing any handicap from the administrative side.

Organisation of Defence

(a) Defence positions to be established at Vulnerable and Important Positions:

The defence positions which can be called outer defence of Ladakh should be established at the vulnerable and important points. These defence positions must have the following requisites.

(i) Source of Water Supply

Each defence position should have some sort of source of water supply within its defence area. It, therefore, follows that defences of the position should be sited in such a way that source of water supply comes well within its area. The question of water supply becomes very important in picquets at the hill tops and adequate arrangements should be made in advance to stock water or make arrangements for its regular supply.

(ii) Reserve stocks of Ammunition and Supplies

These outposts as suggested above should be stocked with reserve ammunition and other necessary supplies enough to last for six months. In winter the passes often get blocked and consequently the stocked supplies can come in handy. Besides in case of an enemy attack the outposts can hold out till the aid reaches them.

(iii) Good Communication

Each defensive position should be provided with powerful signal sets so that communications with the rear areas can be kept up at all times.

(iv) All Round Defences

These defence positions must have all round defence. It is because the defence positions have to hold out till aid reaches them.

The main aim and task of these defensive positions is to stop or delay the attacking forces till reinforcements from the rear areas can come to grips with the invading forces. The strength of the troops manning these defensive positions cannot be a fixed one. It all depends upon the strength of the forces that the country on the other side of the border is likely to deploy.

(b) Mobile Reserves to be held at Strategic Places

After the outer defences have been organized by holding defences at vulnerable and important points, it is essential to have mobile reserves ready to rush to any threatened area at a moment's notice. These mobile reserves must be kept at strategic and important points. The following two places are considered suitable for keeping mobile reserves.

- Leh: For Eastern and Northern Ladakh
- Kargil: For Western Ladakh

As is clear from the map, from Leh roads go to Tibet, Sinkiang (Xinjiang) and Kashmir. Consequently Leh is ideally suitable for holding mobile reserves for Eastern as well as Northern parts of

Ladakh. However, Kargil which is now right on the Indo-Pak border assumes a great importance, for its capture by Pakistan will cut the line of communication between Srinagar and Leh. Consequently mobile reserves must be kept at Kargil to safeguard the line of communication as well as to hold Kargil and the surrounding areas. Here, again exact strength of troops that should be kept at these bases cannot be fixed as it will depend upon the forces which the adjacent countries are deploying in their areas.

(c) **Development of Landing Grounds and Dropping Zones**

The communications in this highly mountainous country being extremely difficult, it is essential that the landing grounds and dropping zones should be established in Ladakh and Kargil regions at proper places.

If landing grounds or even air strips are established at proper places it will go a long way in solving the difficulties of communications. It will help in solving not only the problem of communication of this area but also of defence, as it will then be possible to rush in reinforcements at a short notice to any part of Ladakh.

(d) **Stocking of Supplies**

As the line of communication between Srinagar and Himachal Pradesh to Leh is long and difficult, it is essential that supplies must be stocked well in advance to meet any emergency at important and central places. While stocking supplies of various kinds, one important point must be kept in mind. That the reinforcements can be rushed in to Leh as well as Kargil at a short notice as air fields exist there but administrative arrangements must be made in advance so that these forces can go into action immediately. If the supplies for these forces have also got to come along with the forces, the build up and move out of the forces to the threatening front will take much more time. In order to tide over this problem, it is suggested that supplies and ammunition at Leh and Kargil should be stocked at the ratio of two times the strength of the forces that are at present garrisoned there. It would mean that even if twice the strength of the forces that are at present stationed in Ladakh arrive at a moment's notice, these can go into action straight away as all the necessary supplies would be available.

Organisation of Guerilla Battalion

During J&K Operations, it was proved beyond doubt by the daring exploits of Major Prithi Chand later Colonel and MVC, that Ladakh area is ideally suitable for guerilla warfare. He organized small groups of Ladakhi personnel into efficient guerilla bands and with little training was able to achieve notable successes. However, it is important to note that personnel from India cannot be of much advantage as guerillas. The guerillas will have to operate cross country and often at heights varying from 13,000 feet to 15,000 feet. Besides, the soldiers will have to carry their rations and provisions on their backs as country can supply nothing by way of supplies. Thus it will be very difficult for those personnel who are not accustomed to the high altitude and severe winter to operate as guerillas. The locals of Ladakh are ideally suitable to be trained as Guerilla soldiers. They are used to living on high altitude and can easily perform the cross country movements. Besides, the locals can live surprisingly on the small scale of rations. A handful of parched barley with saltish tea is good enough for an average Ladakhi for a day. Consequently, the Ladakhis can easily carry rations to last for a week on their backs, and at the same time can be able to move cross country with ease which is beyond the imagination of an average plains-man.

Conduct of Operations

It has already been discussed that the lack of communications, paucity of supplies, severe weather conditions and high altitude of the area present special difficulties for the conduct of operations in this part of the country. However, as the communications improve, and the more roads and air fields are constructed the operations with large forces are possible during the summer months.

Around 1953-54 the Chinese started road construction in a big way. The Chinese have constructed good roads from Tibet to Ladakh as well as from Xinjiang in the north to north eastern Ladakh. So they can now operate with much larger forces in Ladakh region. The Chinese have also constructed a road which runs up to border of Himachal Pradesh which can affect Indian communications with Ladakh. Secondly, we now have a Corps Headquarters at Leh, this affects the strategic dynamics greatly. However, the fundamental issues of tactics and strategy in a disputed area remain the same.

APPENDIX "A"

(Refers to Chapter II – Geographical Survey)

AREA OF LADAKH

Mean Length and breadth	Extreme Length and breadth	Total Area	Total Area measured at assessment	Uncultivated Fit for cultivation/ Not fit for cultivation		Cultivated	Total of colns (e) (f) and (g)
(a)	(b)	(c)	(d)	(e)	(f)	(g)	(h)
170x124 Sq miles	268x191 Sq miles	21,080 Sq miles	88,993 miles	15,517 acres	55,626 acres	20,107 acres	91,250 acres

Chapter IX

SOME PERSONAL RECOLLECTIONS

When one stays at an interesting and engrossing place like Ladakh for two years, one cannot but have some experiences which leave a lasting impression. Ladakh IN 1952 was an isolated far off place in the North West corner of India which was totally neglected both by the J&K Government as well as the Indian Government. After the 1947-48 J&K war, the Indian Army had withdrawn from Ladakh, so when I arrived in 1952 at Leh, the main town in Ladakh, I found myself quite alone. It had however, the 7 J&K Militia Battalion which had two companies of J&K Muslims and two companies of Ladakhi Buddhists (This Militia was not an integral part of the Indian Army at that time).

The officers of 7 J&K Militia Battalion were from India as well as J&K, remember this was a young nation at that time and still integrating. The Commanding Officer, a Lt. Col and the second in Command, a Major, Adjutant and Quarter Master (Captain) were the Indian Officers in the unit while the remainder four or five officers were from J&K. They were selected by the J&K Government from amongst the so called freedom fighters from the valley, from amongst those who had taken part in the struggle against the Pak invaders, when they invaded the valley from Pakistan in 1947-48. Most officers and JCOs were from the Valley, many were members of Sheikh Abdullah's political party and were opposing the Maharaja of J&K's rule in the State. They were keen to have a democratic type of Government in the valley, preferably to be formed with Sheikh Abdullah as the leader. Sheikh Abdullah as the Chief Minister of J&K had the implied sanction of Government of India to raise a few Militia Battalions which would be the responsibility of the Indian Government by way of all expenditure like pay etc. including the provision of all weapons and equipment as authorised to the Indian Army

Infantry Battalions. However, their command and control was not fully defined in that J&K Government claimed that the Militia Battalions were under their command in the valley but the Indian Government would be responsible for all their expenses. However, when a Militia Battalion would be deployed in the field area on the border like Ladakh, it would be under the command of the Indian Army.

In Ladakh, 7 J&K Militia was deployed only along the Indo-Pak border with its Head Quarter located at Leh. When I landed at Leh in 1952, as Army Head Quarter Liaison Officer, I reported to the officer commanding 7 J&K Militia. There was great paucity of accommodation, as there were no barracks or any Mess building in Leh. The small fort at Leh which was constructed by General Zorawar when he captured Leh a few centuries ago was used by the Militia Battalion personnel while their officers had occupied a big building which was once Head Quarter of the British Resident who used to look after the British interests against the Chinese activities in Xinjiang border as well as the Ladakh-Tibet border. This was also the best building in Leh district in 1952 and boasted of a nice garden around the big building.

The British used to send a strong military patrol to Western Tibet very frequently and these patrols used to travel inside Western Tibet for weeks together. The British patrols used to patrol very close to Xinjiang region also along the northern border. The Indian traders mainly from Hoshiarpur and Amritsar districts of Punjab, were quite active and their large convoy of camels and ponies used to make regular trips to Xinjiang province from Ladakh. Many Indian traders had actually settled down in the two well-known cities of Xinjiang like Yarkand and Kashgarh.

The Chinese authorities welcomed them as they helped in trade between India and China. Many of them had married the local women also though they were Muslims while the Indian traders from Punjab were either Hindus or Sikhs. They had purchased houses and shops also in Xinjiang particularly in the districts of Yarkand and Kashgarh of Sinkiang (Xinjiang).

However, the Chinese authorities suddenly decided in 1952 that there would be no trade between Ladakh and Xinjiang and that all Indian traders from Xinjiang would have to leave Xinjiang immediately. Consequently, the Chinese Government ordered the Indian traders to wind up their businesses and to do so within a week at the most. Incidentally, the Chinese can be very harsh in their treatment of what they perceive to be a weaker community or nation. The Indian traders therefore lost not only their houses and shops but all their belongings and wealth also as they were allowed to take minimum luggage only. The Indian trade commissioner in Xinjiang was posted in Urumachi, Capital of Xinjiang province and tried to help the Indian traders in Xinjiang but all his efforts failed. He was also ordered to leave Xinjiang at short notice. His request to travel along with the Indian traders to Ladakh was also turned down. He had to go back to Shanghai and then travel to India via the sea route.

I met the expelled Indian traders at Leh in Ladakh in the local bazar and later talked to them in the Sarai in Leh. A few traders told me that they had to sell all their goods as well as their belongings in their houses at the minimum possible price, as they were permitted to carry limited stock only. Each trader was allowed to take back only stocks which could be carried by one camel while he was allowed to take one horse for travelling back to India via Ladakh.

The traders knew that they would be searched for valuable items like golden ornaments which they may like to take back to India. They knew that the costly items like golden ornaments would be confiscated by the Chinese guards at the border who would search their belongings before allowing them to cross the border. So many of them carried Hookas (the typical Indian method of smoking tobacco) they melted their golden ornaments and then poured the melted gold into their hookas, particularly into the bottom part of the Hooka, which normally contained only water. I was shown some of the golden bottom hookas by the traders. The Indian traders certainly possess ingenuity of high order, no wonder they are so successful. However most of the traders I met had lost heavily and were certainly not backed by the Central Government adequately.

Another interesting episode I can remember is that of officer commanding 7 J&K Militia Battalion which was the only unit posted in Leh Ladakh. There was one Infantry Battalion of Indian Army located at Kargil but there were no regular troops located in the whole of Ladakh region in 1952, even though the Chinese had moved large forces into Xinjiang in the North and Tibet in the East and were improving their road communications in both these regions having common borders with Ladakh.

The Chinese had their border out post at the border with Tibet at Demchok which was manned by the Chinese soldiers. On the other hand, the Indian border out post at Demchok area was occupied by the J&K police personnel only. Similar was the case in the northern part of Ladakh as well where the Chinese had their last outpost just north of Karakoram Pass. India had no military outpost in the northern part of Ladakh either in 1952 for the reasons best known to the authorities concerned. The 7 J&K Militia had their troop's mostly facing Pakistan border in the north western portion of Ladakh. There was obviously no danger perceived from the Chinese side in the north as well as from the East.

The Militia Battalions had two companies of Ladakhi Muslims and two companies of Ladakhi Buddhists. As stated earlier the Ladakh Buddhists had fought very well during 1947-48 in India-Pakistan War in Ladakh region. Lt. Colonel B.U. Desai was the officer commanding of 7 J&K Militia Battalion. What was his religion was not known to me but he somehow did not like the Ladakhi Buddhist troops being part of his unit. He mentioned his doubts about their loyalty to me as well as to few other officers of the Militia Battalion also. He felt that the Chinese being mostly Buddhists and their occupation of Tibet meant that the local Buddhist Ladakhis in the 7 J&K Militia would not be very loyal to the Indian Army during any future war. I told him in the course of many discussions that his doubts were not really logical, as the Chinese Govt. and the people were communists and they had occupied Tibet after defeating the local Buddhist forces of the Tibetan Government. The Chinese were obviously against the Buddhists I tried to explain repeatedly but he had his own views. I dismissed the subject in due course from my mind as of no importance.

A few months later, a Brigadier from the Army Head Quarters at New Delhi visited Ladakh. On the first day of his visit, he was busy discussing the situation in Ladakh as well as the activities of 7 J&K Militia Battalion. The second day he asked me to come for a walk and went on asking me questions regarding the 7 J&K Militia Battalion including the activities of the Commanding officer and his views regarding Buddhist soldiers of 7 J&K Militia. Finally he asked me whether I felt any doubt about the loyalty of the Ladakhi Buddhist soldiers of 7 J&K Militia towards India in case of a war against China or Tibet. I told him that the Ladakhi soldiers had fought well against the Pakistan soldiers in 1947-48 war and would do so again in any fight against Tibetan or the Chinese forces. He did not say anything in reply. The next day he left for Srinagar. I did not talk about my discussion with the Brigadier to any 7 J&K Militia officer either.

A few weeks later Lt. Col. B.U. Desai was suddenly posted out to a staff appointment in Maharashtra, though he had served in 7 J&K Militia Battalion for a few months only. It came as a great surprise to all other officers at Leh also.

In August 1952, the 7 J&K Militia Battalion held a parade to celebrate the Independence Day. The Commanding Officer took the Salute at the dais where the flag which was hoisted was not the Indian National Flag. When I asked about the identity of the flag, I was told that it was the flag of the J&K Nationalist Party of Sheikh Abdulla, the then Chief Minister of J&K. I was taking photographs of the parade and felt strange that the 7 J&K Militia Battalion was not showing any respect to the Indian national flag even on the occasion of the Independence Day. I therefore just walked away from the parade ground which annoyed the Commanding Officer of the Militia Battalion. When I returned to where the Militia Battalion officers mess was located, I was told that I should vacate the room where I was staying, as it was meant for the Militia Battalion officers only. So I had to find an, accommodation in Leh city. However, the unit allowed me to take my meals in the mess which was indeed a great favour in 1952. Today Leh boasts of so many hotels and restaurants as it has become a great attraction for the tourists but in 1952 it had only a few proper houses, the rest of the town had mostly small houses or huts for most of the inhabitants. There was no restaurant, only Sarais for travellers where one could live and eat some food. I had to report my concerns about the apparent disloyalty of the Commanding Officer to Army HQ's at Delhi, such incidents and friction kept me quite busy.

I, after my being forced out, sent a letter to Army Head Quarters requesting them to arrange for a house for myself and a staff of four persons and to also kindly arrange a peon to work in the office as well as for general cleanliness of the house in which I and four members of the staff would have to stay. The Ministry of Defence generously approved the appointment of a peon for the office. They also sent the uniform which was generally worn by the peons in the offices of the Govt. of India. Then I selected a peon and told him the salary as well as the clothes which included a turban and long flowing coat, he was so happy that he brought his entire family to serve in the office because the salary paid by the Ministry of Defence was much more that he could imagine in Ladakh in 1952. I had to explain to him that the salary being offered to him was only for his services and none of his family members would have to work in the office or at the house. This shows the level of poverty that existed in the region in the early fifty's. But it also showed the high level of honesty and integrity of Ladakhi people.

After moving out of the JK Militia Camp, I moved to a house wherein the other staff were also located, kind courtesy the Local Army Unit. I had a staff of four personnel, One was Mr Kaul, a resident of the valley, an astute translator in Ladakhi and Tibetan languages. He was a graduate and also had a law degree, a qualified lawyer; he was a valuable asset while dealing with the civil and religious leaders in Ladakh as also in interacting with Tibetan traders. I also had a Chinese language interpreter, Mr Shibrurkar, belonging to Maharashtra, a graduate, he also had a degree from the Chinese University at Peking (as it was known then). His study of Chinese history and culture for two years was most useful, specially in gathering information and in dealing with Chinese Personnel on the border, as and when I met them. In addition I had a JCO (Junior Commissioned Officer) and a Havildar Clerk (NCO) for official work. I had to send a monthly detailed report to the Army HQ's Military Intelligence Directorate, always to be marked Top Secret. I had to interact with local civil officers as well as political and religious leaders frequently, many a times informally.

I was also asked subsequently to attend to the duties of the Station Staff Officer (SSO) at Leh by the GOC 19 Infantry Division. This duty enabled me to deal with the local military personnel as also the civilian officers regarding the army civil issues and also provided me a convenient platform to meet a wide range of people. A good quality horse was also given to me to travel within Leh Area. Incidentally, in 1952, there was only one jeep in the Leh Region, which was used only by the Officer Commanding the J&K Militia Battalion. There was a track from Leh to the airfield which was meant for use of ponies and camels but the jeep could also be driven upon it. There were no roads as such in Ladakh in 1952, only tracks.

I came across many personalities in Ladakh, some who left a deep impression upon me. There was the well kept Moravian Mission, headed by the gracious Dr. and Mrs Driver, from the UK; they extended medical care inclusive of medicines to the poor. Being missionaries, they were very dedicated and tried their best to spread Christianity while extending medical care. The couple were however not popular inspite of their medical care as they remained aloof from the masses and maintained a distance. They were replaced in 1953 or so by the Swiss couple, Dr and Mrs Vittoz, they mixed well with the population and were certainly more popular but they were also unable to spread Christianity.

Amongst the Buddhist leaders, I found Kushak Bakula the most impressive and capable leader, a sagacious leader who wanted close and abiding relations with India. He was very fond of Prime Minister Nehru as well General Carriappa, whom he met at Delhi, his travels to Delhi were frequent. He preached and advocated openly and clearly that Ladakh was an integral part of India. Kushak Bakula was afraid that the State of Jammu & Kashmir could opt one day for Pakistan or declare its independence and was of the view that it would certainly impact adversely the Buddhist population of Ladakh. Sheikh Abdullah and his close leaders disliked him intensely. Kushak Bakula also used to inform and state that the State Government was certainly communal in attitude and indirectly encouraging the spread of Islam in Kargil, the consequent communal tensions at Kargil were certainly impacting the followers of Buddhism as also creating a divide between the two communities. The fear of losing their majority within the Leh Region preoccupied Kushak Bakula and his followers. His clear viewpoint was that Ladakh would be an integral part of J&K as long as J&K was an integral part of India. In case of any move towards independence by J&K, the people of Ladakh would opt for India by a special dispensation.

Kushak Bakula's letters to General Carriappa were quite interesting, he would consistently invite him to visit Ladakh and be his personal guest. In one of his discussions with me, he was frank and said he did not trust the Chinese at all. According to his judgement, the Chinese would one day ensure that Buddhism as practised in Tibet was finished off and the same fate would be of Ladakh in case the Chinese captured Ladakh too. Whenever I asked him as to why the Chinese would attack Ladakh, considering that both nations wanted and advocated close relations, he would become pensive. He would only say that it is not wise to take things for granted, for nations changed their views and policies as per their changing interests. His oft stated views were to welcome peace but to be simultaneously alert and to have a certain degree of preparation always for any eventuality. I found such statements profound for a Buddhist Monk in an isolated region such as Ladakh. He was a wise saint and leader and I wish he had given this advice to the Indian leaders more vociferously in the 1950s.

Incidentally, Kushak Bakula was a Minister in the State Government for some time. He was later a Member of Parliament and also held the appointment of a Minister. He had the distinction of addressing the meeting of the United Nations also on one occasion. He evolved as a Buddhist Monk as also a successful politician both at the State and Central levels. His list of achievements was long and he was held in high esteem in Ladakh. I certainly found him a remarkable personality. I can add that in time Kushak Bakula left a deep spiritual impression on me and showed me the pathways of spiritual enlightenment. There were quite a few other leaders and monks too, but Kushak Bakula stood out.

The people of Ladakh as such have left the most lasting impression upon me. Patriotic, committed, loyal inspite of being on the most periphery of the then political leadership, they were steadfast in their pride in the young emerging nation. The honesty, truthfulness and good cheer they radiated in such hardships as I witnessed have stayed with me since then. Even today the memories are fresh and firm, each and every discussion with Kushak Bakula have stayed with me as have the monasteries and their silhouettes as dusk would descend. The engrossing mystical element and insight I gained into Budhism as was then practiced at Ladakh has been a wonderful part of my life.

I survived death narrowly during my patrol of the Aksai Chin area. This was the age of minimal radio communications in that region. I actually drifted from the patrol to track rare and exotic wildlife and once snow started falling heavily, getting in touch with the main party became a major concern for me. Without shelter and wet and cold, I was at my wits end. After a few hours, survival itself was a concern and I had actually made up my mind to shoot myself rather than die miserably and alone. It was touch and go as I continued to trudge in the general area where we had agreed to meet. The patrol was equally concerned and was itself looking for me by flashing lights / fires etc. It was a relief to be back with the patrol ultimately and I would still say it was due to the blessings and goodwill of the monks that I was safe.

About the patrol to Aksai Chin itself, I was not permitted to write to my family about the assignment or that we would be out of contact for some time. At a time when writing letters home frequently to my father was absolutely necessary, I was out of touch for some time. Even on return and proceeding on leave to my home at Hoshiarpur in Punjab, I did not tell my parents about my trip and experiences. It was only when the relationship deteriorated with China, did I tell them.

Lastly, the ways of the Central Government always mystify. In 1952-53 the general issue for discussion was the priority for a road to connect Ladakh with Himachal Pradesh (as known today). The need to take up construction of tunnels was also discussed, both directly towards Himachal Pradesh and to the Kashmir Valley. Sixty odd years later we are still discussing the same issue. Infact connectivity through Himachal Pradesh would not only benefit the population of Ladakh but the nation also strategically. The road would reduce considerably the distance as today the route is Leh – Kargil – Srinagar – Jammu – Pathankot while it would be Leh – Kullu – Mandi – Chandigarh and certainly much shorter. We can learn from the Chinese in Engineering (Roads and Railways) and their national priority to integrate the periphery or isolated regions with the mainland.

I must add here that I never informed my parents about proceeding on the patrol. Firstly the letters took a long term and it was as it is classified as Secret. However when I proceeded on leave a few months later, I did inform them. In those days, with tracks and minimal infrastructure only, it was essentially a risky adventure.

Chapter X

INDO PAK WAR 1947-1948 OPERATIONS IN LADAKH

History records that the Maharaja of J&K and his Prime Minister (Kak) did not like Indian leaders, particularly Prime Minister Nehru, due to certain events before independence. They wanted J&K to declare independence but the sudden Pakistani attack in 1947 forced J&K to opt for India. The J&K Government had only six infantry battalions to guard the large frontiers of the state which had mostly a common border with Pakistan. It could spare only one infantry battalion to look after the security of the entire northern part of J&K from Gilgit in the west to Ladakh in the East, while the other battalions were deployed in Poonch-Jammu-Sri Nagar area. However, in addition to these infantry battalions, there was a Scout's Battalion which was stationed in Gilgit and was commanded by the British officers only to look after any threat from Central Asia as well as from Xinjiang region in the north before 1947. The Scout battalion had two companies of the Muslims and two companies of the Sikhs and Dogras. However, when Gilgit Scouts companies rebelled against the Maharaja of J&K in 1947, it had two Muslim companies and only one company of Dogras in Gilgit area while the other company was deployed in the area between Gilgit and Skardu in the East. The Scout battalion could capture Gilgit easily, as large number of Pakistani raiders had also joined the Scout's Battalion who wanted to capture entire northern part of J&K for Pakistan. The Pakistan raiders along with many Scouts Battalion personnel who were Muslims from Gilgit area took part in the battles to capture Ladakh in 1947/48.

The myth that the Ladakhis who are mainly Buddhists may not make good soldiers was exploded as they fought like brave and bold fighters in

1947/48 Indo Pak War when the Pakistani raiders led by Pak officers attacked Ladakh from Gilgit – Skardu area in the West and which now forms the Pak held Northern part of J&K. This needs some back ground information. The Pakistan raiders along with some Pak regular forces attacked J&K which had refused to opt for Pakistan or India on partition in 1947. The main attack came from Rawalpindi side to capture the Kashmir valley. The Pak forces managed to capture the Western part of the Kashmir valley upto Baramula and were advancing towards Sri Nagar when the Indian forces counter attacked and by the time ceasefire was declared on night 31 December, 1948-49, the Indian forces in the valley had recaptured an area upto Uri in the Kashmir valley.

In north Kashmir in the Gilgit-Skardu area Lt Col Roger Bacon, the British Political Agent governing the Gilgit area retired on 3 June 1947 and Brig Ghansara Singh of J&K State Forces took over as Governor of Gilgit from Lt Col Bacon. Some of the British officers of the Indian army were quite pro Pakistan, as only the Congress Leaders like Mahatma Gandhi, Pandit Nehru and others were asking the British to quit India while Jinnah and the Muslim league leaders were never that vociferous in asking the British to leave India. The Gilgit Scouts in coordination with the invasion of J&K by the Pakistani forces played an important part in capturing the northern part of J&K for Pakistan which is known as Azad Kashmir. Later they made a bold and desperate effort to capture Ladakh area also. After the departure of Lt Col Bacon, Lt Col Brown and Captain Mathieson of the British Army were posted to Gilgit Scouts by the British. The British officers and Pakistan had a secret plan to capture the entire northern part of J&K for Pakistan. The code word to start Gilgit Scouts and Pak Raiders operations in the northern part of J&K was "Datta Khel" which was given on 31 October, 1947.

There was only one infantry battalion of J&K state forces which was responsible for defence of Northern Kashmir which was spread from Ladakh in the East to Gilgit-Skardu area in the West, a distance of over 200 kilometers. At Skardu 250 men under command of Lt Col Later Brigadier Thapa had taken a good defensive position. Kargil had about two platoons worth of troops while Ladakh had an infantry platoon only to defend the vast area!

The Gilgit Scouts reinforced by about 2000 Pak Raiders made a bold plan to capture Gilgit, Skardu, Kargil and later whole of Ladakh. One force consisting of about a battalion worth of troops was to capture Gilgit and Skardu. Another force of similar strength was to make a wide right flanking move to South of Gilgit all the way to Guraiz valley in north Kashmir, then move eastwards and capture Kargil from where this force was to mount the main attack on Ladakh.

To start with, the Gilgit Scouts Battalion quickly over came the resistance of J&K troops in Gilgit, then they moved towards Skardu where Brigadier Thapa had taken up a defensive position in the old Skardu fort area. Thapa's soldiers offered a very tough resistance and even though completely surrounded and with no reinforcements or supply of arms and ammunition, continued to fight in a brave manner for nearly five/six months. Brigadier Thapa was awarded well deserved Maha Vir Chakra for his bravery and courage. The end of the gallant siege of Skardu on 14 August 1948 was followed by mass murder and rape, particularly all Sikh troops were killed and all women raped while few women committed suicide by jumping into the nearby river Indus.

In 1947 Major Prithi Chand later Colonel was serving in 2nd Dogras in Kashmir valley which was commanded by Lt Col G.G. Bewoor later General and Chief of Army Staff as well as Colonel of the Regiment of 11 GR, the Regiment I have the honour to belong to. I served under Col Prithi Chand Thakur as his Adjutant in 3/11 Gorkha Rifles in J&K which he took over as Commanding officer after his excellent work in Ladakh. He infact saved Ladakh from the Pakistan troops who tried their best to capture it. He was awarded a well deserved Maha Vir Chakra for his brave and gallant performance during the operations against the Pakistani forces, otherwise India would have lost Ladakh to Pakistan as has been the case with Gilgit and Skardu. He deserves to be treated as a genuine hero of India who saved Ladakh for the country.

The Second Dogra battalion which was located in Sri Nagar valley had one company of Lahauli and Ladakhi soldiers. However, at the end of the Second World War, most of them proceeded on release except for Major Prithi Chand, Maj Khushal Chand, Subedar Bhim Chand and 15 other ranks. All of them felt that unless some more troops are sent to Ladakh and that also quickly, Ladakh would be captured by the Pakistani invaders. So they all volunteered to go to Ladakh as soon as possible to ensure safety of the Ladakhis as well as safety of their monasteries in Ladakh. Finally 16 military personnel led by Major Later Colonel Prithi Chand and Shri Sonam Norbu, a J&K Engineer from Ladakh who was later to construct an air field in Leh, left Sri Nagar for Ladakh on 16 February 1948 during the cold winter season. The party carried 50 extra rifles and ammunition in addition to their personal arms and ammunition. This was for Ladakhi personnel who would be trained to fight the Pakistani raiders. I met Mr. Norbu in Ladakh in 1952 who gave me interesting details regarding construction of the air field in Ladakh using local labour which enabled the Indian Air Force to carry necessary supplies, ammunition and military personnel to Leh from Sri Nagar to fight the Pakistani forces which are generally referred to as Pak raiders by some writers. Mr Norbu is another unsung hero as the undue idealist emphasis on peace and peace only by post independence leaders led to all heroic efforts going unsung.

It is interesting to note the tasks given to a small party of about 16 officers and soldiers who were instructed to look after the security of a large region like Ladakh. The party was to move to Leh, raise an irregular force from Ladakh and train it to defend Ladakh by using guerilla tactics against Pak forces till such time the regular troops arrived there. The party was to live on local resources through local purchase by way of food supplies and clothes. It was indeed a very difficult task.

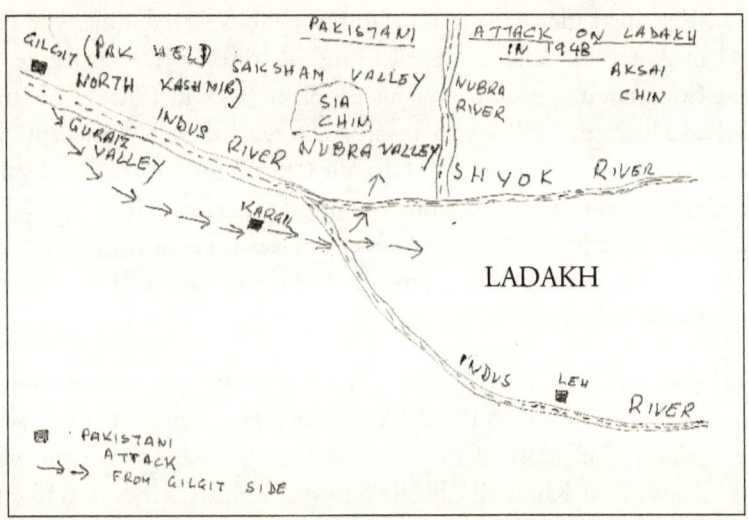

PAK PLAN TO ATTACK IN 1948

The party had to cross about 12000 feet high Zojila pass near Dras in the middle of winter when it was totally covered with snow for miles around the pass with strong winds making life miserable. Incidentally Dras is known as second coldest inhabited place in the world. The party crossed Zojila pass with great difficulty and reached Kargil while the temperature at the Zojila pass had touched minus 60 degree Celsius. The party reached well in time in

Kargil and then moved on to Leh to prepare Ladakh for its defence against the impending Pak attack. The party's morale went up when it was received with great enthusiasm by the Ladakhi villagers.

On reaching Leh, Lt Col Thakur Prithi Chand hoisted the national flag at a ceremony which was attended by almost all the local population of Leh town and where lamas prayed and the one platoon of J&K state forces presented the guard of honour to the Indian flag. After the ceremony, Thakur Prithi Chand addressed the crowd and stated that we have been sent here to help you to defend Ladakh. We would train local young men to fight and defend the area. He also asked them to help Mr. Sonam Norbu, the J&K Engineer to complete the air field quickly in Leh so that we could get supplies, weapons and ammunition to fight the Pak invaders. The local population promised full support to supply recruits for training and fighting the Pak forces and also for the quick construction of the airfield. Thakur Prithi Chand had taken the first and timely step to motivate the Ladakhi population to fight the Pak invaders.

He gave priority to the construction of the Leh airfield near the Indus River for which local labour as well as all available local stores were utilized to complete it as soon as possible. At the same time, Lt Col Prithi Chand started touring various villages in Ladakh to select young recruits who were to be given quick training to use the rifles and learn basic tactics to attack enemy positions and defend their own positions as well as to fight a guerilla type operations against the Pakistani forces which were expected to attack from the Skardu-Kargil side.

Meanwhile, the Pakistani column which was moving along the Southern route to capture Kargil by a surprise attack reached the Kargil area which it managed to capture after a brief battle. But by that time Kargil fell Lt Col Prithi Chand had already got constructed the fair weather Leh airfield by Mr Norbu the Ladakhi Engineer by using the large numbers of Ladakhi volunteers.

Lt Col Prithi Chand was very happy when he saw the first Dakota landing at Leh airfield, particularly when he saw General Thimayya and Air Commodore Mehar Singh getting out of the aircraft. The General asked Lt Col Prithi Chand "Are you afraid of the Gilgit Rats". Lt Col Prithi Chand replied, "Sir I am not afraid of them but I have no regular troops." The general promised him to send some troops and weapons as soon as possible.

It is a well known fact that these two gallant senior officers had flown to Leh against orders from higher Headquarters. But for their timely disobedience, we would have lost Ladakh in 1948.

The Pak column which had taken a long and circuitous route to capture Kargil succeeded not only in attacking Kargil but managed to capture it which gave a large area to Pakistan from Kargil to Gilgit, about two hundred kilometers. The Pakistan troops then started moving towards Leh from Kargil side.

Lt Col Prithi Chand had correctly analyzed that his immediate threat was from Kargil side which had been captured by the Pakistanis. There was only a wooden bridge over the Indus River at Khalatsi which is over 45 kilometers west of Leh. The river Indus flows slowly near Leh as it is passing through the plain area. However, it starts flowing fast as it enters mountainous terrain in the west. When it reaches the Khalatsi area it passes through between the two narrow mountains where it flows very fast. Khalatsi had a wooden bridge over Indus River in 1947. The Pakistani forces coming to Ladakh from Kargil had to cross the Indus River on the bridge only. Lt Colonel Prithi Chand ordered the better part of this wooden bridge to be destroyed. Then he deployed one platoon of troops to inflict casualties on any Pak troops who tried to repair the bridge in order to cross the Indus River. The repeated efforts of Pakistani troops to repair the bridge failed due to our troop's vigilance and accurate firing. The Pakistani troops efforts to cross fast flowing River Indus by boats at Khalatsi were also unsuccessful due to the fast current.

Meanwhile, Leh airfield had been constructed and Lt Col Prithi Chand started getting arms, ammunition as well as troops from Sri Nagar. His thoughtful action of destruction of Khalatsi Bridge over Indus was very successful for it frustrated Pakistani efforts to move troops to Ladakh. Before long two infantry companies of Gorkhas reached Ladakh, one by road from the Himachal Pradesh – Ladakh side and another by air from Sri Nagar. The Pakistani troops numbering about 1500 were waiting in Kargil-Khalatsi area and were planning to somehow attack Ladakh region by crossing river Indus at some other place North West of Khalatsi since the main Khalsi approach had been denied by our troops as well as by the broken bridge.

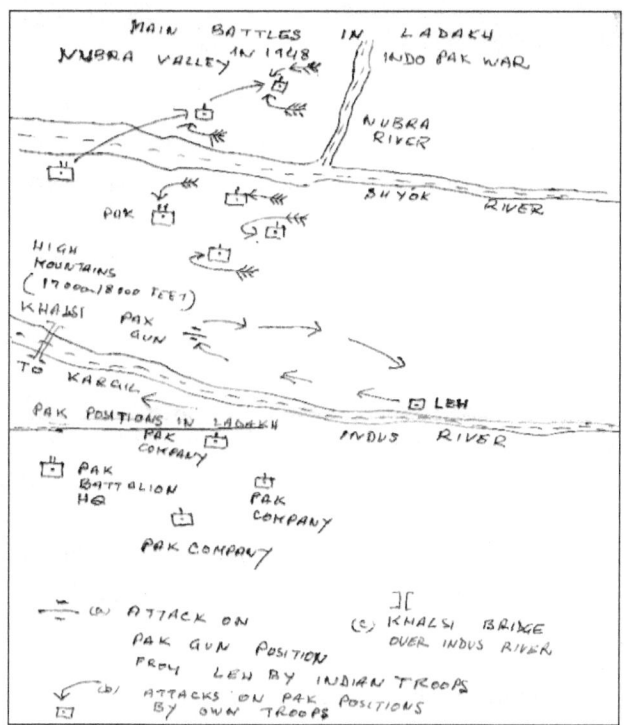

MAIN BATTLES IN LADAKH

At the same time, Maj Khushal Chand and Subedar Bhim Chand and his men were busy recruiting Ladakhi young men while Jemedar Thakur Singh and few NCO's were busy imparting training to them. On the other hand, the Pakistani forces were trying to cross River Indus north east of Kargil and North West of Khalatsi by constructing boats. Eventually they did succeed in crossing River Indus. At least one thousand Pak raiders managed to cross the river Indus and occupied positions at a high altitude in Ladakh region including Nubra valley area as shown on the sketch. One mountain gun was also taken across the River Indus by the Pakistani forces. The Pakistani aim was to make use of this gun to demoralize the Ladakhis in general by firing on Leh town in particular and other neighbouring Ladakhi villages. The Pakistani officers had earmarked platoon (30) personnel to guard it in addition to 10 artillery personnel who were there to make use of the gun to fire at Ladakhi targets. About 100 civilians were used to carry the ammunition necessary for the gun while a few hundred personnel were required to improve the track which was used to move the gun from one place to another in the hilly region of Ladakh. The information regarding the gun as well as its exact location was given to Colonel Prithi Chand by the local Ladakhis.

He devised a plan to destroy the gun and kill the Pak soldiers by a thoughtful offensive action. A special and strong patrol of Ladakhi personnel as well as the Indian soldiers was to undertake this special operation. A cross country move to the place where gun was positioned was devised to attack the Pakistani soldiers who were guarding it carefully. The patrol on its way moved forward during the night and rested during the day. When it attacked the Pakistani position, it achieved complete surprise by attacking it at night.

The Pakistani soldiers fought quite well even though they were taken completely by surprise. The patrol party killed most of them and hardly few soldiers managed to escape by running away. The patrol party destroyed the ammunition as well as the barrel of the gun, before withdrawing to Leh town where they celebrated their success. It was indeed a good start to deal with the Pakistani raiders from the Skardu – Gilgit area who had come to capture Ladakh.

Colonel Prithi Chand believed in attacking Pakistani forces by making use of Ladakhi soldiers' alongwith Indian troops. The Ladakhi personnel were very fit for operations in the high altitude area in Ladakh where Pakistani forces had occupied positions. This offensive attitude of Lt. Colonel Prithi Chand resulted in great success. The Indian troops fought alongwith Ladakhi soldiers and the combination was very successful. The Pakistani positions would be carefully reconnoitered and were always attacked from unexpected directions, mostly either from the rear or from the flanks. The Pak soldiers from Pakistan as well as from Gilgit and Skardu area were nowhere near Ladakhi soldiers who were used to moving fast in high altitude area and would carry out attacks from unexpected and difficult approaches. That is how Pakistani raiders lost their positions in high altitude locations which varied from 13,000 to 15,000 feet in height in North West Ladakh South of the Shyok river.

The Pakistani raiders also crossed river Shyok and occupied few positions on high mountains in Nubra river valley in the North. The Indian troops alongwith Ladakhi soldiers attacked Pakistani positions from unexpected directions. The Pakistani raiders were often surprised but fought well in some positions only. But they could not match the Ladakhi soldiers' capability in high altitude area. The Indian soldiers after few weeks' acclimatization fought for their country as well as the good name and reputation of their Regiments and Nubra valley was also cleared of Pak raiders after a few weeks' battles on the high altitude Nubra valley. The Pakistani raiders withdrew from Ladakh to the Kargil area after suffering heavy casualties.

Lt. Col. Prithi Chand was given deserving award of Maha Vir Chakra for his great contribution for throwing out the Pakistani raiders from Ladakh. He can be called saviour of Ladakh. It is a pity that his services have not been given the recognition at the national level for saving Ladakh by fighting in very difficult circumstances. After the ceasefire in January 1949, 7 Militia Battalion consisting of Ladakh personnel was raised. Now the Indian Army has many Scout Battalions of Ladakhi Scouts who are deployed on the border with China and Pakistan and are rendering good services to our Army and the country.

Operations in Ladakh

As young adjutant, I often requested my Commanding Officer Lt Col Thakur Prithi Chand to explain the details of the battles fought in Ladakh, for he had only a handful of soldiers to fight in a high altitude area to start with. The brave soldier was a very modest officer when it came to describing his excellent performance in Ladakh but which needs to be described for the benefit of our countrymen and Army officers. Thakur Prithi Chand was a Buddhist who belonged to Lahul area which is in Himachal Pradesh and is just South of Ladakh. There was no road in Ladakh, only mule tracks existed in 1948. The Pakistan's main threat was from the West only along track Kargil, Khalatsi (Khalsi) – Leh or along the mule track along high mountainous range just South of Shyok River. North of Shyok River lay the famous glacier Siachen, the highest glacier in the world which has some of its peaks as high as the 25,000 feet. Siachen Glacier lies North West of Ladakh across Shyok and Nubra rivers as shown on the attached sketch. The high mountainous range of the glacier continues south of the River Shyok also, though its height becomes less and steadily starts declining further. From the Pakistani side the raiders could cross the River Indus and Shyok via boats North West of Khalatsi area and then climb this mountainous range. Meanwhile, Pakistan made repeated efforts to attack across the Khalatse Bridge trying to repair it while their troops fired at Indian positions. The battle continued for many days but the presence of Lt Col Prithi Chand inspired our troops which though only of a platoon strength fought bravely and inflicted casualties on the Pakistani troops who tried to repair the bridge or cross it.

As Lt Col Prithi Chand was conducting operations in Khalatsi area, more Pakistani troops crossed river Indus and Shyok by boats and occupied positions on the high mountainous range. Meanwhile, more troops and weapons arrived by air at Leh from Sri Nagar while another company of Gorkhas arrived from Himachal Pradesh by marching through Lahaul Spiti area via the mule track. This column had to cross Rohtang Pass 13,400 feet, Bara Lachala Pass 16,000 feet and Tangla Pass 14,000 feet. These troops were acclimatized for high altitude battles as they had to march for many days enroute along high altitude terrain.

Lt Col Prithi Chand devised a new strategy of attaching one section of newly trained Ladakhi soldiers with each Indian Army Company who fought with great enthusiasm and bravery during various battles in Ladakh. They would also bring useful information regarding locations of enemy positions as they were very good in climbing higher ridges and peaks in a much shorter time, as they were used to the high altitude area being the locals. Some irregulars were under the command of Chewing Rinchen later Colonel Rinchen of Ladakh who was awarded two MVC's and a SM during the various battles that he fought in Ladakh and later in J&K. He personally led troops in various attacks where Pak raiders had occupied positions on mountain peaks which were as high as 15-16000 feet above sea level. Later on, Rinchen Chewing took part in the 1965 and 1971 Indo Pak wars also. The Ladakhi troops fought very well in recent Kargil War also. No wonder, we have more than one Ladakhi Scout Battalions in our Army at present. The Ladakhi troops are performing very well in high altitude area of Ladakh and Kargil.

Incidentally, in 1981, when I was the GOC, Punjab, Haryana and HP Area, I called upon Col Prithi Chand at Kullu where he had settled down post retirement. He had set up a lovely orchard and had a serene prayer room in his house. Well into his old age, he remained ever so humble about his achievements.

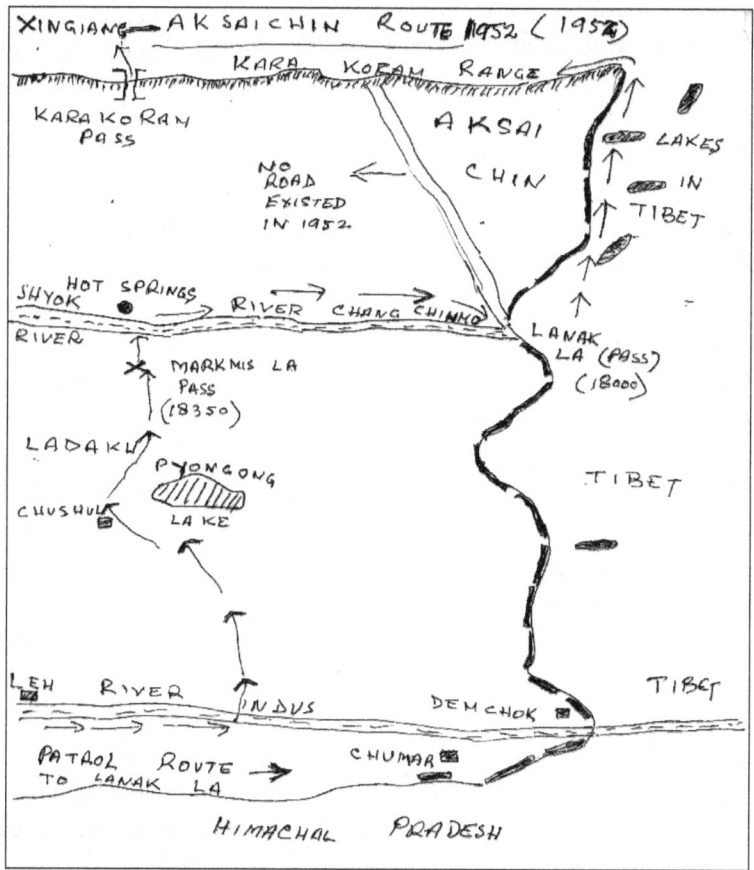

PATROLS TO THE AKSAI CHIN AREA- LANAK LA IN LADAKH:-

Lanak La is located in the north eastern part of Ladakh which is approximately 18,000 feet high. It connects north east Ladakh with Western Tibet. It had only a mule track in 1952 but now it has a proper road and is the most important road link between Western Tibet and Xinjiang through the disputed Aksai Chin region of North Eastern Ladakh. Ladakh has two Chins/Chens. The other Chin is Sia Chen which is a glacier in the North West Ladakh which is the highest glacier in the world with heights reaching upto 25,000 feet above sea level. The Aksai Chin border with Tibet in the North East was not even properly marked on the maps in 1952. It had no land marks like pillars or any sign board on the ground either.

I was working as GSO3 (Intelligence) in Army HQ in New Delhi in 1952 when I was detailed to go on a reconnaissance patrol to Lanak La in the North Eastern part of Ladakh. The pass is located in the Southern part of Aksai Chin area. I was told that Lanak La is on the boundary line of the Ladakh - Tibetan border. I was asked to find out if there are any Chinese troops in Lanak-La pass area. In addition, I was also instructed to ensure that the patrol party should not contact the Chinese troops located in the area. There were other instructions also. The second main task given was to find out if the Chinese were constructing any road from Tibet to Xinjiang located North of Ladakh through Aksai Chin which may be passing through Lanak La. LA means pass in Ladakhi/Tibetan language. Lanak La which is located in the Southern part of Aksai Chin region and was the main pass in Aksai Chin region connecting Western Tibet not only with Ladakh but through Aksai Chin, a road if constructed could connect Western Tibet with Xinjiang also. Please see the attached sketch of Aksai Chin region and Western Tibet to see the large detour that the Chinese road will have to take to reach Xinjiang from Western Tibet by avoiding Aksai Chin / Lanak La. China had to then construct a long road from Western Tibet along the long North Eastern Ladakhi border which had to take a turn to the left and then reach Yarkand and Kashgarh, the main two southern towns of Xinjiang. The short cut route passing through Aksai Chin would be less than half of the longer route. The patrol was to have an Engineer officer also to help the patrol party in its task and also looking for ways to improve communications in North East Ladakh.

Incidentally India did not use its Air Force at all to carry out any reconnaissance of Aksai Chin Area on India - Tibet border area to find out about the Chinese activities along the border for reasons which have never been explained even till today. It's a strategic blunder which has cost us dearly. It was stated by some reporters that a foreign agency had informed the Indian Government not to use its Air Force on the border as it could adversely affect the India – China relations. According to some other observers, it was perhaps due to the fact that the use of the Air Force could unnecessarily escalate the situation along the disputed border with China while the Indian Government wanted to have cordial relations with China and so wanted to resolve the border problem in a peaceful manner. However, in practice it worked against the Indian interests, as in the early fifties, India had no roads at all in Ladakh region and patrolling in the high mountainous region took weeks to travel and observe the new developments in the area which the Air

Force could have done in a few sorties or atleast it could have narrowed the area for detailed observation. Of course the ideal would have been to use both the Air Force to do general reconnaissance and the Army to do the detailed reconnaissance on the ground. But unfortunately, the Air Force was never used to carry out any reconnaissance along the 4000 KM long India China border not only in the fifties but even in the 1962 India–China war which resulted in serious reverses for India. Incidentally, the Chinese also did not use its Air Force to carry out any reconnaissance before the war or even during 1962 war as China had a much stronger army as compared to India. It was for us to use our meager assets optimally, which could have given useful information to our forces regarding the outflanking movements which the Chinese forces made to go around our positions and to establish road blocks or attack our positions from the flanks and the rear, in Eastern India as well as in the Ladakh sector.

But in 1952, nobody in India was thinking of India-China conflict. Our patrol to Lanak La was primarily meant to find out if there were any Chinese troops in that area and secondly whether the Chinese were constructing any road in that area. These were the main tasks for the patrol.

I was shown reports of two patrols led by British Officers of the Indian Army who had crossed into Western Tibet in 1916-1917 as well as in later years. These patrols had been moving in the Western Tibet area for many weeks before returning to Ladakh. However, those patrols were well equipped by way of weapons as well as supplies for a long stay in the Western Tibet. The Tibetan Government had hardly any army troops in the Western Tibet at that time. But the occupation of Tibet by the Chinese forces in 1950 had completely changed the situation and the Indian Government was concerned about their activities as well as the future intentions of the Chinese Government, particularly in the Ladakh region. According to some other reports, the Chinese had decided to first initiate the construction of the road from Xinjiang region well to the East of Yarkand city in Southern part of Xinjiang to Western Tibet in Lanak La pass area.

Incidentally, in the 1962 India China War, the Chinese forces which attacked Ladakh were commanded by the Chinese Army Head Quarters which was also located in Xinjiang region and not in Western Tibet.

The Aksai Chin region was a high plateau where airfields could be built. The present Indian landing ground at Daulet Be Gouldi near Aksai Chin area in North Ladakh, is one of them. Consequently, roads can also be easily constructed in Aksai Chin area which has no rivers and this was perhaps the fear of the Indian Government.

Before leaving, I was briefed at Army Head Quarters that the border was not demarcated at all on the ground. Even on the map provided to me, the border was not properly marked. I was told that the Tibetan Government had recognized the Western Tibet-Ladakh border in an agreement with the then British Government, but the Chinese Government did not accept it and so it did not sign the agreement. Hence there was a genuine concern in the Ministry of Defence regarding the Western Tibet-Ladakh border as well as the Chinese activities in Aksai Chin. In the following years, the Indian Govt. fears were proved right.

The Chinese forces in the Western Tibet had to be supplied with their daily requirements all the way from Lhasa in the East which was over 1200 kilometers away while a road joining Western Tibet from the Xinjiang province of China in the north of Ladakh would be only 500-600 kilometers long if it could pass through the Aksai Chin area of North Eastern Ladakh. The other alternative available for the Chinese was to build a road along the long North Western Tibetan-Ladakh border which meant crossing high mountain ranges along this rather long route as shown on the attached sketch.

Besides, the Aksai Chin Area was a high plateau ranging between 13000-14000 feet high which had no rivers or lakes in the area as is the case in Western Tibet. The Aksai Chin region had no population. The Ladakh-Tibetan nomads or shepherds did roam around in the area but they were no permanent huts or villages in this dry region. It had no vegetation or trees either except for small bushes. The Aksai Chin area is a high mountain desert. The construction of road through this area did not pose any major problems.

The J&K Government had no police post or any administrative establishment in Aksai Chin region either which spread from Western Tibet to Xinjiang while it had a police check post at Dem Chok in the south where the Indus river enters the Eastern part of Ladakh from Tibet. However, there were mule paths which connected Western Tibet and Xinjiang province and these were used by the nomads of Tibet or of Ladakhi region.

The area of Aksai Chin lay just north of River Chang Chenmo which originates from the famous pass Lanak La on Indo-Tibetan border which is about 18000 ft. high. The main task given to the patrol was to go up to Lanak La and find out if the Chinese were building a road through the Lanak La pass which would connect Western Tibet with the Aksai Chin plateau and through the Aksai Chin plateau to the Xinjiang province of China. It was indeed a necessity for the Chinese to adopt this short cut approach to send quick supplies to the Western Tibet region. It does not need a strategist to suggest this course but its consequences could be so dangerous for India. That is the reason why the first patrol of Independent India was tasked in 1952 to patrol the Lanak La area which is in the Southern part of Aksai Chin.

The patrol which got delayed at Sri Nagar eventually reached Leh in August 1952 and started collecting supplies, arranging mules, double hump camels and ponies etc. to get ready the patrol to start its journey to Lanak La which is located on Ladakh Tibetan border. It was first week of September when the patrol party left for its destination. There being no road in Ladakh in 1952, the patrol party left Leh via a mule track which went along the River Indus. The first day we covered about 18/20 miles as the going was easy along the river bank till it had to take a turn towards north to travel through high Himalayan ranges. The journey through the Himalayan ranges was slow due to high altitude of the area. In due course the patrol party crossed the high pass of Chang La which was close to 18000 feet. The track after a week took us to village Darbuk which was the last inhabited village in this area in 1952. On the eastern side of Darbuk and about 20 kilometers to the East lies Chushul where the Indian forces had to fight a bitter battle with the Chinese in 1962. Incidentally Darbuk was the Brigade Head Quarters of the 114 Brigade which fought in Chushul area in 1962.

At Darbuk we got few local ponies which were better suited for high altitude area as compared to the ponies which we had taken at Leh which is located at 11000 ft while Darbuk is about 14000 ft above the sea level. From Darbuk the patrol party headed northwards but was held up for 2/3 days on the Southern side of Mars Mik La – 18350 ft. due to continuous snow fall for the next two days. It was now end of September but the snow can fall at such altitudes in September also. After crossing Marsmik La, the track was quite bad till we reached the Chang Chenmo River which gets most of its water from the high mountainous range where Lanak La is located. It took the patrol party a few days to reach the Chang Chenmo River from

Marks Mik La. The mule track was not only quite narrow but was difficult to travel particularly by the mules. After crossing the Chang Chenmo River, the patrol reached the Hot Spring area on the Northern side of the river. From there, the patrol followed the track East wards on the north side of the river Chang Chenmo for few days. It was a steady climb and the track was in bad condition. We did not come across any huts or any human habitation in the entire area. The weather was now becoming quite cold and the winds were also blowing rather fast. There were no trees at all in the mountainous terrain. The small bushes in the hills could be plucked easily and we used to make tea with these bushes as these were quite dry and would burn quite well too. It gave an immense feeling of being alone. The high mountains in the area were quite dry and had no snow though their height was about 14000-15000 feet. The Aksai Chin area starts from East of the Hot spring area and continues Eastward till Lanak La which is on the border of Tibet and Ladakh according to the our (Indian) claim. The Aksai Chin area is quite vast and continues till the Kara Koram Range in the north along which the boundary between India and China runs according to our (Indian) claims. The whole of Aksai Chin area can be called a Mountain Desert, according to what our patrol observed during their reconnaissance. Incidentally, the Ladakhis do call Aksai Chin area as Chang Than or Mountain Desert.

The patrol party reached Lanak La area when it was almost end of October 1952. The weather had become cloudy and it was snowing also in the Eastern Ladakh. Lanak La being a pass about 18000 feet high was getting heavy snow fall. It was quite obvious that the mule track was passing through the pass, though it was becoming narrower as it approached Lanak La. There was no road at all not only in Lanak La but in any area near about it. The patrol party which went up the pass area in the morning returned in the evening. On its return journey to the Hot spring area from the Lanak La area, we came across Ladakhi/Tibetan shepherds with their herd of sheep. According to them, there were no Chinese barracks or huts in the area. The shepherds did say that the Chinese forces seemed to be also similarly reconnoitering the area. The patrol party did not see any huts nor met any personnel whether Ladakhis, Tibetan or Chinese in or around Lanak La area. There was no road in that area either in 1952. The patrol report sent quite detailed information in its report to Army HQ on its return to Leh, it took a couple of weeks to write it.

I was given a letter of congratulation from Army HQ which was signed by the officiating Chief of General Staff in 1952 (this appointment does not exist now). A copy of letter is reproduced.

From: Maj Gen SPP THORAT, DSO

No 16372 / D / GSI (z)
CHIEF OF THE GENERAL STAFF,
ARMY HEADQUARTERS,
NEW DELHI
Aug 52

Dear Rajendra Nath,

    I have read with considerable interest the book on LADAKH prepared by you and your staff. I have, no doubt, you must have taken considerable pains in collecting all the material and putting it together in the manner you have done. This is a good effort on your part and I wish to congratulate you for it.

    The book is, at present, being scrutinised by us and you will be informed of any changes or corrections necessary before it is officially published.

Yours Sincerely,

Capt RAJENDRA NATH,
Army HQ Liaison Officer,
LEH

The Ministry of Defence complimented me separately; I received a letter signed by the Deputy Secretary of the Ministry of Defence.

Brig RAJ BIR CHOPRA
A/CGS

DO No 18245/GSI(a)
CHIEF OF THE GENERAL STAFF,
ARMY HEADQUARTERS,
NEW DELHI,
9 Jun 53

Dear Rajendra Nath,

I have read with interest your reconnaissance report of the track Leh-Lanakla. This report will be very useful in bringing uptodate our information regarding this important track. I wish to record my appreciation of the work you have done not only in carrying out the reconnaissance, but also in compiling this comprehensive report.

Yours sincerely,

Capt Rajendra Nath,
GSO3 GSI(k) MI Dte.
GS Branch, Army HQ.

Letter of Appreciation from Ministry of Defence

MINISTRY OF DEFENCE (D/GS)

Subject:- RECONNAISSANCE PARTY - LEH/LANAKLA

Reference General Staff Branch note No 18245/GSI(a) dated the 29th April 1953.

2. The reconnaissance report submitted by Captain I.N. Suri, 84 Fd Coy Engrs and Captain Rajindra Nath Pandit, LO (Leh), has been read with interest in the Ministry. Ministry of Defence would like their appreciation of the work done by these officers to be conveyed to them.

SD/ K C JAIN
UNDER SECRETARY
8.6.1953.

GS Branch (MI Dte)
(Lt Col NK Chatterji)
Def Min u/o 2940/S/D-GS dated 9-6-53.

No 18245/GSI(a)

GENERAL STAFF BRANCH
GSI(a)

A copy of the above is forwarded for your information and retention.

Capt
GSO3 GSI(a)
Jun 53
(NA DAVE)
Tele 41/449

Captain I N Suri,
84 Fd Coy Engrs C/O New Delhi 56 APO

Captain Rajindra Nath Pandit
GSI (k) MI Dte.

This would underline the seriousness accorded by the senior most echelons of the then Government to our patrol. Later, I wrote this book and forwarded it to Army HQ's for permission to publish it. I received a letter from the Chief of General Staff (General Thorat) in 1953 appreciating the book and stating the Army HQ's would publish the book but this did not fructify.

However, consequent to our report and briefing, the Government whether J&K or Indian took no action what so ever to establish a police check post in that area to monitor the future movements of Chinese troops in Aksai Chin area. In the South, the J&K Govt. had established a police check post at Dem Chok along the track from Tibet as soon as it enters the Indian Territory. In 1952, the whole of Ladakh had only one battalion of J&K Militia which had its outposts towards the Western border. As is well known, Ladakh has two Chins, the Aksai Chin in the East and the Sia Chen in the West which is infact the highest glacier in the world. Till 1952, India had completely neglected both the Aksai Chin in the East and Sia Chen in the West.

In later years we could have easily flown an aircraft or helicopter over Aksai Chin area from Leh airfield. In half an hour or so the aircraft could have reached the Aksai Chin area to carry out an aerial reconnaissance. We did not send any patrol either to carry out any reconnaissance of Aksai Chin region for four years after our patrol in 1952. The next patrol led by Maj later Brigadier Tugnait was sent in 1956 which reported that the Chinese had built a road through Aksai Chin which connected Western Tibet with Xinjiang province which is located north of Ladakh. This was too little too late, even then first we did not grasp its strategic and national impact immediately, secondly, we misread the Chinese intentions consistently even knowing the evidence and lastly we refused to build up forces in Ladakh even after observing their intentions.

India China Relations 1959-1961

The Indian leaders were completely surprised when China declared that it had constructed a road through the Aksai Chin area in Ladakh in 1959 which India rightly believed was part of Ladakh. The Indian Govt. was criticized by other political parties in 1959-1961 for its pro China attitude while China had actually constructed a road through India's territory. China replied that if the road was in the India's territory, how come the Indian Govt. was not even aware of the fact that China was constructing the road in its territory for so many years.

China had occupied Tibet in 1950 by moving its troops from main land China. After quickly overcoming resistance offered by the Tibetan soldiers, it spread out its forces all over Tibet particularly in the Western region which was far away from Lhasa. Since sending supplies to its forces in Western Tibet from Lhasa, took lot of time, it was decided by China to send the same from its Xinjiang region which was situated just north of Ladakh. A road from Xinjiang passing through North East Ladakh in Aksai Chin via Lanak La would solve the logistical problem of the Chinese forces located in Western Tibet and that is what China did. The J&K administration based in Leh did not have any administrative control of Aksai Chain area which is the highest plateau in the world in North East of Ladakh. Since the road through Aksai region was of strategic importance to China, the Chinese Govt. refused to accept the Aksai Chin region of Ladakh as part of Ladakh. There were press reports that the China's Prime Minister Chou En Lai in 1960 was prepared to accept McMahon Line as the border in the Eastern region of Tibet with India in exchange for India's acceptance of Aksai Chin as part of Tibet. But India did not agree to this proposal, according to these press reports. However, officially the Indian Government has not commented on these press reports.

China wanted to teach India a lesson in realpolitik apparently as India was militarily week and had no reliable allies either to help it in case of any conflict because of its non aligned policy. No wonder, the Indian forces were defeated in 1962 China-India war, as the Indian forces were neither equipped nor trained for mountain warfare. The Indian Air Force which could have given India an adequate warning regarding the concentration of Chinese forces in Tibet/Xinjiang or their forward movements to attack the Indian forces was never used for the reasons which have never been explained officially. India had airfields in North Eastern India as well as in Ladakh from where it could operate its aircrafts to carry out reconnaissance over Tibet as well as in Aksai Chin area. Our aircraft could actually support our troops in the battle also. In the Eastern India, our airfields were in the plains where our aircrafts could carry more bombs and ammunition as compared to the Chinese aircrafts which had to operate from Tibetan airfields which were located at much higher altitude. But the Indian leaders were obviously scared of the Chinese Air Force and so did not deploy the Indian Air Force at all during the 1962 war.

The main reason for the Chinese attack seemed to be wide differences of opinion between the Chinese leaders and the Indian leaders of that time. Mao Tse Tung, Chou En Lie, Chu Teh and others were not only political but also military leaders. They had led the Communist Chinese Army in war against the Japanese forces for many years, and later defeated the Chiang Kai Shek's forces in central China in 1949. They believed that the ends justify the means and that the successful leaders should use any means to attain their goals and their actions require no moral sanction. India actively supported China's entry into the Security Council even though it annoyed USA no end at that time. Hindi-Chini Bhai Bhai became a familiar slogan in India (only in India). The Indian leaders trusted the Chinese leaders completely. The only exception was the then Home Minister, Sardar Patel who felt suspicious about the intentions of the Chinese leaders. He wrote a letter to Prime Minister Nehru warning the Indian Government regarding trusting the Chinese Government as regards China's intentions towards India. This letter to Prime Minister Nehru sent by Sardar Patel was published by newspapers as well as by Brig. Dalvi in his book. Dalvi commanded the 7 Indian Brigade which was deployed along McMahon line in North East India in 1962 and suffered heavy causalities before withdrawal in 1962.

Ladakh's Impact on India-China Relations

Ladakh, particularly the Aksai Chin region of Ladakh which has a common border with Western Tibet played a notable part in the India-China confrontation during 1950-1960 which later resulted in the 1962 India – China War. According to the Chinese, the Aksai Chin region which has a common border with Western Tibet had not been demarcated on the ground when the British ruled India. A treaty regarding the Ladakh-Tibet border was signed by the then British Government of India with Tibet. But this treaty was never signed by the Chinese Govt. according to the Chinese Govt. and its historians. It also suited the Chinese Government to say so. There were no land marks like stone pillars etc on Ladakh – Western Tibet border either. There was no population or even vegetation in the Aksai Chin area in 1952.

Perhaps it suited the then Tibetan, Chinese as well as the British Government of India also. I have read reports of British Army officers carrying out detailed reconnaissance of Western Tibetan region across Lanak La for many weeks at a stretch as early as 1916. The British officers used to take a large party which was well equipped with weapons also. The Tibetan authorities did not raise any objections either while the Chinese Government and their regional authorities also did not do so in those years. But according to Indian historians, a proper treaty between the then British Indian Govt. and the Tibetan Govt. was signed in 1920 regarding the border between the then Indian Government and Tibet in which Aksai Chin area in the North East Ladakh was accepted as part of Ladakh. However, no pillars or other land marks were erected on the ground, perhaps because the area was so large and climate so difficult. May be it also suited the then British Government, for the British military strength was much superior to Tibet or China. But after the Communist Govt. took over China and became militarily and economically strong, it refused to accept past agreements which did not suit them. For example the Chinese Govt. does not accept the McMahon Line in north east India as the border but it accepts the same McMahon Line in Myanmar as an international border between China and Myanmar, for it suits its strategic interests, for through Mynmar, China gets access to the Indian Ocean.

The Indian Government genuinely wanted to have good relations with China and went out of its way to help it wherever it could possibly do so. For example, China wanted to become member of the United Nations after defeating the Chiang Kai Shek Government's forces in China but USA did not want to accept it, as it wanted to support the Chiang Kai Shek Govt. which had control over Taiwan only. The Indian govt. went out of its way to support China's case in UNO even though it meant spoiling its relations with USA which was the leading power in the world at that time. Mr. Pannikar the Indian Ambassador to China at that time also went out of his way to convince the then Govt. of India to trust China in its friendly policy towards India. The Indian political leaders sincerely if naively believed in China's peaceful intentions towards India.

In 1950, the Chinese forces attacked Tibet and quickly overran it's territory with its much superior military strength. It was an important development which needed careful attention of our leaders. What would China do next? Our leaders genuinely wanted peace with China which was a big and upcoming country in Asia. The Indian national leaders had fought a successful non violent movement to achieve independence, though the impact of the Naval Mutiny etc on British Government to leave cannot be discounted. They were well meaning national leaders who wanted to develop India using peaceful means only. They did not think in terms of developing India as a militarily strong country as they believed in peaceful methods to develop its economy and also look after its security. They believed that by following a thoughtful but peaceful foreign policy, they would have no need to have strong armed forces for India's security also. Consequently India could earmark more funds for economic development. We also adopted a non aligned policy in order to have peace with all countries. This naïve formulation of policy did not take into account the integral role of armed forces in maintaining peace and in projecting a nation's prowess alongwith its economic might. The armed forces were out of the loop of consultation also in those years.

No wonder when Chief of Army Staff Gen Thimayya asked Prime Minister Nehru for India's defence policy, he was told that Indian Army should look after Pakistan with which India had fought a war for a year or so. As for China which was a bigger and more powerful country militarily, India would like to deal diplomatically and by adopting a peaceful and thoughtful foreign policy. Unfortunately, for the intelligent but peace loving Indian political leaders who believed in morality and peaceful means to resolve national and international problems, the Chinese leaders had quite opposite views for they had gone through difficult times where they had to fight bitter wars for years first against Japan and later they had to fight against the Chinese forces led by Chiang Kai Shek which were backed by USA by way of supply of weapon systems as well as financial assistance. So they really understood the value of strong armed forces. They were great leaders like Mao Tse Tung, Chou En Lai and Chu Teh and other such military cum political leaders who believed in military might to solve not only country's internal problems but also to deal with foreign policy issues.

The Indian political leaders made a virtue unnecessarily about adopting peaceful means to deal with internal as well as external problems with neighbouring countries. They could have read what Dr. Nagendra Singh ICS, onetime India's Defence Secretary stated thoughtfully in his book the "Defence Mechanism of the Modern State" - "The control over external affairs has been one of the essential attributes of a fully sovereign state, but foreign policy is so intimately related to defence considerations that it tends to be weak or strong according to defence capabilities". He further adds "Defence considerations lie at the root of the existence of the state, its sovereignty, its independence as well as maintenance of internal peace and law and order". Actually defence, economic development and pragmatic foreign policy go together which has not been fully appreciated by the Indian leadership sadly even now. Maybe it is due to our cultural heritage. China has incidentally achieved great power status by integrating defence and economic development with pragmatic and thoughtful diplomacy. India needed but failed to develop a long term strategic response to various security challenges which faced the country after 1947. No wonder, we have fought multiple wars and also faced strong internal security problems in which our armed forces have also got involved in one way or another.

Back in 1950, when China occupied Tibet, the Indian policy makers did not obviously factor in and analyse the security aspects of this new development which led to the 1962 India China War. The Indian Government was advised by its then Foreign Secretary to demarcate the border with Tibet as soon as the Chinese forces occupied Tibet in 1950. His aim was to avoid future border problems with China, as there were differences of opinion regarding the actual border alignment between India and China both in the Eastern border as China did not recognize the McMahon line as well as the Western border where the Chinese had a different perception of border in Ladakh particularly in Aksai Chin area. But his advice was ignored as India's Defence Minister Krishna Menon and India's Prime Minister Nehru were having personal and close relations with their counter parts in China. But the occupation of a large country like Tibet and its close linkages with China which included road communications between China and Tibet was to create serious problems between the two countries later on.

This required serious consideration as well as proper coordination between the Foreign Ministry, Home Ministry and Defence Ministry including advice from Chief of Army and Air Staff which was essential. In India, the Defence Secretary who is a Civil Servant, as then and even now, gives advice to the political leadership regarding all important defence issues. The Defence Secretary strangely acts more or less as Chief of Defence Staff, a system which is prevalent in the USA, UK and all Western countries while in erstwhile communist countries like Russia and China, the Defence Minister is normally from the Defence services like Army, Air Force and Navy. The moot point, it's not a career civil servant in both systems.

In 1960 the Indian Government was not consulting Military officers regarding India – China border problem. The loop of discussions was purely civilian. In India, then as now, the Chief of Defence Staff system has not been introduced for reasons which do not look logical, for a bureaucrat can never be so competent in matters Military as are the serving Military officers.

The bureaucrat normally serves in various ministries like Home, Finance, Transport, Social Justice, Environment etc. So when he becomes Defence Secretary, he is not as thorough in matters concerning military as are the Defence officers. Yet he is at present more or less acting like the Chief of Defence Staff and gives advice to the Government of India regarding various Defence issues which is not correct for India's security. Maybe it's a cultural issue, for academics in India normally are more vociferous in stating that its economic progress which indicates a nation's strength, the idea of parallel pillars of strength escapes many even today.

(Note – Refer to the flight to Ladakh by senior air force and army officers actually disobeying the orders. My Book Military Leadership in India states the role of (some) British Officers in India in assisting the Pakistani forces in 1947-48 War, Field Marshal Cariappa himself told me that the undue importance given to the British Officers by the then senior most Indian Political Leaders has cost us heavily in Kashmir, it was sheer naiveté by the then top political leadership to repose our trust in them so sincerely).

Chapter XI

1962 INDIA – CHINA WAR IN LADAKH – SOME BACKGROUND INFORMATION

According to many experts, one of the important causes of the India – China war in 1962 was the construction of the road by China in the Aksai Chin Area. China wanted India to accept Aksai Chin as part of Tibet and consequently accept the road constructed by China through the Aksai Chin region as a part of the overall settlement of India China border dispute. This was a unilateral offer in a way by a more powerful nation, more so a nation willing to use military power to suit its objective. But the Indian government could not accept or consider the offer as all the opposition parties in the Union Parliament were very critical of India's prolonged policy of peace (some would say idealistic peace) towards China inspite of the reports of intrusions etc. At the same time, India was not prepared for war at all, logistically, diplomatically or militarily. Because of its non alignment policy it had no strong country like USA to back it, in the world as we realistically know it, a weaker nation looks for allies. Actually India's non aligned policy had annoyed most of the militarily powerful countries of the Western world, the USA in particular and also other militarily strong European countries like U.K. India had no alternative but to try and persuade China to vacate the Aksai Chin region and also accept the McMahon line in the north eastern part of India by peaceful means. Its own oft proclaimed peaceful policy towards all countries; particularly towards China; was based on the premise of a totally ruled out possibility of conflict with China. So India's armed forces were neither mentally prepared for a possible conflict with China nor was any effort made to equip our armed forces with modern weapon systems in case war with China did break out. It was obvious that the Govt. policy was that our foreign policy was to sort out India-China differences regarding the border issue only through peaceful means, which seemed as the only alternative in the existing circumstances of under-equipped and under manned forces any way. The Indian Govt. had infact committed a serious mistake, particularly the Ministry of Defence, should have been concerned about the presence of the large number of the Chinese forces in Tibet. These forces had later fanned out towards the Eastern part of Tibet as well as the Western part of Tibet, particularly on the Ladakh border which was far away from Lhasa. How would the Chinese authorities supply their forces in the Western Tibet area which would have to be supplied all the way from Lhasa region, a distance of over 1200 kilometers.

Ideological Divide

India became independent in 1947 after a long freedom struggle which was based upon the satyagraha type of movement and peaceful non violent struggle. The communist party of China obtained power to rule China in 1949 after a long and bitter fight which included war with Japan till 1945 and later on another war against Chiang Kia Shek's Chinese Army which was backed by USA till 1949. The Chinese leaders believed in the use of military power to achieve its aim to make China a great power while the Indian leaders believed in peaceful negotiations and mutual understanding to solve international problems. So there was great difference in the approach, it could be called an ideological divide, in the approach to tackle mutual problems like the border problem between China and India. Unfortunately the Indian leaders had not really understood that the Chinese leaders believed in the use of military power as much as negotiations to tackle problems with the neighbouring countries.

The Chinese Government decided to send armed forces to Tibet in 1950 to bring it under its full and complete control, and impose its ideology and to spread the communist culture in Tibet which had so far followed the Buddhist religion and Buddhist culture and was considered an autonomous region of China. Many observers actually accorded it an independent status. Actually the British Indian Govt. always had a greater influence in Tibet than China as well as enjoyed good relations with Tibet till 1947 (Indian Independence). The British Indian Government obviously implied the backing of the British Empire. In 1950 the Chinese forces attacked and quickly defeated the Tibetan troops who offered resistance to the Chinese forces when they tried to impose their full control over Tibet. The Chinese leaders then tried to spread their forces to all parts of Tibet by quickly dispatching their forces to the Eastern as well as Western parts of Tibet. This naturally affected India as Tibet has a long border with India starting from Ladakh in the West to the Eastern Indian border with Myanmar, which is approximately 4000 Kilometers long.

Unfortunately, the Tibetan – Indian border was not fully defined and demarcated on the ground. In the Eastern Tibet there was the McMahon line which was according to the Indian Govt. the border between China and India but the Communist Chinese Govt. did not accept this as an international border. However, the same Chinese Government later accepted McMahon line as border between China and Myanmar. It was obvious that the Chinese Govt. under the strong Communist Govt, experienced in warfare, was ideologically prepared to settle issues with the use of force if diplomatic negotiations were failing or even otherwise. The Indian leaders considered negotiations as the only method to solve the international problems.

There was a complete mismatch and world of difference between the Chinese and the Indian leaders in their style of approach to the national and international problems. This was to play a greater role in the days to come.

The information regarding the road could have been easily obtained if only India had carried out an aerial reconnaissance of the northern part of Aksai Chin which was then very much a part of Ladakh or sent a long range patrol to the Ladakh – Xinjiang border which is to the north of Aksai Chin region, a distance of over 350 kilometers. Considering the scenario at that time, such a decision would have required senior most level approvals. The lack of aerial reconnaissance of Aksai Chin region which occupies a large portion of North Eastern Ladakh was to cost our country dearly, as the occupation of the Aksai Chin region by China eventually led to the India – China War in 1962.

Incidentally Lt. Gen Thorat has written a book entitled "Reveille to Retreat" which generally gives account of his personal life. However his account of an interaction with the then Prime Minister reveals the ideological underpinnings, which we can contrast with the Chinese. Gen Thorat describes the visit of Prime Minister Nehru to HQ Eastern Command in Calcutta when he was the Army Commander Eastern Command. Eastern Command deals with the North Eastern part of India which includes area from Sikkim to Myanmar along the McMahon Line which was not accepted by China. Actually, China was claiming a large area in Arunachal Pradesh in North East India. India had posted para military troops of Assam Rifles along the disputed borders and was making plans to deal with the developing situation as the Chinese activities along the McMahon line were increasing.

Lt. Gen. Thorat explained to Pandit Nehru, the Prime Minister the growing Chinese threat to North Eastern India as well as the counter measures that India should adopt to deal with it. He generally recommended a plan under which India should start building defences along a line in the mountains midway between the plains and the McMahon line on the disputed border with Tibet. He further recommended that we should start sending forces to these defence positions and also start making proper road communications to the areas where we intended to occupy positions so that we could quickly send reinforcements and the necessary supplies in case necessity arises, as the Chinese were developing roads in Tibet which were leading upto the border with India. They were also constructing houses and barracks for their military personnel in Tibet on a large scale while claiming a large area in Arunachal Pradesh while also refusing to accept the McMahon Line as a border. So the plan recommended by Gen Thorat to prepare defences as well as accommodation for troops and develop roads to those defence positions was sound, for it takes years to prepare defences in the Himalayan mountains. However, Prime Minister Nehru did not accept General Thorat's plan. He remarked that he was busy trying to improve relations between the two super powers like USA and USSR. He felt that it would not be proper for him to be seen moving forces towards the disputed border while he was trying to have rapprochement or develop peaceful relations between the two superpowers. General Thorat's only comment in the book was that our Prime Minister was perhaps taking himself too seriously or words to that affect. In any case it was a clear message to the Eastern Command not to think in terms of any defence preparations near the India – China border. The Prime Minister was obviously unaware that it takes years to construct roads and prepare defences and accommodation for the troops in the high Himalayas along the India – Tibet border as also more importantly the need to signal to an inimical neighbour that we were also preparing suitably.

The granting of asylum to Dalai Lama earlier by the Indian Government (The Dalai Lama is the respected Buddhist leader of not only Tibetan Buddhists but the Buddhists living in other countries like Thailand,

Myanmar, Cambodia, Japan and Sri Lanka) was a serious mistake on the part of Indian Government for it adversely affected India – China relations which eventually led to the 1962 India - China War. Buddha lived and preached in India all his life and at one time Buddhism in ancient India was as popular as Hinduism. Perhaps Prime Minister Nehru acted in a civilized manner and in a democratic tradition when he gave asylum to Dalai Lama and his other senior Buddhist leaders of Tibet. But it upset the Chinese leaders considerably, they, by virtue of their mindset, wrongly interpreted this action of the Indian leaders as an interference in the internal affairs of China, as Tibet to them was a part of China though it has been acting more or less as an independent country for centuries.

A pertinent fact to consider is the British Indian Government could sign a treaty with the Tibetan Government regarding the boundary between Western Tibet and Ladakh as well as the McMahon line as the border in the Eastern part of Tibet only because it was an independent nation. But the Communist Chinese Govt. with its strong military leadership was greatly upset by India granting asylum in India to Dalai Lama and other members of the Tibetan Government. This was unfortunately to play an important role in adversely affecting India – China relations.

At that time, USA was the most important economic power in the world as well as the most powerful military country in the world, we managed to annoy it while pleading for China's entry at the UN. This would have been considered by the Chinese leadership while exploring the alternatives (military, diplomatic etc) to deal with India. The Chinese military leaders knew that China was militarily much stronger than India. In addition, India had to cater for possible confrontation with Pakistan also, as India had fought a year long war with Pakistan over Kashmir issue in 1947-48. So India was in no position to engage in a battle with China over a 4000 kilometer long border with Tibet. The strong Chinese leadership kept up the façade of Hindi-Chini Bhai Bhai but actual relations with India started deteriorating between the two countries.

The Secretary General of India's Foreign Service now Foreign Secretary strongly recommended to the Indian Government that we must demarcate the boundary between Tibet and India. But for some reason, the then Indian Government did not take any appropriate action to ask the Chinese Government to demarcate the border quickly between India and Tibet for the reasons best known to it. They did not anticipate that the border problem could create strategic problems for our country in due course.

Actually throughout the Indian history, our Kings or Rulers had ignored the security of our borders. That is why India has been repeatedly attacked from Afghanistan. The Indian Kings never thought of strong defences along our Western border with Afghanistan or Iran. China built the famous China Wall to look after its Northern borders. The Indian rulers never thought of a wall or other fortifications in North West frontier. The only exception was Maharaja Ranjit Singh who constructed few forts like the one at Jamrud, in South West of Peshawar in Pakistan.

The Indian Government in the country was organized in a peculiar manner in 1950 when China occupied Tibet. Prime Minister Nehru was not only the Prime Minister; he was also the Foreign Minister of India throughout his tenure as Prime Minister. He seldom met or consulted any Chief of Army Staff on any Foreign policy issue even if it had serious bearing on security aspect of the country like the border settlement with China. Prime Minister Nehru would consult only his Defence Minister Krishna Menon who also acted as his close foreign policy advisor. Krishna Menon, an intellectual, was anti USA and pro Communist, who was fond of USSR according to many experts. Krishna Menon did not like the senior military officers for reasons best known to him but was rather kind to young military officers. When I was a Captain I met him in 1959 when he was Defence Minister and when I was proceeding to Canada to do Canadian Army Staff College course. He called me to his office for interview and gave me good advice as to how I and my wife should behave in an advanced Western country like Canada.

India was then following a Non Aligned policy and had serious differences of opinion on foreign policy issues with the USA, and other Western countries (including Pakistan) who were anti USSR or anti Communist. The nations allied to the USA joined in military pacts like NATO/SEATO which were meant to contain the USSR, the leading and most powerful communist country in the world in 1950-60. In fact, militarily and politically India was alone, for all other non aligned countries were weak countries that lacked both military as well as economic strength.

It was unfortunate that the Indian Government did not realize that the Chinese Government was really upset with Dalai Lama being given asylum in India. The serious differences between India and China over the Aksai Chin road, McMohan Line and the Dalai Lama led the Chinese to plan a military response to India. The fact that the Chinese Government had sent large forces to attack US – South Korean forces in the Korean War just a few years ago and could possibly use its strong army against India in the North East and Ladakh region also was never appreciated by the Indian Government and its advisers. Unfortunately, it did not listen to the advice of General Thimayya who was then the Chief of Army Staff as well as capable generals like Thorat who were advising the Indian Government to make preparations for a possible Chinese operations in Arunachal Pradesh in the East and Ladakh in the West.

The Chinese leaders had actually planned to mount an attack in Arunachal Pradesh region in the East and Ladakh area in the West and full scale preparations had also started in Eastern Tibet and Xinjiang region just North of Ladakh in the West where China had already constructed a road joining Xinjiang with Western Tibet. A Chinese military HQ had been established in Xinjiang province for this purpose to plan and later mount the attack in Ladakh region to occupy more area in Ladakh region in particular as also to drive home their superiority.

Meanwhile, the Chinese strategy was to continue peaceful negotiations with India regarding the border issue with India and also to continue the full scale preparations for an attack on India at the same time. A high level plan was devised to hide the Chinese preparations for an attack by adopting a peaceful posture in order to convince the peace loving Indian Government who was not even consulting the Indian Military leaders on the India - China border issue. While the Indian Government and the Indian Army was therefore totally unprepared for war, China was going ahead for large operations for a war, if it came to it. To them it was just one of the alternatives to consider keeping India in place.

China's Prime Minister Chou En Lie during his visit to India in 1960-1961 asked the Indian Govt. to accept Aksai Chin as part of Tibet while China would accept McMahon line in Arunachal Pradesh. But the Govt. of India could not do so due to severe public pressure. The Chinese had not only constructed the road but had concentrated its forces in Aksai Chin region. The Indian Army was totally ill prepared for war. The Indian Government as well as the country faced a serious situation in Ladakh while in the Arunachal Pradesh region; China was not accepting McMahon Line but had not occupied any large area in this region unlike in Ladakh.

At the same time, the Chinese false propaganda war against India was continuing to convince the Indian Govt. that it would not attack India under any circumstances even though minor skirmishes had taken place in Ladakh as well as in Arunachal border areas, between the Indian and China's para military forces as well as regular army units.

While this was the situation on India – China border, the Chinese had started their peace offensive against India in a big way. India's Ambassador to China was shown extra courtesy by the Chinese Government and was brainwashed to believe that China would never attack India. Meanwhile, India's Defence Minister Krishna Menon who was pro China and anti US was given ample promises by the Chinese Defence as well as Foreign Ministers that China wants peaceful relations with India and would solve border problems through normal diplomatic negotiations only. What is worse, the Indian Government started believing in the Chinese assurances that it would never attack India. At the same time, there were serious differences of opinion between the Defence Minister Krishna Menon and the Chief of Army Staff General Thimayya regarding the situation on the India – China border as well as in the day to day functioning of the Army.

General Thimayya resigned due to his differences with the Defence Minister Krishna Menon due to the continued neglect of the Army and the approach to the India China border dispute. Kirshna Menon did not believe in the Army's perception and analysis that the Chinese may attack India for which the Indian Army was not prepared. He strongly believed that China was unlikely to attack India. Krishna Menon believed in promoting the officers whom he liked like such as promoting General Kaul to the rank of Chief of General Staff, a position inappropriate for him, by virtue of his prolonged service in the Army Service Corps.

Unfortunately, General Thimayya withdrew his resignation later on after Prime Minister Nehru asked him to do so. It was a mistake, for after his withdrawal of the resignation; Krishna Menon's attitude became worse towards him. When General Thimayya retired, everybody expected that General Thorat who was Army Commander Eastern Command and considered the most capable officer of the Army would be promoted to this position. But he was retired and the hardly known General Thapar who had reportedly connections with senior politicians was promoted as the Chief of Army Staff. He was an indifferent Chief of Army Staff and resigned after the Indian Army suffered serious reverses in 1962 war. However, he was still appointed as the Ambassador to Afghanistan. An additional point, Krishan Menon started the practice of senior political leaders playing an important part in the promotion policy particularly to the senior ranks in the Army which was very unfortunate.

Chapter XII

1962 - INDIA CHINA WAR – FOCUS ON LADAKH

By 1962 India had evolved as country of some standing in Asia and also the most important leader among the non aligned countries in the world. These nations looked up to India for advice. It was also attempting to play an important role in the United Nations and was considered an important member of the United Nations even though it was not developed industrially and economically. It had only weak armed forces as its leaders were not prepared ideologically to expend more funds to equip their forces adequately. By defeating India in a short war in the high Himalayas for which the Indian armed forces were neither equipped nor prepared, China would become the most powerful country in Asia. This was their analysis, as they perceived India to be projecting itself much above its actual strength. Any defeat for India would certainly lead to its losing its respect among the non aligned countries in particular and in the World and United Nations where it was striving to play an important role. India would have to pay dearly for its confrontation with China regarding the Indo - Tibetan border, all because India had neglected its defence forces completely since 1947. Besides, India followed a non aligned policy, developed by its leadership, and had no strong country like the USA and USSR to assist it in case it was attacked by China. This suited China very well. It could therefore plan to attack India, keeping in view the various factors mentioned above.

The plan for China was to attack in the East in Arunachal Pradesh. The aim was to defeat the Indian forces in Arunachal Pradesh but then withdraw just close to the original positions across the McMahon Line. However, in the West, in Ladakh the Chinese army was not only to capture the important positions in the region but to further enlarge the already occupied area in Ladakh which would provide additional depth to their roads in Aksai Chin. This was by defeating the comparatively smaller Indian forces deployed in Ladakh; this would also enable the Chinese to show their superiority. The Chinese forces were not to withdraw but to stay put in the captured area in Ladakh.

China did not use its Air force in the war as its army was much superior to the Indian army in strength, in weaponry and equipment and had developed new tactics of establishing road blocks behind the Indian positions before attacking them. It had carried out necessary preparations for war while talking of peace with India at the same time. By not using its air force in the war, India committed a serious mistake for our air force would have provided valuable inputs regarding the forward movement and concentration of the Chinese forces from the rear to their forward positions both before and during the war. In Ladakh in particular our air force would have given us necessary information regarding the large scale movement of the Chinese forces all the way from Xinjiang region in the north across the high Himalayan ranges to the northern, central as well as southern part of Ladakh which is about four hundred kilometers south of Xinjiang. Incidentally all the Chinese forces that attacked Ladakh came from the Xinjiang region and not from western Tibet. The overall command and control in Ladakh region was also to be exercised by the Xinjiang military command which was located in the southern part of Xinjiang province just north of Ladakh. It was tasked to carry out operations in Ladakh, defeat the Indian units and capture more area in the northern and north eastern part of Ladakh. This would provide additional depth to the Aksai Chin region, where it had already completed a road joining Xinjiang with western Tibet sometime in 1953-1956. Incidentally, China had also developed roads to the northern and central part of Ladakh which it used to move forward its forces as well as its equipment and the necessary stores for the war. The Indian forces were unaware about the large scale movements of the Chinese forces as the Air Force was not deployed to carry out any reconnaissance of the area in possession of the Chinese nor aggressive patrolling taken up. In fact, immediately after the completion of Aksai Chin road, the Chinese troops had moved forward to the northern as well as central part of Ladakh to quietly capture more area in the region.

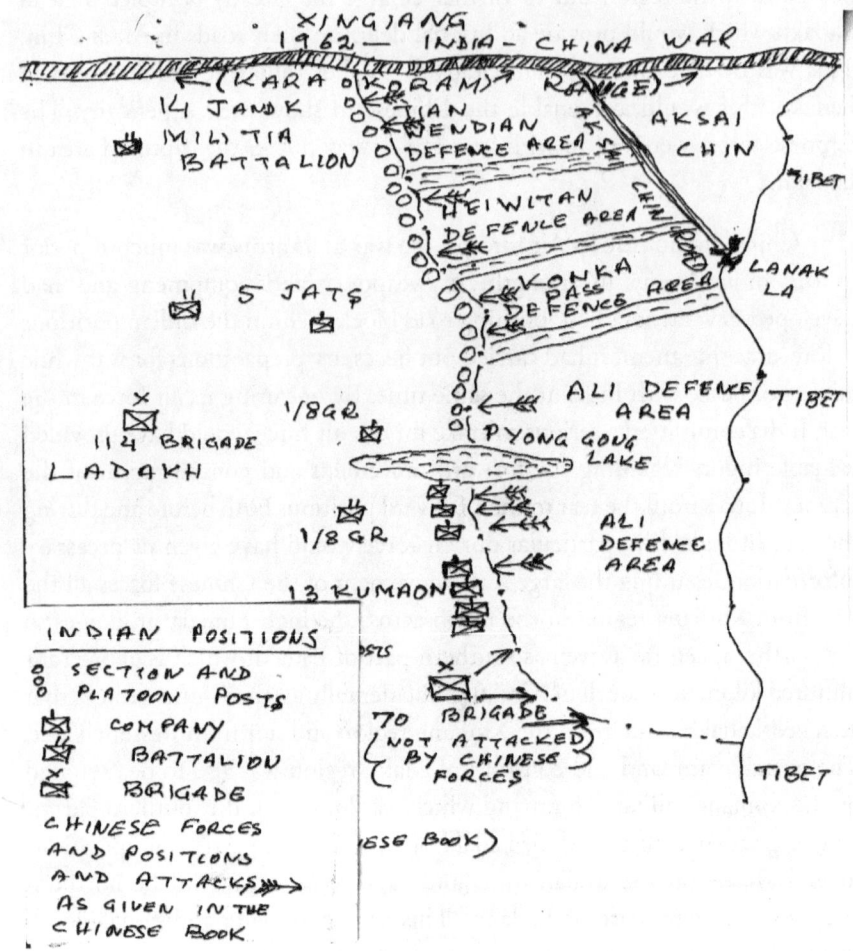

CHINA ATTACKS ON INDIAN POSITIONS

China starts its Offensive in Ladakh Sector

China started attacking Indian forces on 20th October, 1962. However, before this main offensive China had already not only occupied Aksai Chin but moved forward its troops to capture more area upto the Galwan River which is in the Northern most part of Aksai Chin and extends close to DBO (Daulat Beg Oldi). China had also already moved forward its troops to occupy more areas in the South Western part of the Aksai Chin area. It meant China had more or less occupied the better part of North Eastern Ladakh before it even initiated its main operations on 20th October, 1962. Pertinently, the Chinese claim line in Ladakh was a very flexible one. As they went on occupying more areas, they went on increasing their claim line!

This was one of the main factors for India to adopt the so called forward policy where Platoon or Section posts were deployed in the forward area so that the Chinese forces could not advance any further without physically attacking them. These small posts were established only to show on the ground that the area belonged to India but the small detachments were in no position to deal with the Chinese attacks because of their meager strength, which varied from ten to thirty men only on each forward post. These posts had no artillery or mortar support either. Importantly, these posts were not mutually supporting as there were located well apart, about two kilometers or so from each other. A fundamental premise signalled from the top was major hostilities would actually not occur.

Before dealing with the Chinese offensive it will be logical to describe the dispositions of the Indian forces in Ladakh. India had deployed the 114 Infantry Brigade which consisted of four battalions (14th J&K militia, 1/8 GR, 5 Jats, and 13 Kumaon.) This brigade was deployed to cover a large border area starting from Kara Koram pass in the North to Chushul area in the South, a distance of over 150 kilometers. The 70 Infantry Brigade was deployed south of the 114 Infantry Brigade covering the Southern part of Ladakh including the Indus River. But it was not involved in the war, as the Chinese forces did not attack its positions.

The Chinese strength and the way operations were conducted from the Chinese side are described in the a book by the Chinese named "History of Counter Attack War in Self Defence along Sino-Indian Border," Academy of Military Science Publications 1994 Chapter 3. According to this book, only one infantry division known as the 4 Infantry Division along with additional artillery and mortar regiments took part in the operations. However, studying the course of battles and the manner in which the Chinese deployed their forces for various attacks, it becomes obvious that the Chinese had utilized atleast two if not more divisions during the operations in Ladakh in 1962 war. In any case, the Chinese believe in using strong over whelming forces to ensure victory in a war.

On the Indian side, the 114 brigade which took on the main brunt of the battle was deployed in an area starting from the Kara Koram Pass in the north to the Chushul Area in the south. It had deployed the 14 J&K

Militia Battalion along with one company of 5 Jats to occupy the area in the northern part of its sector which covered an area upto Chang Chenmo River in the south, as depicted in the sketch attached, 1/8 GR was deployed in the area north as well as south of Pongong Lake including Chushul Area while 13 Kamaon was deployed in the southern part of Chushul Area. Actually only one company of the 13 Kumaon was attacked by the Chinese during the war while the remainder battalion did not take part in the battle, as it was withdrawn.

14 J&K battalion and one company of 5 Jats was deployed in the northern most area of Ladakh. Only one company of 5 Jats had taken up proper defensive positions on a high ground from where it could adequately dominate the surrounding area. 14 J&K Militia battalion had infact deployed itself all along the border and was deployed in small posts which were having only 10 personnel (section post) or 30 persons (platoon post). One company of 1/8 GR was also deployed along the border north of the lake in platoon posts. However, the remainder 1/8 GR was deployed south of the lake where all three company positions were properly prepared to fight a battle. Similar was the case of four companies deployed in the south by 13 Kumaon.

The Chinese forces on the other hand had started doing active patrolling all along the border with the main intention of obtaining maximum information regarding the Indian positions by way of their locations as well as their patrolling pattern and activities along the border. The Chinese plan was to do so without giving any indication that their patrolling was in fact the preparation for an attack by them. The Chinese had divided their area of operations in Ladakh into various sectors which they called Areas as shown on the sketch (page 196).

(a) Tianwendian Defence Area with HQ at Point 5243.

(b) Heweitan Defence Area with HQ at Heweitan.

(c) Kongka Pass Defence Area with HQ at Point 5408.

(d) Ali Defence Area with a Forward HQ southeast of Spangur Lake.

The overall command and control in Ladakh sector was to be exercised by the Xinjiang Military Command. While all the above preparations were being made to attack the Indian positions, the Chinese authorities were informing India in particular and the nations observing the developments in general that they had no intention of attacking India or starting a war with India. Our own political leadership contributed to it by somehow believing that the war just would not occur.

India in Ladakh had deployed about two brigade worth of troops, it had only very limited artillery support. It had only one Artillery Regiment in the Chushul area to support the Indian forward positions. Obviously it was too inadequate to give the necessary artillery support to the Indian troops deployed along the large border. By and large the Indian forces knew they had to fight with very limited artillery support, this would not have encouraged them. The Chinese on the other hand had deployed a number of artillery regiments, equipped mostly with Mortars. In the hilly terrain mortars are more effective as compared to guns for giving necessary fire support to the infantry units. This was a highly adverse development because the Indian forces could not possibly fight effectively without having proper artillery support. The Chinese obviously out gunned and outnumbered us in Ladakh in 1962.

As discussed, air support was not made available to the Indian Army for reconnaissance or ground support. Yet we had a few helicopters available which were later on used to evacuate the wounded Indian soldiers from the forward area during the war. It's still not clear nor are explanations available for denying the Indian forces air support to find or obtain information about the deployment and activities in Ladakh of the Chinese forces before the actual battle started. It's a fact that the Indian government as well as senior military officers (including the Air Force Senior ranking staff) failed to provide air cover even for reconnaissance purposes in Ladakh area. When the Chinese started their attack all along the front, the Indian forces were taken completely by surprise and in the process suffered heavy casualties as well as serious reverses.

The Chinese started their attacks from the North and quickly over ran the small section / platoon posts in the 14 Militia Battalion area. According to the Chinese accounts, some of the small section posts were attacked by their engineer sub units even. However, the company of 5 Jats offered severe resistance and fought very well as it had occupied proper defensive positions near the 14 Militia Battalion HQ. The Chinese troops attacked from two sides, the Chinese troops had established a road block position behind the Jat company area also. The 5 Jat Company could withdraw only after suffering high casualties. 1/8 GR fought a fierce battle when the Chinese forces attacked its positions on both sides of Pong Gong Lake. The strong Chinese forces which attacked 1/8 GR (Gorkha Rifles) positions were brought forward from a rear area for this operation while existing forces were deployed along the border, this is as per the Chinese account. The Chinese troops first attacked the 1/8 GR company which was deployed north of the lake. The Gurkhas fought well but the much superior Chinese forces attacked in force with good artillery support and eventually captured the Gorkha Company positions. Then strong Chinese forces attacked 1/8 GR positions south of the lake. The first attacks were repulsed after fierce fighting. The Chinese attacked once again with strong forces the Gorkha positions south of the lake. Their attacks were well supported by their strong artillery and mortar fire. The Gorkha companies had to fall back due to strong and repeated Chinese attacks with stronger forces even though the Gorkhas offered fierce resistance. The Chinese artillery and mortar Regiments gave very good fire support to their forces while there was only one artillery regiment with the Indian Brigade in The Chushul area to give fire support to 1/8 Gorkhas and other battalions.

The Chinese forces had to fight a fierce battle to capture 13th Kumaon's northern most company position in Chushul area. This company was commanded by Major Shaitan Singh. The Chinese were holding a strategically important position opposite this company's position, this was much higher than the Kumaonis position, and so the Chinese were fully aware of the dispositions of this company. The Chinese observed that the trenches dug up by the troops had no over head cover so their artillery or mortar fire on such positions would inflict a lot of casualties on the Indian troops.

The Kumaon Company had no artillery support at all for the reasons which are not known. Probably this was due to a shortage of artillery fire support, considering that one artillery regiment was only deployed over such a large area. But then after the battle of 1/8 Gorkha Rifles, the guns of the artillery regiment should have been available to give the fire support to the Kumaon's company positions also. Actually, there was no Artillery observation post established in the area defended by the company which could bring down artillery fire against the Chinese. This was unfortunate indeed. Hence this company had no artillery support. What is worse, there seems to have been no support either from the Battalion 3 inch Mortar platoon to the brave troops of this company, for reasons still not clear. The Chinese had occupied higher positions on the opposite hills from where they could over look Kumaon's positions.

In spite of these crucial disadvantages, the brave troops of this company under the courageous company commander Major Shaitan Singh offered fierce resistance, even though their positions were known to the Chinese troops, they still fought extremely well indeed. According to the book authored by the Chinese, this company was attacked from three sides, from the north, south as well as from the rear side. There was no frontal attack at all. The Chinese attack was fully supported by their heavy mortar fire. Inspite of all the disadvantages, the brave Kumaon troops fought very well indeed. The company commander and 95% of the troops were killed or seriously wounded in the fierce battle. However, according to the Chinese account of this battle, as stated by them, their troops did not suffer much casualties in this battle, though it is difficult to believe. After this battle, 114 Brigade withdrew 13 Kumaon to the rear area.

This was the last major battle in Ladakh. Infact only one Company of 5 Jats, the 1/8 GR Battalion and one company of 13 Kumaon Battalion had fought very well in the battles of Ladakh, as these were deployed properly on the battle field. The platoon and section posts deployed in the north along the large frontage could not possibly and logically have faced the large Chinese forces in Ladakh. The Indian Army needed to have at least two Divisions worth of troops in the large Ladakh region to offer any worth while resistance in the 1962 war. In addition, we should have given our troops the crucial and adequate artillery or mortar support. We had only one artillery regiment to give fire support. The actual fact is that the Indian Army was not really prepared to face the large scale Chinese attack while the Chinese forces were fully prepared for the war.

Incidentally, this abject defeat, individual battles being well contested notwithstanding, led the nation into a mode of defeatism and mourning for the martyred soldiers. The well known and widely sung song at most patriotic meets, "Ae Mere Watan ke logon", is more a lament for the well fought and contested in battle but ultimately martyred soldiers. This hurt the nation's and army's psyche very adversely and was a collective trauma for the nation. This song, which is an outpouring of grief, is also a signal to the political class and bureaucracy about the overall costs of losing a war; it's not only about the soldiers. A song celebrating victory and respect for the fallen and reverberating in the nations' psyche still eludes us.

Post the 1962 war, the nation's standing at the international level took a major hit and the then political leadership lost credibility within the nation. This aspect must be factored into all decisions relating to the military though unfortunately, it is not understood even now in this context, maybe it is due to our deep rooted cultural mindset.

Chapter XIII

SIACHEN GLACIER AND LADAKH

LADAKH AFTER HEAVY SNOW FALL

Ladakh as a region has special characteristics of its own which are not found in other parts of the world. It has Aksai Chin, the highest mountain desert in the world with average height of 13,000-14,000 feet in the East. In the West, it has Sia Chen. Sia Chen is the highest glacier in the world, its peaks reaching upto the heights of 25,000 feet above the sea level. Sia Chen is approximately 71 kilometers long and has river Shyok in the South and Nubra River in the East. In the West of Sia Chen is Pakistan's territory. In the north of Sia Chen glacier is the Saksham Valley and the north of Saksham Valley is the Chinese region of Xinjiang. The Saksham Valley was part of Pakistan's occupied territory in the northern part of J&K since the 1947-48 Indo-Pak war. But Pakistan willingly handed over the Saksham valley to China after the 1962 India-China war, in 1963 to be precise, for the reasons which have never been formally disclosed by Pakistan. Later on China has built a highway to northern part of J&K from Xinjiang and has also positioned 10,000 or so troops in Pak occupied J&K in Gilgit – Skardu area which can cause serious security problems for the J&K state also in due course of time. It is obvious that Pakistan has been courting China to help it in case of any future war with India. China may also help Pakistan in annexing Sia Chen in return in due course of time, therein lies its' importance to Ladakh region.

The Indian government lost the Aksai Chin area some time between 1953-1956 when the second Indian patrol to Aksai Chin in 1956 found that the Chinese had infact completed the road joining Xinjiang in the North with Western Tibet. With this India had lost the whole of Aksai Chin area in the North Eastern part of Ladakh which is a large area indeed. The Indian military in particular and the Indian govt. in general has been quite anxious to ensure that the Sia Chen glacier area does not meet the same fate as was the case of Aksai Chin. However, some Indian politicians and social workers / peaceniks have been at times talking of the unnecessary loss of lives and the expenditure required for maintaining the Indian forces in the Sia Chen glacier area, without realizing the strategic implications or its importance.

The Indian troops moved into Sia Chen in 1984. But India's Siachen adventure had begun six years before that when Colonel Narendra Kumar, a well known mountaineer of our country and a courageous Army officer led the first army expedition in 1978 to the glacier and to the vital Saltoro Ridge on its South Western flank. He mounted another expedition in 1981, leaving behind army squads at key points this time to ensure the security of the area. Colonel Kumar (nickname Bull) and his team later scaled many other high peaks in the glacier region to fully explore the Sia Chen glacier. He has since been acknowledged as the first person to reach "Indra Col" a key feature on the northern most tip of the Saltoro ridge line in the Sia Chen Glacier.

The credit for India having the Sia Chen area under its control goes mainly to the "Bull" as stated. He was Commandant of the Indian Institute of High Altitude Warfare. He was the right choice too to go to Sia Chen Glacier area for he had already climbed most of the highest Himalayan peaks in India. He was to climb and reconnoiter the better part of the unknown glacier on the North Western part of Ladakh beyond which the area belongs to Pakistan. Would Pakistan not claim it or try to quietly occupy the better part of Sia Chen as did the Chinese in the case of Aksai Chin in the north eastern part of Ladakh, was the main worry for India. The Army HQs deserves to be complimented for its selection of Col Bull, to take Indian troops properly trained in climbing high mountains to Siachin Glaciers.

Colonel Kumar, who first gained fame as the deputy leader of India's first successful Everest expedition in 1965, learnt that by mid 70s, Pakistan has been issuing permits to foreign mountain expeditious to Sia Chen glacier. Pakistan was also showing Sia Chen as part of Pakistan in its maps too. Actually, in 1949 India and Pakistan ratified a cease fire line (now called the Line of Control also) in J&K that ended South of the Sia Chen glacier's base at the point known as NJ9842. Some map makers in Pakistan made this point NJ9842 not only as the last point on the Line of Control but also all area north of this point as no man's land and later claimed that this area which meant Sia Chen also belonged to Pakistan. By mid 1970s, Pakistan started issuing scores of permits for mountain expeditions to Sia Chen glacier and earning money also. It is the persistent efforts of officers like Colonel Kumar and a few other army officers that later some senior Indian Army Generals such as General Krishna Rao and General Chibber flew over the Sia Chen glacier and observed for themselves its strategic importance to Ladakh and India. That is how the Indian troops moved to occupy the Sia Chen region in 1984, when a Pakistani Special Forces unit was also trying to move up the glacier. After that Pakistani forces have tried more than once to capture the strategic Sia Chen glacier but all their attacks have so far failed due to the valiant efforts of the Indian Army and the Indian Air Force which are jointly looking after security of this area. From Leh, a road goes north to Sia Chen, the Army does use it. The Indian Air Force is also playing an equally useful role to ensure that Sia Chen remains a part of Ladakh no matter what stratagem Pakistan adopts. However, as is their wont, some peace loving Indian leaders want serenity in the high altitude Sia Chen area by withdrawing Indian troops. The issue of funds, loss of lives, the extreme cold and Pakistan's attacks are stated to be reason enough to withdraw. Strangely, this was the same argument to rationalize the loss of Aksai Chin in 1962.

The post independence Indian leaders have always been rather kind to neighbouring countries by handing over the Indian Territory to them for gaining their goodwill. In early 1950s the Indian government handed over a small island between Andaman Islands and Myanmar as the Myanmar government had been repeatedly requesting the Indian government for the

COLONEL NARENDRA KUMAR
(PVSM, KIRTI CHAKRA, AVSM, PADAM SHRI, ARJUN AWARDEE AND MACGREGOR MEDAL)

same. Today, the Chinese scientists and technologists stationed on this small island are reported to be monitoring the launching of Indian missiles and rockets from coasts of Odisha in Eastern India. After independence and the 1947-48 Indo-Pak War, we did not post any civil police personnel or position any Army troops in Aksai Chin area of North East Ladakh. We know the consequences. Another PM gave away an island to Sri Lanka. We are also inclined to hand over some enclaves to Bangladesh.

However, to return to the glacier, the Line of Control as laid down by the UN after the 1947-48 Indo-Pak war in J&K finishes South of Sia Chen glacier. So the glacier was not a part of any country according to UN's verdict on J&K by way of the Line of Control as laid down in J&K. Pakistan being led by ambitious and aggressive rulers was bound to occupy it one day or another, unless India took the initiative. Moreover its Defence Ministry is not civil servant dominated, as in India. Pakistan started giving permission to foreign mountaineering expeditions to climb the Sia Chen glacier and to explore its large number of high peaks; the highest peak is little over 25,000 feet high, the Pakistan government wanted to later claim the Sia Chen glacier by this ruse. The Pakistan rulers were learning from the Chinese government's policy in the Ladakh area.

Luckily for India, as already discussed, some Generals like General Krishna Rao, General M.L. Chibber and others flew over the Aksai Chin area and understood its strategic importance for the North Western Ladakh. The Army knows India has already lost the better part of North Eastern Ladakh which amounts to hundreds of kilometers of our area. Thus Army HQs as well as the Indian Government permitted Colonel Narinder Kumar "Bull" to mount an expedition to reconnoiter important peaks from southern part of Sia Chen to the northern part of the Sia Chen glacier. He readily volunteered to carry out the expedition to the Sia Chen Glacier, for he fully understood the strategic location of the glacier for the security of north, western and central part of Ladakh.

We have discussed earlier in 1947-48 war that the Pakistani raiders had crossed Shyok River by boats and landed in Nubra valley, just east of Sia Chen glacier. Actually most of the water of Sia Chen glacier forms part of Nubra River which supplies maximum water to Shyok River which is an important distributary of Sind River. From Siachen glacier, mule tracks come down to Nubra valley which has many villages which have a fair number of Muslims and this made the Pak raiders in 1948 establish a few bases in Nubra valley. If the Sia Chen glacier had become a part of Pakistan, Nubra valley would have become a part of Pakistan's held J&K like Gilgit and Skardu. Colonel Kumar and his brave team had to carry out many reconnaissance's of this rather long and highest glacier in the world to ensure that the Indian troops could later occupy it, particularly all the important and highest regions of this glacier all the way from the Shyok River in the South to the northern part of the glacier. Incidentally, Colonel Kumar is the only Indian who has travelled from Southern end of the glacier to the northern most part of the glacier which touches Saksham valley.

India has now troops stationed on the highest glacier and that too well in time to deal with various Pak attacks on India's forward most positions in Sia Chen. In the last many years, the Pakistani forces have made repeated efforts to capture Indian posts by attacking from the Western side of the Sia Chen glacier which have resulted in many casualties to Pakistani as well as some casualties to the Indian troops also. Many Indian soldiers have earned well deserved awards in the bitter battles against the repeated Pakistani attacks on Indian held posts on the Sia Chen glacier, importantly our posts are generally higher. The important point to remember is that both China and Pakistan are interested in capturing more area in Ladakh. The Pakistanis are trying to capture Indian held peaks in the Sia Chen glacier area, whenever there is the opportunity to do so. China always flexes its muscles in Ladakh. So India has to be on the guard. Meanwhile, we must remember with pride that our brave soldiers and their officers are constantly watching the security of the world's highest glacier with determination.

Chapter XIV

CHINA'S FUTURE STRATEGY - IT'S IMPACT ON INDIAN SECURITY

China has officially stated that Tibet belonged to China from the time of Yuan Dynasty which means for well over one thousand years ago. Actually, Tibet which existed independently till 1950 comprises approximately one fourth of China's land mass. The Chinese Govt. does not accept the 1918 Shimla agreement or any other agreement regarding Tibet, which was signed between the British and the Tibetan Government. It was very necessary for the Indian Government to demarcate the border with China in 1950 when the strong Chinese forces quickly defeated the small Tibetan army and established their full control over Tibet. But we failed to appreciate the affects of the likely Chinese attack on Tibet. Since China had defeated Chiang Kai Shek's army only in 1949, India did not expect China to attack Tibet in 1950 and capture it so quickly. It was mainly because the peace loving Indian leaders failed to appreciate that the Chinese leaders were bold and militarily oriented and understood the utility of military strength to achieve strategic objectives.

The Chinese Government has now significantly tightened its control over Tibet by large scale Chinese migration as well as by the strict measures undertaken by the Communist Party's "Long reign and perennial stability" policy in the restive Tibetan region. China has started large scale logistics development in Tibet by building highways right across Tibet. China's main achievement of building the railway line to Lhasa in Tibet at a staggering cost of US 4.2 Billion dollars has really integrated Tibet with China. Now China is trying to expand its railway network both on the eastern as well as western side of Lhasa. China has informed India that it will bring the railway line to the Tibetan town of Dromo close to Nathu La Pass in northern Sikkim. China is aiming to project Tibet as a major trade hub between China and South Asia.

China has developed Xinjiang just north of Ladakh by constructing good roads, airfields and by setting up small scale industrial units in the region. Since Xinjiang region is well connected with Western Tibet by the Aksai Chin road which the Chinese have converted into a modern highway, there is more traffic between Tibet and Xinjiang region of China. In addition China has also constructed a good road in Western Tibet which goes upto Demchok, the last Indian outpost in Eastern Ladakh. The main population of Xinjiang is Muslim and resent the strict control of Communist China's Government which does not believe in any religion. There are often clashes between the Chinese Army and local Uighur Muslim population. The Central Asian states like Tajikistan, Uzbekistan, Turkmenistan, Kyrgyzstan and Kazakhstan are Muslim states and do not like the Communist Govt. of China's attitude towards the Muslim population of Xinjiang. Incidentally a large part of Xinjiang is a desert known as Takla Makan in local Uighur language, this occupies the central part of Xinjiang.

The Communist Government's anti Muslim attitude towards the local Muslim population of Xinjiang often results in clashes between the two sides. The Central Asian Republics which follow the Muslim religion are not very fond of the Chinese Government, though they have signed agreements regarding sale of gas and oil with the Chinese Government for trade purposes.

Meanwhile, China has built up a network of internal highways and subsidiary roads in Tibet and Xinjiang to connect strategically significant border areas with India, Nepal and Bhutan. It has also constructed the Kara Koram highway which starts from Kashgarh in Xinjiang and connects important places in Pakistan held northern part of Kashmir like Gilgit and Skardu. Incidentally, Kashgar in Xinjiang region is over 2000 KM away from Lhasa by road. This large road connectivity gives China lot of flexibility to move forces in South Asia from one part of China to another. In addition, there are large number of lateral roads leading to passes on the Tibetan – Indian borders from Tibet.

There are five operational airfields inside Tibet and as many as dozen airfields surrounding these are being upgraded slowly. The construction of new airfields and up gradation of advanced landing grounds and helipads in Tibet and Xinjiang is likely to enhance the capability of the Chinese Air Force. It also gives the Chinese Air Force the ability to strike or engage targets in India on a broad front and in depth. India did not use its Air Force in the 1962 War but China would definitely use its Air Force in any future war with India, as it has now built adequate facilities for its air force both in Xinjiang and in Tibet.

China has also moved motorized Divisions in Tibet as well as in Xinjiang region. These motorized divisions have tanks and armoured personnel carriers, as well as modern artillery guns to give close fire support. According to some reports, China has also deployed in Tibet medium range missiles having nuclear capability which can hit targets upto 2500 kilometers. This means India, Pakistan, Afghanistan as well as most South Eastern countries of Asia also come within their range.

China has made fantastic economic progress. The Chinese leaders have taken thoughtful and strong measures to make China's economy the fastest developing economy in the world. It has also developed its armed forces and has equipped them with the latest weapon systems including nuclear and thermo nuclear weapons and missiles including intercontinental missiles. Infact China is considerably more advanced than India both militarily as well as economically. Recently China has announced that it had increased its military budget for 2014 to almost 132 billion which means a 12% rise over last year's defence budget. This was expected as China has made no bones about its desire to emerge as a dominant military power in Asia as well as in Pacific region. It has been systematically working towards that goal by increasing its military budget consistently for the past several years so as to project its power across the Asia and Pacific region.

The Chinese Prime Minister Li Keqiang said at the opening session of National People Congress that China will comprehensively enhance the strength of its armed forces and further modernize them to upgrade their performance. China's military spending is the second largest in the world behind that of only the USA. It is obvious that as a growing economic power, China is concentrating on improvement of its military might to enhance its strategic interests in Asia.

According to some military experts China has the largest standing military in the world which is 2.3 million strong. It is also concentrating to make lot of improvements in its nuclear force. At a time when India's own defence modernization programme is moving very slowly, China's military transformation should be taken seriously by Indian defence planners. China has started asserting its military strength more than ever before. It has claimed the South China Sea as under its control. It has deployed an aircraft carrier as well as other warships and has also tested a stealth fighter which gives more strength to its air force. The Chinese military officers are openly talking of building the world's strongest military in due course of time which would even displace the US as the strongest military power. This sort of talk might be premature at the present moment as the US military is far more advanced than China's. But it should cause us concern.

China's Defence Budget for 2014 was three times the size of the Indian Defence Budget which is 40 Billion according to our defence experts. However, according to many Western Defence experts, the Chinese Government hides the actual defence budget by quoting lower expenditure figures. Whatever may be the reason, India has to face an increasing security threat from China. A number of measures are required to be undertaken if we have to improve the capability of our armed forces to look after the security of our country. We should attach more importance to the development of weapon systems in India and to modernize our armed forces keeping in view the main threat from China as well as Pakistan's known hostility towards India.

According to strategic experts China's rapid military growth is also affecting and shaping the nation's broader foreign policy objectives like laying more claims over Indian territory particularly in Arunachal Pradesh in the East. While China is growing rapidly its military strength, in India its defence establishment has been reduced to repeatedly requesting from its civilian masters both politicians as well as bureaucrats for adequate funds to hasten the modernization of the Indian armed forces. Such things do not go unnoticed around the world particularly in countries like Pakistan and China. Infact, it can have grave consequences for India's ability to defend its borders. The recently elected new BJP government needs to look into this problem seriously and expeditiously.

Meanwhile, the problem of demarcation of the India – China border remains unresolved. China has recently stated that Arunachal Pradesh is also a part of Southern Tibet. It is a new demand. How should India deal with an economically and militarily much stronger China, which consistently increases its demands on Indian Territory is a difficult problem indeed.

In this connection, General Thimayya who was Chief of Army Staff made a profound statement in 1961 when he said "Where as in the case of Pakistan, I have considered the possibility of War, I am afraid I cannot do so in regard to China. I cannot as a soldier envisage India taking on China in an open conflict. It must be left to the politicians and diplomats to ensure our security." This statement is as true today in 2015 as it was in 1961. Our leaders and the country must think deeply about the security of our country for which they have not accorded priority since independence. The past five years have seen a consistent pattern of neglect of modernization of the forces. This when the present Indian security scenario is very disturbing indeed with powerful China breathing down India's neck from the North while, Pakistan is waiting for a rare chance to annex J&K from India in case there is a war between India and China.

The Indian diplomacy has to ensure that India has really good relations with powerful countries like USA, Russia, Japan and Australia so that they and other strong countries help India in facing upto the Chinese threat till we can catch up. India's first priority should be to make the country militarily strong, inspite of ideological and cultural biases to the contrary. Lastly, India should discuss the demarcation of the border with China (Tibet border) and attempt to resolve the problem as best as it can.

Meanwhile, the Chinese probes across the Line of Actual Control particularly in Ladakh will continue to keep the Indian Government as well as the Indian Army on their toes. Ladakh, a paradise for the visitors is also facing serious threats from the Xinjiang in the North and Western Tibet from the East. So India as well as its armed forces have to be ready to face the border problem with China which can be escalated by China whenever it suits its national interests. So India has to in addition to improving its armed forces focus upon upgrading its logistical and communications infrastructure along its northern borders. This is a priority.

The Defence Ministry needs a major overhaul since in a complex scenario it oversees the three services, The Army, Navy and Air Force. There is a need for Chief of Defence Staff System to coordinate the working of all three services. All Western Democratic countries like USA, UK, France and Germany have integrated their service HQs with Ministry of Defence and have created the Chief of Defence Staff system for providing military advice to the Government. India the largest democracy must also do so. But this would require political sagacity and their visible determination. The political leadership must overcome their irrational suspicion of our armed forces as well as overcome the bureaucrats' obduracy to delay the long overdue measures to improve our national security. In a truly integrated Ministry of Defence the civil and military would accept joint responsibility for national security instead of engaging in futile blame games. When I had the opportunity to visit the Pentagon in USA, it was a pleasure to go around the joint defence HQ where the officials from the Army, Navy, Air Force and personnel of the Ministry of Defence were working smoothly in a joint HQ.

However, at present the civilians starting from the Defence Minister to the bureaucrats, who may logically lack defence knowledge, run the Defence Ministry. The truth is that the relations between the Ministry of Defence and the Armed forces are and have been deeply flawed. It is because the three Chiefs of Army, Navy and Air Force in the guise of civilian control carry the full burden of responsibility for their services operational and administrative work but lack standing and authority within the Ministry of Defence. Their actual access to the top echelons is filtered. Strangely, senior most military officers are not allowed to give direct advice to the Prime Minister on matters pertaining to Indian security and particularly to military affairs.

On the other hand, the Defence Secretary in India is invested with authority for Defence of India and for the three Armed Forces HQ's, but has no accountability, particularly when things go wrong. In practice, every single decision regarding weapons, equipment, infrastructure and personnel impinging on Army, Navy and Air Force's operational efficiency needs the approval of a bureaucrat. The bureaucrats keep on changing in the Ministry of Defence from other ministries and are not experienced enough or aware regarding the problems facing the three services, yet they are the one's who take the final decision. The recently elected BJP government must review this aspect. Somehow successive governments overlooked this, deliberately or otherwise. With ministers engrossed in electoral politics and bureaucrats lacking comprehension of complex military issues, decisions are delayed for years. It is the indifference of the politician, the bureaucratic inefficiency and the civil military divide that are stalling the much needed armed forces modernization programmes which in effect undermines our national security.

The above scenario has resulted in a situation where our Defence Forces are massively under equipped. India produces only 30% of its defence equipment and 70% is purchased from the other countries. India is now the biggest importer of Defence equipment in the world; this has its own issues such as scams and a sudden clamp down on purchases. According to defence experts, it is due to the incorrect policy of bureaucrats and the politicians who have been running the Defence Ministry that no large scale defence industry has come up in the country after 68 years of independence. It again could be a mindset issue, whether to involve the private sector in defence. The new BJP government must look into this problem expeditiously.

Moreover, we ourselves as a nation attempt to obfuscate the issue of national security by setting up Councils on National Security and adding layers of complexity without addressing the core issues. There is no denying that national security is a complex issue comprising of multiple strands but a stress on scholarly approaches while neglecting the main pillar can only be to our detriment. It also seems the National Security Advisor or his Deputy can only be an IFS, IAS or IPS Officer, as Military Officers in India very obviously lack the intellectual rigour and application to take it up, there can be no other logical explanation. This also stems maybe from as much as bureaucratic dominance, as also the comfort levels of the politicians with the bureaucracy and importantly our age old historically rooted cultural biases and moorings, about matters military.

The integration of the Border Forces (Paramilitary forces) along the borders with the Army is also a major area of concern. Lack of integration impacts adversely on coordination and deployment as also command and control. The ITBP is deployed along the border with China, strangely it operates under the Home Ministry while performing the role of border guards. One reason could be since the police officers took over all the border forces, they preferred to have the border forces under the Ministry of Home rather than the Defence Ministry. The impact on security due to a lack of integration was ignored or rather in keeping with our ethos at that time, not even attempted to be understood. The same incidentally applies to the BSF also. We can only observe that obviously the Police Officers did not like serving at sea so thankfully the Coast Guard is atleast operating under the Ministry of Defence.

India needs to improve its infrastructure development in Northern states urgently so that we can improve our capability to defend our borders. We have constructed a road from Himachal Pradesh to Ladakh but it is blocked for 5/6 months due to non completion of tunnel in Rohtang Pass even though over 13 years have passed on its construction. After this tunnel is completed, the road from Himachal Pradesh to Ladakh would be open for almost all the year around. The Indian Government must allot priority to the construction of roads to the northern border of India with China. Similarly the roads to the India – China border in North East India are not in good condition and in comparison to Chinese roads, they are sub par. This requires the immediate attention of the Central Government, for the states concerned are not taking due interest. The Central Government has also not accorded this crucial aspect its attention. The attention on the central regions or regions away from the borders is understood, but the outer edges have to be safe for the hinterland to develop unhindered. The development of infrastructure along the borders also embeds loyalty amongst the citizens.

India also needs to improve its relations with other countries to deal with a great power like China. China plans to be the most powerful country in Asia and obviously finds satisfaction if India remains engaged in resolving problems with other South Asian countries, thus impacting its economy and its ability to develop its military capability. China has made Pakistan it's all weather friend on this premise and is supplying it technology to develop not only nuclear weapons and missiles but also help in manufacturing tanks, guns and aircrafts. A quid pro quo is China accessing gas and oil supply from Iran via the Gwadar port in Baluchistan which will subsequently pass through the Pakistan held J&K to Xinjiang, which is North of Ladakh. Hence China remains alert and aggressive about the Ladakh region of India. As a part of this strategy it keeps expanding its claims, now China claims more areas near Demchok – Chumar which is located in Southern part of Ladakh, just north of Himachal Pradesh. China is developing ports in Pakistan, Sri Lanka as well as in Bangla Desh so that its expanding navy can in years to come have naval bases to dominate the Indian Ocean. China is already in the process of dominating the South China Sea which will affect countries like Philippines, Vietnam, Indonesia, Thailand and Malaysia. This action of China has alerted even USA which is considering bringing US fleet from European countries to South Eastern Asian region.

While maintaining good relations with China, India should improve its relations with Japan. Japan can help India in developing its logistics and communication systems. Ideological barriers to India interacting with Japan or the USA or any other well developed country to improve its economy and industry must be reduced, as these will generate financial surpluses to develop latest weapon systems.

Incidentally Indian history tells us that the armies of Indian kings which fought the invaders were invariably equipped with inferior weapon systems. No wonder the Indian forces were defeated and India was ruled by foreigners for long periods. Babur who defeated the Indian kings did so with the help of guns and muskets which his army possessed while no Indian king had thought of developing a gun and a musket. Babur came from a comparatively backward Afghanistan, yet he could develop guns and Muskets which no Indian king could do so, even though India possessed iron and steel for years which is evident from the famous Ashoka pillar which was built hundreds of years before Babur's invasion of India in 1526 A.D. It is time we learnt from our past history and develop India's industry, encourage scientific development and produce quality weapon systems.

China is a world power. It has much stronger armed forces as compared to India. China's economy has made excellent progress. It has a strong Central Government which governs effectively. China's aim seems to be to dominate India, big country in Asia but a weak state as compared to China which should accept China's superiority in South Asia. It has made Pakistan an all weather friend and is giving it economic as well as military aid. When the US troops move out of Afghanistan completely, China is likely to assist Pakistan to dominate Afghanistan in order to possess strategic depth, which Pakistan has always desired but China also stands to gain economically. Afghanistan possesses a large quantity of Iron and Copper ores as well as some other metals. China can get the iron ore as well as other metals from Afghanistan also once US troops vacate Afghanistan.

Pakistan using its own agents or the Afghan Talibans loyal to Pakistan can enable Pakistan to annex areas in Afghanistan which are closer to Pakistan border. Pakistan desires to have control over the better part of Afghanistan in order to have strategic depth in case of a war with India. This is Pakistan's strategic concept. With China's help Pakistan can dominate Afghanistan, and also facilitate China in dominating South Asia.

A combination of a militarily powerful China having a major border problem with India and Pakistan, which again has the Kashmir Issue with India, is a dangerous combination for our security. Besides improving its defence capability and economy, India has obviously to further improve its relations with powerful countries like Japan, South Korea, USA, Australia and Russia to look after its security as well as its economy. In this connection, Prime Minister Modi's visits to USA, Japan and Australia have been very successful. The Russian President's recent visit to India and the agreements to purchase the latest weapon systems from Russia as well as purchase of nuclear plants from Russia are developments which augur well for us. President Obama's visit to India in January 2015 indicates the growing relations between India and USA, which should benefit India's security. The visit by PM Modi in May 2015 to China has been well received and acknowledged, but the border issue will not be resolved easily unless as is obvious from the Chinese commentary, we agree to their terms and viewpoint. The Dalai Lama factor, though now too late apparently to be discussed within India as to its impact, has been a major concern for the Chinese and needs analysis.

India must seek clarification from China regarding its policy towards Kashmir, for it has deployed about ten thousand troops in Northern part of J&K, as China considers Kashmir a disputed territory. As a matter of fact, India should convey its concern to China regarding the presence of the Chinese troops in North Kashmir. In bilateral talks with Pakistan on J&K, India must not forget that China now looms large on J&K. It seems that China's strategy is to use Kashmir as a bargaining chip for Arunachal Pradesh in the East besides keeping India busy and pre occupied in the Western sector in J&K.

The presence of the Chinese forces in Northern part of J&K has boosted the morale of Pakistani Military leaders as well as Pak terrorist organizations that often infiltrate terrorists into J&K to create security problems. Such actions keep the J&K problem alive and help Pakistan leaders to claim more concessions from India in order to maintain normal trade relations with India. Pakistan is also sure that India can take no large scale military action against Pak held Northern Kashmir, nor start a large scale campaign against Pakistan along India – Pak border because India cannot afford to fight on two fronts. Pakistan feels that China being its closest ally it would never let it fight alone against India. This has created a situation for India where the Indian leaders have to improve its economy, its military preparedness as well as its relations with strong countries of the world.

Main Chinese Approaches to Ladakh

When the Chinese President came on a recent visit to India he was first taken to Gujarat where special arrangements had been made to look after him and also display Indian hospitality. While the Chinese President was going around in Gujarat, enjoying the Indian hospitality, the Chinese troops in Southern part of Dem Chock were asking the Indian troops to vacate what they claim to be the Chinese territory in Southern part of Ladakh. As is well known the Chinese Line of Actual Occupation keeps on increasing in Ladakh as its troops occupy more areas in Ladakh. The Indian troops in Southern part of Ladakh refused to vacate their positions and so the Chinese and Indian troops continued to face each other, shouting slogans and threats to tell the opposite side not to move forward and claim further area. It looked strange that while the Chinese President was enjoying the Indian hospitality, the Chinese troops were threatening the Indian troops to vacate their positions in Southern Ladakh. When the Chinese President returned to China he is reported to have made a statement asking the Chinese armed forces to be ready to fight a regional battle in Asia.

The Chinese President may have been referring to a future incursion into Ladakh to capture more area and to further downgrade India in its standing amongst nations. The visualization of scenarios and the moves of an enemy are a soldier's prime duty and this must be grounded on maps and anticipated and planned for. In case China decides to capture more area in Ladakh it can move its forces from the North starting from the Kara Koram Pass. The route from Kara Koram Pass to Central part of Ladakh has no roads presently to ensure the proper maintenance of large forces by us. China has also the option of capturing more area through the central part of Ladakh south of the Chang Chenmo River upto the Chushul area. This area has roads which can be used by the Chinese forces to fight a proper war and to push us back.

In the South Chinese forces can advance either along Indus River or they can also come via a road which has been recently developed by the Chinese which starts from Western Tibet and comes to the Tangste Pass area and joins the Indus River approach. China can also attack Southern Ladakh via the Shapkila Pass which lies on the border of Western Tibet and Himachal Pradesh. The Chinese can advance into the Northern part of Himachal Pradesh, then cut off the Himachal Pradesh – Southern Ladakh road and later attack Southern Ladakh along with other Chinese forces advancing from Demchok along the Dem Chok approach. This approach would not only surprise the Indian forces and can be very dangerous as Ladakh would be cut off from Himachal Pradesh, as shown on the attached sketch.

Lastly, the Chinese forces may try to help Pakistan to capture the Siachin Glacier area by attacking it from the Northern side. There is already a road which passes through Kara Koram pass and later joins the road which runs along Saksham valley which lies North of Sia Chin Glacier. India therefore needs to earmark adequate forces to protect Ladakh from Northern Central as well as Southern approaches.

Prime Minister Modi has had a much publicized trip to China in May 2015. But China, if media reports are to be noted, has virtually turned down our Prime Minister's proposal seeking clarifications on the Line of Actual Control (LAC). India, it seems, had sought to clarify where each side stood physically on the border to avoid incursions. Beijing's refusal only complicates the issue and minimizes any possibility of an early solution. China of late has also stated that the dispute involves only 2000 kms, mostly in Arunachal Pradesh, but India would say certainly that the dispute is over 4000 kms of the border. It may be noted the incursions due to any "confusion" are by China only, this is another crucial aspect to be noted in terms of our response.

Lastly, I must emphasise that while we have certainly neglected our forces and security scenario, but this is not 1962. We now seem to have a more energetic and security conscious government, though its actual actions and budgetary allocations need to be studied for some time. The nation now has a young demographic profile; it's a younger more assertive generation, confident about its future and economic progress. This generation will not readily acknowledge its nation being under confident or under equipped militarily. This should in due course encourage the political leadership to be more decisive, as the political class will attempt to reorient itself to its constituency. A strategic mindset is also developing amongst some leaders and they are aware about the need to prepare for two adverse neighbours. To be decisive and prepared is not to wage war, but to be conscious that sophistry and moral philosophy apart, a nation's security and standing is dependent upon both its economic progress and military strength. They must move in tandem and complement each other.

The Army, while definitely under equipped, is certainly not the Army of 1962. It's a battle hardy force, more professional in orientation and well trained. Unlike the disjointed efforts of 1962, any future skirmish or war will be certainly well contested. As regards Ladakh, the Army now operates from a Corps HQ's in Leh. China will most certainly continue its regular aggressive posturing towards us, notwithstanding summits and seminars. Our Government while being judiciously cautious, should not be seen to be micro managing with temerity the Army as regards our responses. We have the Air

Force also well integrated now for any war or area specific incidents against China unlike 1962, but we must be ready to use it as a force multiplier in any eventuality. China also would be obviously aware about these developments. While we build good relations with the Chinese and simultaneously seek allies in tandem with the enhanced modernization of the armed forces, China must be kept aware always and consistently that the costs this time of any misadventure will be heavy. That in itself is a deterrent.

Changing Situation in South Asia

In the last few years great changes have taken place in Asia. China has become a very powerful country both economically and militarily. Pakistan has developed close relations with China economically as well as militarily. China has given Pakistan military aid as well as economic aid. It is giving Pakistan latest technology regarding production of nuclear weapons as well as development of tanks, guns and aircrafts. China needs Pakistan to get oil and gas from Middle East countries via Pakistani ports so that energy supply like oil and gas from Middle East can be supplied directly from Pakistani ports to Xinjiang the western province of China, which is located north east of Pak held northern part of Jammu & Kashmir.

On the other hand, the Pakistani government does not find it easy to rule over northern part of Kashmir like Gilgit-Baltistan because most of the population of this area is of Shia origin. Pakistan is a Sunni state by and large and Shias find it very difficult to live in Pakistan. The Pakistani rulers of northern part of Kashmir are set to be quite indifferent to the development of Gilgit-Baltistan region. So they are quite happy that China is spending billions of dollars to develop roads, bridges, dams and hydro projects to produce electricity for this region. China has also deployed about 10,000 troops in Gilgit-Baltistan area which has created serious security problems for India particularly for the J&K state. This suits Pakistan.

Ever since, the Chinese troops have spread out in Gilgit-Baltistan region, Pakistan has developed more confidence to create security problems for the J&K as well as the Indian government in various parts of J&K. More Pakistani trained and equipped jihadis or militants are infiltrating in various parts of J&K creating more security problems for India. As China's military and economic aid to Pakistan would continue to grow, Pakistan is bound to create more security problems for India particularly in J&K.

It suits China if Pakistani relations with India remain strained so that Pakistan continues to depend more on China for economic as well as military aid. Meanwhile, China is developing the Pakistani port at Gwadar which is located in southern part of Baluchistan, which is posing great security problem for Pakistan as Baluchi's are agitating for an independent state of Baluchistan. Meanwhile, China has declared that it would build modern warships as well as submarines for the Pakistani Navy. The Chinese pipeline as well as the road from Gwadar port to Rawalpindi in the north is bound to pass through Baluchistan. It is very likely that China would give additional aid to Pakistan's military to deal with the Baluchistan problem so that the pipeline remains safe and petrol and gas reach Xinjiang province of China via Gilgit and Baltistan.

China has already constructed good roads from Xinjiang province to Gilgit Baltistan region. One of the roads passes via Saksham valley north of Sia Chin glacier in Ladakh and goes to Xinjiang in the north through the famous Kara Koram pass. No wonder, China is taking keen interest in Ladakh where its line of occupation keeps on moving forward. That is why the Chinese forces did not withdraw after 1962 India China War from the Ladakh region in the West while the Chinese troops withdrew from the Eastern theatre. With the passage of time, the Chinese interest in Ladakh region is likely to grow and India should be prepared to face more problems in Ladakh region.

At present China sends all its supplies to Xinjiang by road to Kashgarh (old name Kashi) which is located in Western part of Xinjiang. From Kashgarh, 1300 kilometre long highway has been developed to Gilgit-Baltistan which passes through the Kara Koram Mountains via Khunjerab Pass. The Chinese have made many tunnels in Kara Koram for this highway to Gilgit-Baltistan or Pak held northern part of Kashmir which was captured by Pakistan during 1947-1948 Indo Pak War. Now that China has built a railway line upto Lhasa in Tibet, it can send supplies to Xinjiang via Lhasa also as Western Tibet has been connected by a big highway from Lhasa. There in lies China's interest in Ladakh. The Chinese have already displayed their interests in Southern Ladakh when they sent their troops to area South West of Demchok which they claimed to be part of Chinese territory. The Chinese have already built a proper highway connecting Western Tibet with Xinjiang via Lanak La in 1955-1956 which has been improved still further. So China can easily send supplies to Xinjiang from more than one route. From Xinjiang it has more than one highway to send goods to Baltistan – Gilgit area, in Pak held

China's Future Strategy – Its Impact on Indian Security

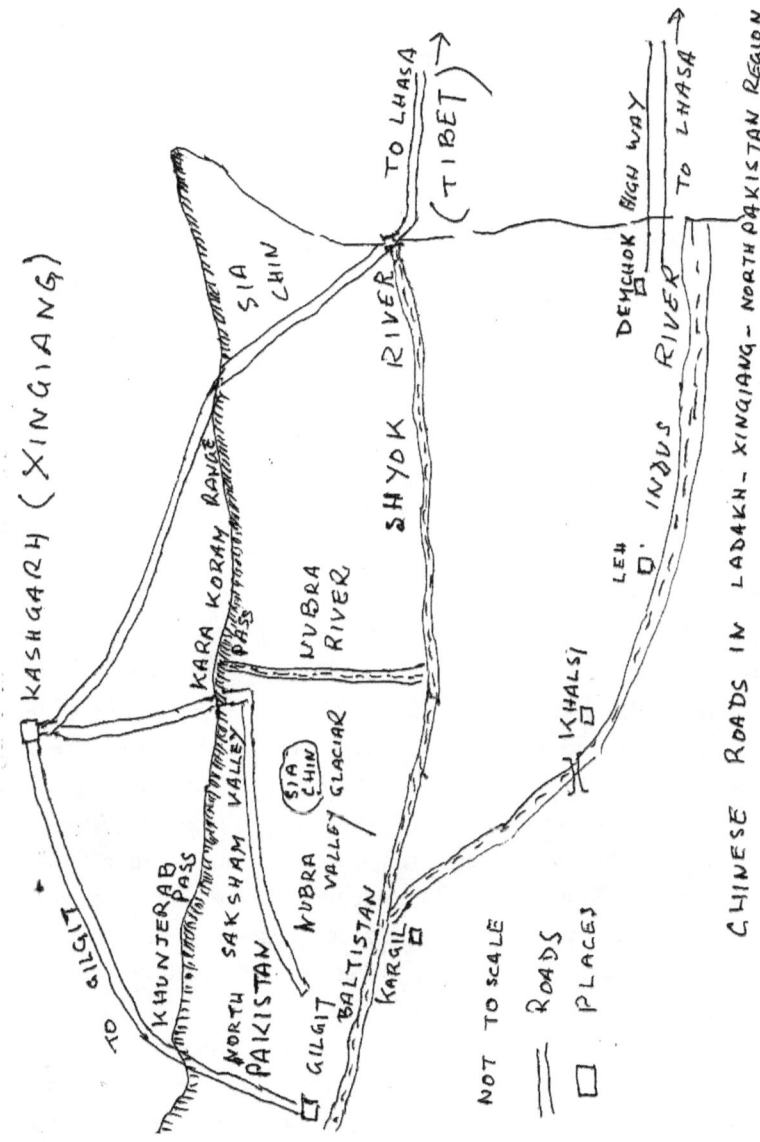

CHINESE ROADS IN LADAKH-Xinjiang-NORTH PAKISTAN REGION

northern part of J&K like highway along Saksham Valley in north Ladakh as well as via Khunjerab Pass through Kara Koram Mountains, as indicated in the attached sketch.

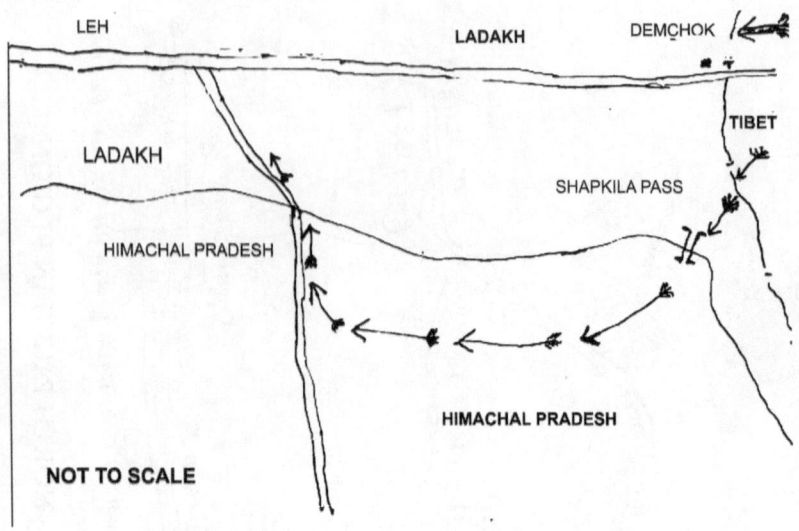

When the Chines President visited India, for the first time, he was taken to Gujrat and was given outmost regards. He seemed to be quite happy with the respect shown to him by the Indian leaders, particularly by the Indian Prime Minister Shri Modi. But while the Chinese President was getting maximum attention and given due regards in Gujarat, the Chinese troops in the Southern part of Ladakh, South West of Demchok to be precise, were asking the Indian troops to vacate their positions. The Chinese troops were shouting that the area belonged to China and hence the Indian troops should vacate their positions and leave the area for the Chinese troops to occupy it. But the Indian troops occupying the positions in Ladakh refused to vacate their positions and so the Chinese and Indian troops continued to face each other, shouting slogans and threats to tell the opposite side not to move forward and claim further area. It looked strange that while the Chinese President was enjoying the Indian hospitality, the Chinese troops were threatening the Indian troops to vacate their positions in Southern Ladakh. When the Chinese President returned to China he is reported to have made a statement asking the Chinese armed forces to be ready to fight a regional battle in Asia.

China's Future Strategy – Its Impact on Indian Security

The Chinese President may have been referring to a future incursion into Ladakh to capture more area and to further downgrade India in its standing amongst other nations. The visualization of scenarios and the moves of an enemy are a soldier's prime duty and this must be grounded on maps and anticipated and planned for. In case China decides to capture more area in Ladakh it can move its forces from the North starting from the Kara Koram Pass. The route from Kara Koram Pass to Central part of Ladakh has no roads presently to ensure the proper maintenance of large forces by us. China has also the option of capturing more area through the central part of Ladakh south of the Chang Chenmo River upto the Chushul area. This area has roads which can be used by the Chinese forces to fight a proper war and to push us back.

In the South, the Chinese forces can advance either along Indus River or they can also come via a road which has been recently developed by the Chinese which starts from Western Tibet and comes to the Tangste Pass area and joins the Indus River approach. China can also attack Southern Ladakh via the Shapkila Pass which lies on the border of Western Tibet and Himachal Pradesh. The Chinese can advance into the Northern part of Himachal Pradesh, then cut off the Himachal Pradesh – Southern Ladakh road and later attack Southern Ladakh along with other Chinese forces advancing from Demchok along the Dem Chok approach. This approach would not only surprise the Indian forces and can be very dangerous as Ladakh would be cut off from Himachal Pradesh, as shown on the attached sketch.

Lastly, the Chinese forces may try to help Pakistan to capture the Siachin Glacier area by attacking it from the Northern side. There is already a road which passes through Kara Koram pass and later joins the road which runs along Saksham valley which lies North of Sia Chin Glacier. India therefore needs to earmark adequate forces to protect Ladakh from Northern, Central as well as Southern approaches.

Prime Minister Modi has had a much publicized trip to China in May 2015. But China, if media reports are to be noted, has virtually turned down our Prime Minister's proposal seeking clarifications on the Line of Actual Control (LAC). India, it seems, had sought to clarify where each side stood physically on the border to avoid incursions. Beijing's refusal only complicates the issue and minimizes any possibility of an early solution. China of late has also stated that the dispute involves only 2000 kms, mostly in Arunachal Pradesh, but India would say certainly that the dispute is over 4000 kms of the border. It may be noted the incursions due to any "confusion" are by China only, this is another crucial aspect to be noted in terms of our response.

Lastly, I must emphasise that while we have certainly neglected our forces and security scenario, but this is not 1962. We now seem to have a more energetic and security conscious government, though its actual actions and budgetary allocations need to be studied for some time. The nation now has a young demographic profile; it's a younger more assertive generation, confident about its future and economic progress. This generation will not readily acknowledge its nation being under confident or under equipped militarily. This should in due course encourage the political leadership to be more decisive, as the political class will attempt to reorient itself to its constituency. A strategic mindset is also developing amongst some leaders and they are aware about the need to prepare for two adverse neighbours. To be decisive and prepared is not to wage war, but to be conscious that sophistry and moral philosophy apart, a nation's security and standing is dependent upon both its economic progress and military strength. They must move in tandem and complement each other.

The Army, while definitely under equipped, is certainly not the Army of 1962. It's a battle hardy force, more professional in orientation and well trained. Unlike the disjointed efforts of 1962, any future skirmish or war will be certainly well contested. As regards Ladakh, the Army now operates from a Corps HQ's in Leh. China will most certainly continue its regular aggressive posturing towards us, notwithstanding summits and seminars. Our Government while being judiciously cautious, should not be seen to be micro managing with temerity the Army as regards our responses. We have the Air Force also well integrated now for any war or area specific incidents against China unlike 1962, but we must be ready to use it as a force multiplier in any eventuality. China also would be obviously aware about these developments. While we build good relations with the Chinese and simultaneously seek allies in tandem with the enhanced modernization of the armed forces, China must be kept aware always and consistently that the costs this time of any misadventure will be heavy. That in itself is a deterrent.

The main danger to Ladakh comes from the powerful China who has already occupied a large part of Ladakh in north east as well as eastern part of Ladakh. The Chinese troops keep on claiming more area in south eastern part of Ladakh. Their Line of Control in Ladakh is very flexible and keeps on moving forward in various parts of Ladakh as suits China. The Chinese troops have displayed their future intentions in south eastern part of Ladakh by carrying out demonstrations on the border even when President Xi Jimping of China was visiting India for the first time. So the security of Ladakh is in danger and China can escalate the situation on the front whenever it suits the Chinese interests.

Meanwhile, President Xi Jimping of China has become Commander in Chief of the country's new Joint Forces Battle Command Centre, as he seeks to consolidate his power over the Chinese Armed Forces. He is taking keen interest in modernizing the Chinese Armed Forces by equipping them with the latest and modern weapons. China has deployed large number of forces in northern part of J&K held by Pakistan to give more confidence to the Pakistani's forces as well as the Pakistani terrorists who want to operate in J&K against the Indian forces. That is why, the Pakistani raids in J&K have increased in the last few months. The close cooperation between Pakistan and China can be dangerous for India, as it will affect all parts of J&K particularly Ladakh where China is showing more interests at present.

Incidentally, China has nominated one HQ only to look after Defence of Tibet as well as for carrying out any large scale operations in South Asia in general and India in particular. India has four command HQ's for dealing with Tibet like Eastern Command, Central Command, Western Command as well as Northern Command due to our country's different geographical profile.

The present government of India is fully aware of the fact that China is militarily much more powerful than India. Pakistan's close friendship with China poses additional danger to India in J&K in particular and India in general. Prime Minister's Shri Narendra Modi has decided to improve its relations with the powerful USA in order to look after India's security. He has visited USA four times and has also invited US President to visit India. The aim of the present Indian Govt. is obviously to look after the Indian security by getting help from a powerful country like USA so that in case of any Chinese operations against India, like attack in Ladakh in J&K, does not find India all by itself in facing a powerful China. It is obvious that in case of the Chinese attack in Ladakh, Pakistan is bound to join the Chinese forces in J&K to take revenge for their defeat in 1971 Bangladesh War.

Incidentally, Prime Minister of India Shri Narendra Modi is the first Prime Minister of our country who is taking such keen and genuine interest in the security aspect of the country by following a very thoughtful foreign policy which can help our country in improving its security. Because of India's improvement in relations with USA, countries like Japan, South Korea and Australis are also becoming friendlier towards India. The Prime Minister Modi is also trying to establish proper defence industry in India so it can produce better weapon systems for our defence forces within India. In developing new weapon systems in India also, USA can help our country as China is doing in the case of Pakistan. In the past, Russia has produced useful T 90 tanks and mechanized vehicles for the Indian Army, submarines particularly helping India in manufacturing nuclear submarines for the Indian Navy and fighters for the Indian Air Force. As India's economy improves, the Indian government must allocate more money for production of better weapon systems for the Indian armed forces so that they can be equipped with the latest weapon systems for the security of the country which needs maximum attention of our government. Pakistan is getting assistance from China and USA, even though relations between USA and China are not good due to China's aggressive policy to have full control over South China Sea in East Asia. India supports US policy of not allowing China to have full control over South China Sea. Japan, Australia, Philippines and Vietnam are also with USA in this connection and so is Malaysia. So India is in good company in Asia as regard to its security.

Index

A

Abdullah Sheikh 150, 156

Aksai Chin viii, 3, 27, 123, 126, 138, 157, 169, 170, 172, 173, 174, 178, 179, 180, 181, 183, 185, 187, 190, 191, 195, 196, 203, 204, 205, 207

Alchi Kargog 13

Allenby, General 1

Anjuman Imamia 98

Anjuman Mamin-ul-Islam 98

Araq 59, 60

B

Balti Muslims 49

Baltistan 16, 27, 35, 49

Balti Wars 16

Banihal Pass 4

Battle of Lankartse 21

Battle of Pashkyun 21

Battle of Sanku 20

Bewoor GG, Lt Col 161

Brahmi language 11

Buddhism 3, 7, 8, 10, 11, 12, 13, 14, 15, 22, 23, 93, 94, 101, 116, 156, 189

Buddhist preachers 10, 11

C

Carriappa, General 156

Chang Chenmo River 126

Chang La 126, 139, 141, 173

Chanthang breed (dog) 59

Chheng (rice wine) 59, 60, 62, 64, 65, 98

Chiang Kai Shek 180, 181, 182, 209

Chomos (nuns) 94, 102

Chortens 8, 14, 18, 22, 110

Chou En Lie 180, 191

Chushul 84, 126, 136, 137, 138, 139, 140, 141, 173, 197, 198, 199, 200, 219, 225

Ctesias 8

D

Darbuk 173

Dards 10, 11, 12, 13, 14, 66

Daulat Beg Oldi 196

Demchok 32, 33, 140, 141, 152, 210, 216, 219, 222, 224, 225

Dras 12, 28, 89, 162, 229

Dras River 28

E

Eisenhower, General 1

F

Festivals
- Mela Chimrrey 103, 106
- Mela Dosmochey 103, 105
- Mela Hemis 107
- Mela Losar 103
- Mela Mashro 103, 106
- Mela Phiang 103
- Mela Phyang 106
- Mela She Shubla 104
- Mela Spituk 103, 105
- Mela Trikse 103, 105
- Puja Kagyur Stangyur 104, 108

Foreign travellers or Writers
- Ctesias 8
- Herodotus 8
- Hieun Tsang 8
- Megasthenes 8

Fotula Pass 30

Funeral Ceremonies 67

G

Galwan River 196

Gartok 138, 140

Gilgit 10, 11, 12, 14, 16, 25, 122, 159, 160, 161, 163, 164, 166, 204, 207, 210, 221, 222, 229

Goncha 53, 54, 55, 58

Gulab Singh 19, 21

Gushri Khan 17

H

Herodotus 8, 12

Hieun Tsang 8

Hooka 152

Hot Springs 66

I

Indus River 1, 15, 26, 27, 28, 29, 34, 35, 43, 44, 45, 48, 50, 89, 122, 123, 124, 125, 134, 135, 138, 139, 140, 161, 163, 164, 165, 167, 168, 172, 173, 197

J

Jalandara 10

Jamyang Namgyal 16, 18

K

Kalon Chhewang Rigzin 113

Kangadi 53

Kanishka 10

INDEX

Karakoram Pass 26, 134, 153

Kargil 26, 30, 41, 48, 49, 86, 91, 93, 113, 115, 116, 120, 122, 123, 136, 139, 140, 141, 144, 146, 147, 152, 156, 158, 160, 161, 162, 163, 164, 165, 167, 168

Kashgarh 32, 123, 132, 151, 170, 210, 222

Khalatse Bridge 167

Kishtwar 19

Krishna Menon 183, 190, 192

Kumdun 31, 130, 132, 133

Kushak Bakula 3, 98, 101, 102, 113, 114, 117, 118, 156, 157

L

Ladakhi nomads 10

Lahaul and Spiti 27

Lahul 167

Lamaism 8, 11, 12, 23, 24, 93, 94

Lamas 3, 64, 65, 67, 68, 72, 93, 94, 98, 101, 102, 105, 106, 107, 108, 163

Lanak La 126, 138, 169, 170, 171, 173, 174, 179, 180, 222

Lankartse 21

Leh viii, 3, 4, 8, 13, 15, 16, 17, 21, 22, 26, 28, 29, 30, 31, 32, 33, 37, 39, 42, 44, 46, 47, 48, 50, 80, 84, 88, 91, 93, 98, 102, 105, 107, 108, 111, 113, 114, 115, 116, 120, 123, 124, 125, 126, 127, 128, 133, 134, 135, 136, 138, 139, 140, 144, 146, 147, 148, 150, 151, 152, 154, 155, 156, 158, 161, 162, 163, 164, 165, 166, 167, 168, 173, 174, 178, 179, 205, 220, 226, 231

Lhasa 8, 15, 18, 23, 59, 138, 172, 179, 186

Losar (New Year) 103, 104

Lughzhun 29

M

Maha Bodhi Society 102, 103, 120

Maharaja Ranjit Singh 19, 190

Malthusian Law 49

Manas 8

Mana Walls 110, 111

Mansarover Lake 29

Marksmik La Pass 126

Marriage Customs 64

  bagma 64

  magpa 63, 64, 65

McMahon Line 179, 181, 188, 191

Megasthenes 8

Monastries 8

Mons 10, 11, 12, 13

N

Namdas 47, 58

Namgyal Dynasty 15, 16, 17

Niabats 86

Nubra River 1, 26, 28, 29, 30, 35, 40, 43, 45, 50, 67, 84, 89, 122, 123, 124, 125, 126, 130, 134, 135, 165, 166, 167, 203, 207

Nyatril Tsanpo 14

O

Old remains for past history 8

  Chortens 8

  Manas 8

  Monastries 8

P

Pabbu (local shoes) 52

Pairak (women headgear) 55

Pataliputra 10

Prithi Chand, Major 148, 161, 163, 164, 166, 167, 168

Pyong Gong Tso 17, 126

R

Rajatarangini 8

Raj Bodhi Mahasabha 102

Rudok 27, 138, 139, 140

Rupshu 30, 36, 40, 50

S

Saksham valley 204, 207, 220, 222, 225

Shaitan Singh, Major 200, 201

Shias 99, 114, 116, 221

Shiraks (shawl) 53

Shrub-Zhing 63

Shyok River 1, 26, 28, 29, 31, 43, 50, 89, 122, 123, 124, 125, 126, 128, 129, 134, 135, 136, 139, 140, 166, 167, 168, 203, 207, 230

Siachen Glacier vii, 167, 203

Sinkiang 13, 26, 27, 29, 31, 32, 40, 42, 46, 47, 57, 82, 95, 123, 125, 126, 127, 132, 133, 141, 146, 151. *See also* Xinjiang

Skardu 25, 26, 29, 33, 44, 122, 123, 125, 139, 140, 159, 160, 161, 163, 166, 204, 207, 210, 231

Spituk clay 88

Sunis 98, 99, 114, 116

Suru Valley 30, 45, 89

T

Tang dynasty 13

Tangtse 126, 141

Thimayya, General 163, 182, 191, 192, 213

Tibetan nomads 9, 12, 172

Tonktse 36, 40

Treaty of Leh 21

Trigtse monastery 15

Tsepal Namgyal 17, 19

Tsing dynasty 8

Tsongkapa 15

INDEX

U

Uighur 210

Urumachi 152

W

Wavel, Field Marshal 1

Western Tibet 9, 10, 13, 16, 23, 29, 42, 46, 90, 121, 122, 123, 138, 151, 169, 170, 171, 172, 173, 178, 179, 180, 186, 189, 191, 204

X

Xinjiang 13, 26, 27, 31, 42, 45, 46, 47, 57, 88, 90, 92, 95, 96, 121, 123, 124, 125, 126, 127, 132, 133, 138, 141, 146, 148, 151, 152, 159, 169, 170, 171, 172, 173, 178, 179, 187, 191, 195, 198, 203, 204, 210, 211, 213, 216

Y

Yarkand 32, 47, 131, 132, 151, 170, 171

Yarkandi woollen blankets 58

Z

Zangskar 10, 11, 30, 41, 42, 45, 89, 116, 136

Zojila Pass 19, 26, 42

Zorawar Singh 15, 19, 21

www.ingramcontent.com/pod-product-compliance
Lightning Source LLC
Chambersburg PA
CBHW022010220426
43663CB00007B/1027